FREEDOM IN MESSIAH

A MESSIANIC JEWISH ROOTS COMMENTARY ON THE BOOK OF GALATIANS

Freedom In Messiah
A MESSIANIC JEWISH ROOTS COMMENTARY ON THE BOOK OF GALATIANS
Copyright © 2015 By Richard Hill
Cover design by Michael Durant of Creating Genius
www.creatinggen.com

$\wp$

S-E-L-F PUBLISHING

Simple-Effective-Literary-Focusing on Publishing
10120 W. Flamingo Rd.
Suite 4 #228
Las Vegas, NV 89147
Visit us at www.yourpublisher.org

All rights reserved. This material is protected under the copyright laws and may not be copied or reprinted. No portion of this book may be reproduced in any form or by any means including information storage or retrieval system, electronic, mechanical, photocopying, scanning, recording or otherwise, without the written permission of the publisher.

Unless otherwise noted, all Scripture quotations taken from the King James Version of the Holy Bible, (KJV). Copyright © 2003, Thomas and Nelson, Inc. Used by permission. www.thomasandnelson.com.

ISBN 978-0-9969201-2-4

Printed In The United States Of America
10 9 8 7 6 5 4 3 2

FREEDOM IN MESSIAH
A MESSIANIC JEWISH ROOTS COMMENTARY ON THE BOOK OF GALATIANS

Dr. Richard Hill

𝓟

S-E-L-F PUBLISHING
Simple Effective Literary-Focusing on Publishing

Dedication

I dedicate this book to my Adonai Yeshua Hameshiach (Lord Jesus the Messiah). He is worthy of all honor and glory and power as Rev. 5:12 states, *"Worthy is the Lamb that was slain to receive power and riches and wisdom and might and honor and glory and blessing."* He is the One that writes the names of all believers into the Book of Life and therefore we should live our lives for Him.

Acknowledgments

I would like to acknowledge and thank the following for their help with the making of this book.

First and foremost, all the blessing, honor, glory and dominion go to my Adonai Yeshua Hameshiach (Lord Jesus the Messiah). He is my everything and without Him this book would never have been written! I hope and pray He will use it to His glory.

My wife Oanh, who I love very much. She is the epitome of a Proverbs 31 wife who had to deal with a husband working into the late hours of the night writing this book. She is a true tireless servant of the Lord; I am a blessed man for having such a wonderful helpmate.

My children, Stephanie, Rebekah and Isaak who I love very much as well, and who have been greatly blessed by the Lord with growing up in a Godly home. They have had to learn patience and perseverance from the Lord as we traveled this great country of ours preaching the good news message of Yeshua and teaching the Jewish Roots in the churches and Messianic congregations.

All of the members of Beth Yeshua Messianic Congregation in Las Vegas, Nevada, who have greatly encouraged me. We are *mishpochah* (family)! We have persevered through the tough times and been blessed in the good times. We continue to walk with the Ruach (Spirit) right down the straight and narrow path to Yeshua no matter what comes our way.

CJF Ministries, in my estimation, by far the best Messianic Jewish ministry in the world to work for. The management, administration and the missionaries have been great and a pleasure to work with. The Lord is definitely using our ministry to reach the "lost sheep of the house of Israel" and the Gentiles around the world.

Gloria Wade, who so diligently typed out the first manuscript of this commentary using cassette tapes of my verse-by-verse sermon series through the book of Galatians. I guess that tells you how long this book has taken to get published (cassette tapes are the dinosaur!). From that sermon series in 2004, a dissertation was written for my PhD and from that dissertation this book was birthed. It took a total of 10+ years but it was well worth the wait. Tod (thanks) goes to the Lord!

Foreword

Virtually from the time it was written, Paul's letter to the believers in ancient Galatia was controversial—and that controversy continues into the 21st century. Contrary to what one might expect, however, the dispute about the epistle has little if anything to do with its Pauline authorship. The fact that the Book of Galatians came from the pen of the Apostle Paul hasn't been seriously questioned, other than in the scant writings of a handful of critical scholars in the 1800s, some of whom postulated "layers" of text where later editors amended what Paul originally wrote. But the scholarly community generally found those arguments unpersuasive; so the controversy since that time has been mainly about the letter's contents rather than its authorship.

What, then, did Paul say in Galatians that so many religionists over the past 2,000 years have found so threatening? It's the same issue that prompted Paul to write the letter in the first place: salvation purely and exclusively by God's grace, apart from human works or merit. The Apostle declared: "But that no one is justified by the law in the sight of God is evident, for 'the just shall live by faith' " (3:11, NKJV).

There is something about our fallen human nature that compels us to want to do something to contribute to our salvation. But it's an impossibility because even our best works are like "filthy rags" in comparison to God's righteous standard (Isa. 64:6). In another epistle, Paul wrote, "Not by works of righteousness which we have done, but according to His mercy He saved us, through the washing of regeneration and renewing of the Holy Ghost" (Titus 3:5). There are certain things that we can "add" *after* we are saved

(2 Peter 1:5-8); but there is nothing we can add to salvation itself.

Paul refers to the notion that anyone—whether Jewish or Gentile—can be justified by any legalistic means as "another gospel" (1:6). My friend and colleague, Dr. Richard Hill, points out in chapter 2 of the present volume that the Greek word for "another" in this verse is *heteros*, signifying "another of a different kind." *Heteros* stands in contrast to another word, *allos*, meaning "another of the same kind." The gospel of the legalists, then, is "not of the same nature, form, class, (or) kind" as Paul's Gospel (see the entry for "heteros" in *Thayer's Greek Lexicon*). It is something vastly different! That is why Paul says the purveyor of this false gospel is to be regarded by believers as "accursed" (*anathema*).

So where did this foreign, insidious gospel come from? In his epistle, Paul provides us with a number of clues. In piecing the evidence together, it appears that a first century religious party of "Torah-observant" Jewish Christians had infiltrated the congregations in Galatia—which were predominantly populated by Gentiles—and tried to convince them that they were obligated to keep Jewish rituals and rites, particularly circumcision, for justification and/or sanctification.

In *Freedom in Messiah*, Dr. Hill wades fearlessly into this churning sea of controversy and shines the light of God's Word on issues that are just as relevant today as they were 2,000 years ago. I predict that this much-needed book will enjoy a wide readership because it defends the true Gospel of God's amazing grace while renewing in a 21st century context the urgency of Paul's warning against believers embracing "another gospel."

                            Dr. Gary Hedrick,
                            President & CEO
                            CJF Ministries
                            San Antonio, Texas USA

Preface

The theme of this book is "Be free in Messiah and be led by the Ruach." It is a rather simple statement to make but a rather difficult goal to reach. I say this because we humans that have been found by God's grace do not make it easy on ourselves to reach this goal. We tend to set up other masters in our lives to worship like the Torah (Law), crosses, baptismals, legalism, our own rules and regulations, stumbling blocks and Hasatan's temptations. You can add anything else to your list. We certainly can easily become our own worst enemies!

The Messianic Jewish Movement (MJM) is certainly no stranger to this dilemma as well. My family and I have been in the MJM for 20 years. We love the MJM, worshiping in a Messianic Jewish way and learning about our Jewish Roots. It is a blessed continuous lifelong process. Our Messiah Yeshua (Jesus) is Jewish, the apostles are Jewish, the Bible was written by Jewish people for the Jewish people with the Jewish writing style and customs in mind. It is everything Jewish. So we as believers should by our connection with the Jewish Messiah be enjoying these Jewish Roots of our faith no matter whether we are Jewish or Gentile.

However, legalism has reared its' ugly head and has revealed itself in many shapes and forms. I have seen this legalism increase dramatically over the last 20 years within the MJM. It seems to me that it is like a runaway train that has no brakes and is running straight for disaster. That's why this book was written: to help those Messianic Jews and Gentiles to see the light of legalism in their lives and their congregations' lives. Legalism can be very enticing and it is not a simple thing to see in one's life.

This book was also written for all believers to enjoy the richness of the Jewish Roots found in Galatians.

Over the last 20 years, I believe the MJM has more fully developed two branches within its' sphere. The Torah Observant group and the New Covenant Freedom group. The Torah Observant group is the larger of the two. Its' premise is simply stated: keep the Torah (the Law, the first 5 books of the Bible) because these are our roots and God commanded us to keep the Torah. Therefore, the Messianic Jewish lifestyle is then set around the commands of the Torah. Implied is the idea that Torah is the more important set of Scriptures of the Bible. They are more important than the rest of the Tenach (the Writings and Prophets; the rest of the Old Covenant) and even the Brit Chadasha (New Covenant Scriptures). The theological idea of keeping Torah then becomes a person's life. Then the idea that we all need to keep Torah for our salvation or our sanctification becomes dominant in individual and congregational life. We all have to keep Torah to please God, to draw close to the Lord and to receive His blessings.

This is the great error that plagues the Torah Observant movement. Sha'ul wrote this letter to the Galatians to dispel all of these notions and this is what is discussed and developed in this commentary. The New Covenant Freedom group believes just as Galatians preaches that all believers are free in Messiah and we should live our lives being free and being led by the Ruach. The Lord dictates exactly what He wants each and every person to do with their lives and He does this through the whole Bible. Those in the MJM have the option to choose (led by the Lord) how much Jewishness or Jewish Roots they want in their lives. This Freedom group believes that the New Covenant has superseded the Mosaic Covenant whereby the commandments of the Law have no authority or mastery over our lives since the death and resurrection of Yeshua. The Torah is no longer our master showing us what we need to do in life. Yeshua is our new Master and He is the One we all need to follow.

In no uncertain terms does this New Covenant Freedom position believe that the Jewish Bible (the Old Covenant Scriptures, aka Tenach which includes the Torah) has been abolished! In fact, there are two verses in the New Covenant Scriptures that proclaim the Torah was written for our instruction. There is much to glean from the Torah. We simply believe that the Lord wants us living in freedom under the New Covenant and not in bondage to the Torah.

It is my humble hope that all who read this book will listen, consider and reason with the Lord over its' contents. The Lord has spoken through Sha'ul in Galatians. He has written a very clear and straight forward message. It is much more important for believers of Yeshua to be free in Messiah and led by the Ruach than to be in slavery to the Torah and led by the Law. Shalom!

About the Author

Dr. Richard Hill is the Messianic Pastor of Beth Yeshua Messianic Congregation in Las Vegas, NV since 2003. He is also a Ministry Representative with CJF Ministries since 2000. He received his Ph.D. from Antioch Baptist Seminary in 2010. Rich's great desire is to share the good news message of Yeshua Hameshiach (Jesus the Messiah) with the apple of God's eye - the Jewish people.

For more information, please contact:
Richard Hill
P.O. Box 36156
Las Vegas, NV 89133
(702) 256-0840
www.bethyeshualv.org
www.cjfm.org

Contents

Dedication
Acknowledgement
Foreword
Preface
About the Author

1. Introduction	15
2. Truth or Consequences (1:1-10)	25
3. The Good News Transforms (1:11-24)	39
4. The Truth of the Good News (2:1-10)	48
5. The Good News Confronted (2:11-21)	62
6. Righteousness is by Faith not by the Law (3:1-9)	83
7. Abraham's Blessing and the Law's Cursing (3:10-18)	103
8. Why the Law Then? (3:19-29)	119
9. Sons of God and not Slaves under the Law (4:1-11)	137
10. Maintain Your Freedom from the Law (4:12-20)	153
11. Listen to the Law (4:21-31)	166
12. Messiah has Set Us Free (5:1-12)	181
13. Messiah Called Us to Freedom (5:13-18)	202
14. Keep the Fruit of the Ruach (5:19-26)	219
15. You Reap What You Sow (6:1-10)	234
16. Walk in the Lord not in the Flesh (6:11-18)	251
17. Summary	271

Chapter 1

Introduction

The Messianic Jewish Movement (MJM) of today is under great spiritual attack. Those Jewish and Gentile believers who desire to worship God in a Jewish way are being put through the test of a lifetime. The very root of our Movement is being challenged and the very essence of our traditional theology is being disputed. Many leaders in our MJM are alarmed and concerned. Messianic Rabbi Jonathan Cahn strongly warns:

> *"Woe to us should we forget whose love, whose life, and whose blood it was by which we were washed, forgiven and raised to new life. It was not Jewish culture that gave its life for us, not Jewish tradition that was crushed for our iniquities, not the Torah that hung bloodied on the execution stake for our salvation. It was Messiah alone. To Him alone, the Holy One of Israel, we owe the full measure of our love, our devotion and our lives."* [1]

Rich Robinson and Ruth Rosen nicely summarize the problem areas in the MJM. They state,

"There is plenty of room in the messianic movement for different opinions. There is room for people to choose the day or night in which they will worship the Lord. There is room for people to choose what they will or will not eat, what traditions they will or will not follow, what holidays they will or will not celebrate. There is room for some people to hand out tracks to strangers and others to share the Gospel only with those whom they already know. There is room to pray spontaneously, or from a Siddur, in Hebrew or English, or other languages. There is room to sing traditional songs or contemporary choruses. There is even a place for doubts and soul-searching and wrestling for a better understanding of the Scriptures. But, is there room for a changing theology of salvation? Is there room to regard certain Scriptures as more binding on Gentile believers than on Jewish believers? Is there room for the idea that being Jewish is more fundamental to our identity than believing in Jesus? We hope you will agree that there is not." [2]

I certainly agree that there is not. Stan Telchin is another author who agrees as he takes a stand for unity in the MJM. Telchin summarizes his purposes for writing his book, "Messianic Judaism is not Christianity."

He writes,

> *"Simply stated, I want to accomplish three things. First, it is my hope and prayer that the leaders within Messianic Judaism will accept my challenge to question some of the attitudes and practices of this movement in the light of God's Word....My second purpose is to address those who are involved with Messianic Judaism. They need to ask themselves these questions: Are you caught up in the beauty and nostalgia and romance of "Jewishness" to the point that you are ignoring God's clearly stated will that we all are to be 'one new man?'... Do you really understand that in His sight there is no difference between Jews and Gentiles? Finally, because more and more Jewish believers are proclaiming the Messiah-ship of Jesus every day and receiving Him as Lord of their lives, they – as well as pastors and church leaders everywhere – need to understand the nature of the crisis that is emerging."* [3]

As these quotes reveal, there is a crisis emerging within the MJM. I believe there are at least five major issues that are the cornerstone of all the problems within the MJM. These five issues are as follows:

1. The belief that one must be Torah Observant to be saved or sanctified.
2. The belief that Yeshua is not God nor is He co-equal or co-eternal with God the Father or the Holy Spirit.

3. The belief that Jews already have a covenantal relationship with God and do not need Yeshua for salvation (this belief is also known as Dual Covenant Theology).
4. The belief that being Jewish is more important to our Jewish identity than believing in Yeshua and living for Yeshua.
5. The belief that the MJM needs to be the Fourth Branch of Judaism (the three branches are Orthodox, Conservative and Reform).

The first purpose of this book is to address these five concerns within an analysis of the book of Galatians. Rabbi Sha'ul [Hebrew for the Apostle Paul] almost 2,000 years ago addressed and answered all of these problems and concerns that plague our MJM today.

The second purpose is to reveal and thoroughly discuss the Jewish Roots of the book of Galatians from a Messianic Jewish perspective. I believe that many of the commentaries concerning the book of Galatians leave out the richness of its' Jewish Roots. Knowing these roots sheds some much needed understanding and wisdom to Sha'ul's message to the congregations of Galatia and to believers for today.

Rabbi Sha'ul wrote the letter to the Galatians anywhere from 48-55 A.D. Within the scope of addressing these Messianic concerns, he dealt with four major themes: grace versus law; freedom versus bondage; faith versus works; and Spirit versus flesh. These four themes are additionally examined throughout this book.

The question that has sparked historical controversy over the book of Galatians is, "Who are the Galatians?" Josephus tells us in his "Book of Antiquities" that Antiochus the Great had settled 2,000 Jewish families in Lydia and Phrygia, which is in Galatia prior to the time of Sha'ul's first missionary journey. ⁴ J.B. Lightfoot, a Jewish theologian writes,

> *"With these attractions [great opportunity in commercial enterprise] it is not difficult to explain the vast increase of the Jewish population in Galatia, and it is a significant fact that in the generation before St. Paul, Augustus directed a decree granting special privileges to the Jews to be inscribed in his temple at Ancyra, the Galatians metropolis, doubtless because this was a principal seat of the dispersion [of the Jews] in these parts of Asia Minor."* ⁵

The Encyclopedia Judaica confirms the quotes of Josephus and Lightfoot and adds more historical documentation that shows there were many Jewish people living in the Asia Minor region. It states,

> *"At the end of the third century B.C.E. Antiochus III issued a command to transfer 2,000 Jewish families from Babylonia to Phyrgia and Lydia in order to settle them in the fortified cities as garrisons. The first synagogues in Asia Minor were apparently built at that time. Important evidence of the distribution of Jews in Asia Minor has been preserved in the Roman circular of 139 B.C.E. to the Hellenistic cities and states. It mentions Caria, Pamphylia, and Lycia as places of Jewish settlement (I Macc. 15:23) Cicero's account of the confiscation of the*

> *money which the Jews of Pergamum, Adramythion, Laodicea, and Apamea had designated for the Temple in Jerusalem, during the governorship of L. Valerius Flaccus, provides additional evidence of the spread of Jews in Asia Minor. Philo of Alexandria testifies that in his day in Asia Minor, as in Syria, there were many Jews. But the most extensive and detailed information on Jewish settlements throughout Asia Minor is furnished by numerous inscriptions and documents preserved by Josephus in Antiquities (book 14), and by accounts of the Jewish communities in the New Testament – in Acts and in Paul's Epistles. According to these inscriptions, Jews were settled in the following regions of Asia Minor: Ionia, Mysia, Lydia, Caria, Lycia, Phrygia, Lycaonia, Cappadocia, Galatia, Bithynia, Paphlagonia, Pisidia, Cilicia, and other localities.* [6]

These quotes reveal a thriving Jewish population among the cities in Galatia where Sha'ul shared the good news of Yeshua in his first missionary journey. What is amazing is the Encyclopedia Judaica quotation stating that portions of the New Testament were historically accurate in accounting for the Jewish communities in Asia Minor! The Encyclopedia Judaica is an Israeli publication from an unsaved Jewish perspective. For them to admit that the New Testament is the best source on this topic is significant.

The point thus far is to show there was

a substantial Jewish population in the Galatian region. As we investigate the following Scriptures we find that as a result of Sha'ul's first missionary journey to the region many Jewish people as well as Gentiles were saved and thus started the local churches in Galatia. This in turn reveals the answer to the question, "Who are the Galatians?" They are Jews and Gentiles who were saved through Sha'ul's preaching during his first missionary journey.

In Acts 13:13-52 we find Sha'ul and his traveling disciples in Pisidian Antioch, which is in Southern Galatia. In the local synagogue, Sha'ul is invited to share a word of exhortation. He then proceeds to address his audience in verse 16, "... *Men of Israel, and ye that fear God...*" These men are most certainly Jews and Gentile proselytes. They are further identified in verse 43 as, "... *the Jews and religious proselytes...*" who were following Sha'ul and Bar-Nabba (Barnabas). Sha'ul and Bar-Nabba "... *persuaded them to continue in the grace of God.*"

This phrase certainly implies that these Jews and Gentiles were saved through the preaching of Sha'ul. However, in the next town we know for sure there were Jewish and Gentile salvations. In Acts 14:1, Sha'ul preached a mighty message in the Ruach (Spirit) in Iconium that resulted in "... *a great multitude both of the Jews and also of the Greeks believed.*" Iconium is another Southern Galatian city where Jews and Gentiles were saved. In verses 19-20, Sha'ul was stoned and dragged out of the city of Lystra supposed to be dead. But he was miraculously alive and well and went back to Lystra to preach the good news to them again. The next day he and Bar-Nabba went to Derbe to preach. Verse 21 shows us that he made many disciples in Derbe and returned to Lystra, Iconium and Antioch.

The key to this section is verses 22-23 where Sha'ul was:

> *Confirming the souls of the disciples, and exhorting them to continue in the faith, and that we must through much tribulation enter into the kingdom of God. And when they had ordained them elders in every church, and had prayed with fasting, they commended them to the Lord, on whom they believed.*

The disciples of all these Southern Galatian cities were the Jews and Gentiles from the synagogues (with some pagan Gentiles) where Sha'ul preached the good news message of Yeshua. He helped strengthen and encourage them and from this group of disciples some were selected to be elders of the newly founded congregations. The idea here is that obviously some of the elders of the congregations were Jewish as well. Therefore, I conclude that the Galatians (the recipients of Sha'ul's letter) were Jewish and Gentile believers of Yeshua found in the Southern Galatian churches noted in Acts 13 and 14. It is also concluded since Sha'ul is writing his book of Galatians to Jewish and Gentile believers (with many of the Gentile believers being converts to Judaism), then he must be writing with a Messianic Jewish perspective. It is this perspective that I have introduced in this book.

A second question that is pertinent to this introduction is "Who are the Judaizers?" Before I can answer the question, the term "Judaizer" needs to be addressed. This term has and can be used in an anti-Semitic way. Some modern day Gentile believers have even labeled the MJM as being "Judaizers." Dr. David Stern explains the situation:

"Some Gentile Christians say that Messianic Jews are 'Judaizers'... But because the 'villains' of the book of Galatians are commonly termed Judaizers, this word has a strongly negative valence in Christian circles; and for this reason it is necessary to defend Messianic Jews against the charge of being Judaizers.[7] Unfortunately, there seems to be an automatic negative understanding of the word "Judaizer." When in fact, the Greek word *Ioudaizo* means "to Judaize or conform to or live according to Jewish customs or manners.[8]

In and of itself, living like Jews should not be automatically viewed as being evil or bad. Therefore, I am using the term, "Legalizer," which is much more suitable for this situation. To re-phase the question then, "Who are the Legalizers?" The Legalizers were those Jews, saved and unsaved, who desired to put Messianic Jews and Gentiles back under the Torah (Law) through strict observance of the commandments of the Torah so that they could be saved and/or sanctified. Sha'ul describes these Legalizers in the book of Galatians as false brethren (2:4); certain men from Yacov (James) who are of the circumcision (2:12) who distorted the truth of the good news message of Yeshua (1:6-7); tried to control their liberty through bondage (2:4); hindered them from obeying the truth (5:7) by teaching justification through the Torah and the works of the Torah (3:1-5; 4:3-11; 5:1-4). Luke in the book of Acts reveals that these Legalizers were from Judea, were of the Pharisees who had believed in Yeshua and were part of the Jerusalem Council (15:1, 5, 24). It is additionally clear from Acts 15:1, 5 that the Legalizers' teaching included that Gentiles must be circumcised and keep Torah to be saved. The Legalizers were teaching a dangerous doctrine that would spiritually shipwreck any believer that followed it. Sha'ul met this false teaching with the book of Galatians encouraging these new Jewish and Gentile believers to live not under Torah but under grace, to live not by works but by faith and believe not in Jewishness but in Jesus. Today's MJM needs to hear this same message.

Chapter 2

Truth or Consequences
(1:1-10)

1:1 Paul, an apostle, (not of men, neither by man, but by Jesus Christ, and God the Father, who raised him from the dead;)
1:2 And all the brethren which are with me, unto the churches of Galatia:
1:3 Grace be to you and peace from God the Father, and from our Lord Jesus Christ,
1:4 Who gave himself for our sins, that he might deliver us from this present evil world, according to the will of God and our Father:
1:5 To whom be glory for ever and ever. Amen.
1:6 I marvel that ye are so soon removed from him that called you into the grace of Christ unto another gospel:
1:7 Which is not another; but there be some that trouble you, and would pervert the gospel of Christ.
1:8 But though we, or an angel from heaven, preach any other gospel unto you than that which we have preached unto you, let him be accursed.
1:9 As we said before, so say I now again, If any man preach any other gospel unto you than that ye have received, let him be accursed.

1:10 *For do I now persuade men, or God? or do I seek to please men? For if I yet pleased men, I should not be the servant of Christ.*

Have you ever experienced a loved one turn on you for no good reason? It feels like that person placed a knife in your back and started to twist. Sha'ul must have felt the same way as he was writing to the congregations in Galatia. This is exactly what the Galatians had done to him. He helped to save them; was a father to them; labored over them; planted them in congregations; discipled them and loved them. But along came some smooth talking Legalizers and all of a sudden, the world turns upside down. Why is all this happening? The Legalizers were attacking, the Galatians were believing and Sha'ul was defending. Right from the beginning of the book, Sha'ul takes a defensive posture concerning two issues: 1) his apostleship and more importantly 2) the good news message of Yeshua. The Galatians had a choice to make: accept the truth or accept the consequences.

1:1 Sha'ul states from the beginning that he is an apostle. The Legalizers were probably telling the Galatians that Sha'ul was not an apostle at all or was a self-proclaimed apostle. Why? Since Yeshua did not select Sha'ul as one of The Twelve apostles in His earthly ministry then Sha'ul could not be an apostle. However, Sha'ul told the Galatians he was an apostle and to the Jewish people the word "apostle" was greatly understood.

The Encyclopedia Judaica simplifies our understanding of this matter:

> *The term [apostle meaning 'messenger'] is equivalent to the Hebrew **shali'ah** and some scholars have suggested that the early*

> *Christian apostolate was indebted to Jewish precedent (e.g., the custom of sending messengers not singly but in pairs). The alleged similarity between John 20:21 ("As my father has sent me, so I send you.") and the rabbinic rule (Ber.5:5) "A person's messenger is as himself" is more apparent than real.* 2

The important point in this quote is not whether the rabbis believe there is a similarity between John 20:21 and the rabbinic rule but the actual rabbinic rule found in the Talmud. This rule shows the Jewish understanding that when a rabbi or a master sent out his messenger it was as if he were sending himself.

Sha'ul makes the point that he was sent out as a messenger not from men but from God the Father and His Son the Messiah. He states that his authority and commission come from God and no one else. Presumably, these Galatians knew Sha'ul's testimony on the road to Damascus. In Acts 9:1-25, Sha'ul was actually met by the resurrected Yeshua shining as the Shekinah light (glory of God) from heaven. Of course, this is where Yeshua commissioned Sha'ul to bear His name to the Gentiles, kings and the Jewish people. This opening verse of Galatians should have had a big impact on the Galatians.

In Sha'ul's opening defense, he boldly reveals were the power as well as his authority comes from. It comes from God the Father who raised Yeshua from the dead. The resurrection of Yeshua proves how powerful God truly is and He is the One along with Yeshua who called Sha'ul to be an apostle. Now compare that authority and power with whom the

Legalizers state as their authority – the apostles from the Jerusalem Congregation. There truly is no comparison. The ironic part about all of this is the fact that the apostles did not send out the Legalizers as their representatives (Acts 15:24)! So the Legalizers did not have God's authority nor man's authority to perform their ministry.

1:2 Acts 13 and 14 reveal the cities in Southern Galatia where Sha'ul visited during his first missionary journey. They are Antioch (Pisidian), Iconium, Lystra, and Derbe. It is possible other congregations were planted in Lycaonia and other cities in the region due to Acts 14:6. As stated in the introduction, each congregation would have Jewish and Gentile believers as elders and members.

1:3 Keener notes that the standard Greek greeting was the word "greetings" (*chairein*). *Chairein* is related to "grace" (*charis*). Jewish people greeted one another with *shalom* (peace) as we do today. However, the typical greeting in Jewish letters often began with "greetings and peace." Sha'ul adapts this standard Jewish greeting into a blessing by adding the word "grace." [3] However, this greeting becomes even more of a blessing because he says it is from our Lord and God.

Charis means "grace" and "primarily denotes the demonstration of God's favor, mercy and kindness toward mankind." [4] Most believers would say that the meaning of grace is unmerited favor. God bestows his favor on us not because we are such wonderful people and not because we have performed great works in our life. It is solely based on Him and His love for us. *Shalom* denotes much more than just peace. Dr. Stern explains that *shalom* also means, "tranquility, safety, well-being, welfare, health, contentment, success, comfort, wholeness and integrity." [5]

There is quite a lot of meaning when you say the word "shalom!" Sha'ul actually opens up this section with a very nice blessing upon all the Galatians.

1:4 This tremendous statement should remind the Galatian believers of two promises of God: 1) the suffering servant of Isaiah 53 who gave of Himself for our sins; 2) the "woman's seed" would crush the "serpent's seed" and thus the evil one would have no more power. This promise is found in Genesis 3:15.

Both of these promises are reflected in the fact that Yeshua died for our sins and crushed the evil one, Satan, who had power over us (Heb. 2:14; Col. 1:13). Therefore, Yeshua delivered us out of Satan's hand and this present evil age so that we could live an abundant life for God. Here, Sha'ul gets right to the point of the epistle. Yeshua not only died for our sins so that we could be saved, but died for our deliverance from evil. What "evil" is Sha'ul speaking about? In 5:19-21, he lists the evil deeds of the flesh: adultery, fornication, uncleanness, lasciviousness, idolatry, witchcraft, hatred, variance, emulations, wrath, strife, seditions, heresies, envying, murders, drunkenness, reveling, and such things like these. I believe that the evil deeds of the flesh additionally include believing and following the different gospel message of the Legalizers! This evil message included putting the Galatians under the Law with the belief that the works of the Law would sanctify them!

Why is being "under the Law" a part of the present evil age? It contradicts the most important directive from Yeshua that believers walk by the Ruach Kodesh (Holy Spirit) and by faith. This is an "either or" situation that Sha'ul reveals throughout this epistle. Believers either walk by faith or walk by the works of the Law but not both.

The MJM begs to differ since Torah says that believers must be Torah observant! However, the New Covenant (New Testament) says believers cannot walk by faith and by the works of the Law at the same time. Galatians 3:12 gives the reason why: *"And the law is not of faith: but, the man that doeth them shall live in them."* This Scripture clearly states the Law is based on practicing the commandments and not based on faith! They would have to follow the Law by practicing the commandments and this is exactly what the book of Galatians says not to do.

1:5 "Glory" (*doxa*) is "... the true apprehension of God or things. The glory of God must mean His unchanging essence. Giving glory to God is ascribing to Him His full recognition." [6] Another definition states, "With reference to God, it [glory] denotes his majesty (Rom. 1:23) and his perfection, especially in relation to righteousness (Rom. 3:23). He is called the Father of glory (Eph. 1:17). The manifestation of his presence in terms of light is an occasional phenomenon." [7]

Specifically, God is glorified through the fact that His Son saved us from our sins and delivered us from the present evil age through His death on the tree and His resurrection from the dead. In general, God receives the glory from His children because of who He is. If believers of God put themselves back under the Law or under the evils of this present world or whatever takes them away from following Yeshua in faith then God is not glorified. Sha'ul reminds the Galatians that God needs to be glorified in all aspects of their lives living by faith and by faith alone.

A great example of God's glory revealed is Yeshua on the Mount of Transfiguration (Matt. 17:1-8, Luke 9:28-36). Kefa, Yochanan and Yacov (Peter, John and James) saw Yeshua's glory manifested as flashing lightning, bright and white. *Kavod* is the Hebrew equivalent to *doxa* and it also denotes, "the manifestation of light by which God revealed himself, whether in the lightning flash or in the blinding splendor that often accompanied theophanies." 8 The Rabbis of the Encyclopedia Judaica describe the *kavod* of the Lord as His divine presence revealed in an envelope of fire, brightness and radiance. 9

The point here is to show that no matter how God or His Son reveals His glory on earth, believers are to give Him praise, respect, honor and glory in return. Sha'ul may have been thinking of Ps. 29:2 as he wrote verse 5. It states: *"Give unto the Lord the glory due unto his name..."*

Sha'ul then ends verse 5 with the word "amen," a typical Jewish (and Christian) phrase that finishes many prayers. In the Jewish synagogue service, "amen" is intended to prompt a congregational response. When the cantor (prayer leader) recites a prayer (i.e. the Kaddish), "amen" can typically occur a few times within the prayer. When the cantor chants the word "amen" it is expected that the congregational response will be in the affirmative "amen."

Dr. David Stern reveals this connection with Sha'ul's expectation of the Galatians believers. He states, "The Galatians' "Amen" is a public statement of affirmation and agreement with Sha'ul's version of the good news, contrasting with the (Legalizers') version described in the following verses (Gal.1:6-9)." 10

In his opening statement of the epistle, Sha'ul recounts the good news message of Yeshua and the power that it brings in living a life free from this present evil world. This was the plain and simple truth that the Galatians were challenged to accept. Sha'ul then requests that the Galatian congregations confirm these statements with an "amen." In the next section, verses 6-10, Sha'ul contrasts the wonderful good news he shared with them to the distorted bad news the Legalizers were preaching to them. If they continued to accept the Legalizers' preaching then they were going to have to accept the consequences that came with it.

1:6 When a soldier in an Army takes a leave of absence without getting approval from the commander, they are considered to be AWOL which means absent without leave. A soldier that is AWOL is considered to be a deserter and is in much trouble with the Army. Sha'ul had considered the Galatians AWOL and was encouraging them to come back from deserting the Lord. What was the terrible action they had performed? They turned from the good news message of the grace of Yeshua to "another gospel." "Another" (*heteros)* means "of another kind." 11
Sha'ul tells the Galatians with one word that they were deserting Yeshua not for another gospel of the same kind but for another gospel of a different kind. In essence, they abandoned the good news of grace for the bad news of legalism.

Erich Kiehl informs us that before 70 AD, the Jewish rabbis had added 341 commandments, or rules, for daily life. 12 What Kiehl is trying to say is that the Jewish people not only had to follow the 613 commandments found in the Scriptures but had to additionally obey many other commandments found in the Oral Law. The Oral Law is "the authoritative interpretation of the Written Law (Torah, which is the text of the Pentateuch) which was regarded as given to Moses on Sinai, and therefore coexistent with the Written Law. This view of the Oral Law was a fundamental principle of the rabbis. The Written and Oral Laws constitute together 'two that are one." 13 The Jewish people believe that God gave Moses the Oral Law at Mt. Sinai and this Oral Law was passed on down the generations to the present. The Oral Law is viewed as equal with the Written Law. The point of this paragraph is to show that legalism and working for salvation had a stronghold on Judaism in the first century. Some within this Messianic Jewish community had a very difficult time giving up this stronghold. The present MJM has this same issue as well.

1:7 If the Galatians did not understand the idea behind the "another gospel" in verse 6, then they should completely understand in verse 7 because Sha'ul restates the point, "which is really not another." The "another gospel" that they believed in was truly not another good news message but a distorted bad news message. Dr. Stern tells us what that bad news encompassed: "It becomes clear in what follows that the particular bad news to which the Galatians have been exposed is legalism." [14] I define "legalism" as the great desire of Legalizers to put Jewish and Gentile believers back under the Law for the purpose of salvation and/or sanctification. This was the Legalizers' distorted bad news message that was disturbing the Galatians.

1:8 How serious is this Legalism problem? Sha'ul uses very strong language to show God's judgment of cursing (*anathema*) against those who preach false doctrine. The Complete Biblical Library's Dictionary states concerning *anathema*, "This solemn curse was not simply a statement of Paul's viewpoint; it was the sentence of God upon those who preach another gospel." [15] The obvious warning to the Galatians was for them to take notice of whom they were fellowshipping with.

Sha'ul's dramatic statement of cursing is similar to God's judgment of false prophets found in Deut. 18:15-22. Moses writes,

> *"The LORD thy God will raise up unto thee a Prophet from the midst of thee, of thy brethren, like unto me; unto him ye shall hearken; According to all that thou desiredst of the LORD thy God in Horeb in the day of the*

assembly, saying, Let me not hear again the voice of the LORD my God, neither let me see this great fire any more, that I die not. And the LORD said unto me, They have well spoken that which they have spoken. I will raise them up a Prophet from among their brethren, like unto thee, and will put my words in his mouth; and he shall speak unto them all that I shall command him. And it shall come to pass, that whosoever will not hearken unto my words which he shall speak in my name, I will require it of him. But the prophet, which shall presume to speak a word in my name, which I have not commanded him to speak, or that shall speak in the name of other gods, even that prophet shall die. And if thou say in thine heart, How shall we know the word which the LORD hath not spoken? When a prophet speaketh in the name of the LORD, if the thing follow not, nor come to pass, that is the thing which the LORD hath not spoken, but the prophet hath spoken it presumptuously: thou shalt not be afraid of him."

This section of Scripture is infamously believed to be fulfilled in Yeshua. Yeshua is the one and only Prophet who was like Moses and yet many of the Jewish people did not listen to Him. This is unfortunate because God will require it of them! Yeshua, the true prophet who spoke God's word is contrasted with the false prophets who speak presumptuously.

These false prophets were to be sentenced to death [by stoning] and hence understood to be accursed by God. Just as these false prophets were accursed by God in Moses' days, the false prophets/teachers were accursed by God in Sha'ul's days.

It is interesting to note that the false prophets of Deut. 18:22 struck fear into the hearts of naïve people. In Gal. 2:12, Kefa (Peter) fears the false teaching Legalizers, and withdraws his fellowship from the Gentile believers. Not only did Kefa sin but his actions (caused by fear) influenced the other Jewish believers to follow his hypocrisy. No wonder Sha'ul strongly encouraged the Galatians to forsake listening and following the Legalizers. They are the ship wreckers of faith!

1:9 This is the second time Sha'ul makes this most important statement. Not only should these false teachers be accursed in the eyes of the Galatians but they should be rejected as well. 2 John 1:9-10 states,

Whosoever transgresseth, and abideth not in the doctrine of Christ, hath not God. He that abideth in the doctrine of Christ, he hath both the Father and the Son. If there come any unto you, and bring not this doctrine, receive him not into your house, neither bid him God speed.

Yochanan (John) warns believers not to fellowship with false teachers and not to even greet them. Why? Because there are tremendous spiritual ramifications involved. 2 John 1:11 tells us, *"For he that biddeth him God speed is partaker of his evil deeds."*

Sha'ul in restating his emphatic plea with the Galatians is implying the great need for them to protect themselves from the evil teaching of the Legalizers. They should not even greet these false teachers since they would be participating in their evil deeds. Unfortunately, this also happens to the unsuspecting believers of today's MJM. Torah Observant teachers have lured them into legalism either believing they need to keep Torah to be saved or follow Torah to be sanctified. They become enthralled with their new-found Judaism and entangled in its' sinful web of deception. All of this performed because they did not heed the warnings of Sha'ul and Yochanan.

1:10 Sha'ul's obvious answer to the two questions is that he is trying to please God and not man. If he were trying to please man, then he would still be living his former life in Judaism (Gal. 1:13). He most certainly used to believe that it was necessary for Jews and Gentile converts to be circumcised and observe the Law for salvation and sanctification. However, after meeting Yeshua as the Light on the road to Damascus, Sha'ul can say in Phil. 3:7-8 with all certainty,

> *"But what things were gain to me, those I counted loss for Christ. Yea doubtless, and I count all things but loss for the Excellency of the knowledge of Christ Jesus my Lord: for whom I have suffered the loss of all things, and do count them but dung, that I may win Christ,"*

The profoundness of these statements is measured in the fact that the context is speaking of the Law! Sha'ul says in his great zeal to be righteous by following the Law (and undoubtedly the Oral Law as well), that it was worthless and counted as rubbish. He concluded in verse 9 that one could not obtain righteousness through the Law but only by faith in Yeshua. How can a Messianic Jew say such statements about the Law? Especially, since most of the Sanhedrin, rabbis and the Jewish people believed they were sanctified and saved by their own efforts in keeping the Torah. Much of today's MJM believes that if they keep Torah or are performing Jewish customs and lifestyle, they are pleasing the Lord with their good deeds and hence have obtained righteousness and/or sanctification. The fact of the Scriptures remains that no one can obtain righteousness before God by keeping Torah. The only way to please the Lord is through faith!

Sha'ul understood the message that Yeshua gave him – that He suffered and died for our sin and He was resurrected to give eternal life to all who would believe and trust in Him. This is the plain and simple truth! What do we have to do with this simple message? Respond with a heart of repentance. Yeshua said in Mark 1:15..."*repent and believe in the gospel.*" Repentance means to change one's mind. What do we have to change our minds about? Simply put, we need to change our minds about our sinful lifestyles — that we are sinners who have broken God's commandments and therefore deserve His judgment of sin which is living in Sheol for eternity out of the presence of God. We also need to change our minds about who Yeshua is and what He has done for us. Once we realize we are sinners in need of God our Savior, then we are able to take the next step of faith in trusting Yeshua as our Lord. We need to trust that He is God and He cleansed us of all of our sin (past, present and future) by dying on the tree. We also need to believe and trust in His bodily resurrection from the dead that proves He is God and that He can provide eternal salvation to all who believe in Him. Once we are able to repent and believe in the good news message of Yeshua, then He writes our names down in the Book of Life and thus we shall be saved for eternity. This is the good news message of Yeshua!

Yeshua also died so we could be free from this evil world and its' influences over us. However, there were the Legalizers teaching the Galatians the distorted bad news. They were not teaching believers to live by faith in Yeshua, to trust in Yeshua every day, to live by and walk in the Ruach (Spirit), or to give of oneself completely unto the Lord. Instead they focused on adding the commandments of the Law (and commandments of men found in the Oral Law) to belief in Yeshua for salvation. In addition, they taught the necessity of following the works of the Law for sanctification. Sha'ul strongly affirmed that these Legalizers were accursed of God and would face judgment. These are the severe consequences of changing the true gospel of Yeshua. Anyone conforming to the Legalizers' teachings would also face these consequences as well.

Chapter 3

The Good News Transforms
(1:11-24)

1:11   But I certify you, brethren, that the gospel which was preached of me is not after man.
1:12   For I neither received it of man, neither was I taught it, but by the revelation of Jesus Christ.
1:13   For ye have heard of my conversation in time past in the Jews' religion, how that beyond measure I persecuted the church of God, and wasted it:
1:14   And profited in the Jews' religion above many my equals in mine own nation, being more exceedingly zealous of the traditions of my fathers.
1:15   But when it pleased God, who separated me from my mother's womb, and called me by his grace,
1:16   To reveal his Son in me, that I might preach him among the heathen; immediately I conferred not with flesh and blood:
1:17   Neither went I up to Jerusalem to them which were apostles before me; but I went into Arabia, and returned again unto Damascus.
1:18   Then after three years I went up to Jerusalem to see Peter, and abode with him fifteen days.
1:19   But other of the apostles saw I none, save James the Lord's brother.
1:20   Now the things which I write unto you, behold, before God, I lie not.

1:21 Afterwards I came into the regions of Syria and Cilicia;
1:22 And was unknown by face unto the churches of Judaea which were in Christ:
1:23 But they had heard only, That he which persecuted us in times past now preacheth the faith which once he destroyed.
1:24 And they glorified God in me.

I remember over 30 years ago taking a class in college entitled "Western Civilization." The professor discussed the mysterious transformation of one first century man that had a great impact on the whole world. He called this man the greatest man in western civilization history. That man was Rabbi Sha'ul, the Apostle Paul. One moment Sha'ul was on the road to Damascus to round up and jail believers in Yeshua, and the next moment, he became a believer in Yeshua. Through the power of the Ruach Kodesh (Holy Spirit), he then helped to change the world. The professor could historically pinpoint the change in Sha'ul, but could not logically explain this dramatic transformation. This professor was obviously a non-believer. I sat in amazement because the professor even marveled over his lack of explanation of this great phenomenon. It is obvious though, isn't it? The professor did not understand or believe that the good news of Yeshua transforms.

In the last chapter, Sha'ul introduced a defense of his apostleship, the good news message, the Galatians' deliverance from the evil world and his amazement in their betrayal of God. In essence, they had turned from their wonderful transformation in Yeshua for a teaching steeped in bondage. Why had the Galatians gone back to the Law and put themselves back under Torah? Sha'ul does not answer that question in this section of Scripture because he already knows how alluring and beautiful Judaism can be. In verses 11-24, he found it more important in his letter to specifically defend his apostleship and ministry. In so doing, he additionally reveals that Yeshua called him out of a life in Judaism and transformed him into a good news preaching apostle.

1:11-12 It seems that the Legalizers were attacking Sha'ul's calling and commission. They were denying his apostleship, and therefore denying his message of the good news. Sha'ul makes a dramatic declaration that the Lord Himself brought him the good news message, saving him for His own good purpose. This purpose was to take the transforming good news message to the Nations. Acts 9:1-8 summarizes this wondrous transformation.

Sha'ul was so zealous for his Judaism that he hated anything that threatened his way of life. The Way (the new Jewish movement believing in Yeshua) obviously threatened Judaism enough for Sha'ul to persecute it. He received letters from the highest religious authority in the Land, the Cohen Gadol (High Priest), to destroy the Way. On his way to the synagogues in Damascus, Yeshua as a light from heaven suddenly flashed on him. Verses 5-8 reveal Yeshua's declaration of who He is and that when someone persecutes His children they actually persecute Him! Sha'ul's salvation is revealed in his obedience to Yeshua's command to enter the city of Damascus and wait for further instruction. Yeshua called Sha'ul to be His ambassador to the Jews, Gentiles and kings (9:15). Sha'ul's immediate transformation is seen in his great desire to fellowship with the very people he wanted to destroy and his proclamation of Yeshua in the synagogues (9:19-20). This transformation was quite dramatic. One day he is an evil murderous Pharisee and the next day he is a loving, kind apostle of the Lord preaching the good news message.

1:13-14 "Time past" (*pote*), when used in speaking of the past means "once or formerly." 1 This word is the key in understanding that Sha'ul's life of Judaism is a thing of the past. Once his transformation occurred all of what he held dear in Judaism was counted as rubbish when compared to his newfound faith and life in Yeshua. What exactly was counted as rubbish? He regarded performing good works (without love and faith) for salvation and sanctification and his zeal for the ancestral traditions as rubbish. Keener notes that in those days, the Jewish image of zeal was commonly rooted in the models of Phineas or the Maccabbees, who were willing to kill for God. 2 Therefore, when Sha'ul was speaking of his zealousness for Judaism and traditions, he was truly revealing his willingness to kill people for God and believed he was doing the right thing. This is even more directly stated in verse 13. Many Messianic Rabbis today believe they are doing right by God in their zealousness for Judaism and traditions. They too, like Sha'ul, are in need of Yeshua's light of truth.

These Jewish traditions spoken of by Sha'ul no doubt included living a Jewish lifestyle under the Law and the Talmud (Oral Law). The Talmud is the written version of the Oral Law supposedly given to Moses by God on Mt. Sinai and passed on down the generations to today. The Talmud, very simply stated, is a compilation of more rules, regulations and commandments to help explain and live life according to the Torah. For example, a Rabbi would say, "The Torah says to sacrifice animals for sin in the Temple. Exactly how do we do this? The Talmud explains."

Sha'ul boldly proclaims that this was his lifestyle before He met Yeshua but afterward his life was transformed into the life of an evangelist. In Phil. 3:2-6, he even proclaims how great he was within Judaism. He put confidence in the fleshly things of the Law. He was a devout and zealous Pharisee and a Jew of all Jews. Most importantly, he was seen as blameless and righteous in the eyes of his countrymen because they believed he lived according to the Torah. However, in the eyes of Yeshua, Sha'ul's righteousness gleaned through the Law was for naught. He needed righteousness by faith in Yeshua the Jewish Messiah. Something the Law could never give.

1:15 Sha'ul's transformation is a wonderful example of God's election. Sha'ul was set apart for salvation and service unto the Lord before he was even born. I have met many believers asking the question, "You don't really believe in election?" The answer they receive is profound, "Of course I do, I'm part Jewish!" The obvious implication is that all Jewish people believe (or should believe) in God's election. The Jewish people are God's *chosen* people! Therefore, how could anyone not believe in God's election? Abraham did not choose God but rather God chose Abraham to be the father of all the Jews (Gen. 12:1-3). Moses did not choose God but God chose Moses (Exo. 2-3).

Sha'ul shows the reason for God's election in Rom. 9:16: "*So then it [election] is not of him that willeth, nor of him that runneth, but of God that showeth mercy.*" God does not call or elect anyone simply because we think we are wonderful, good or great at following the Torah. God elects solely based on His mercy. God told Moses in Exo. 33:19, "*... I will be gracious to whom I will be gracious, and I will show mercy on whom I will show mercy.*" Actually, in Gal. 1:15 Sha'ul states that God called him through his "grace" (charis). Grace means "unmerited favor." Berger famously teaches on the unmerited part of grace: "People cannot earn it nor do they deserve it!" [3] The Hebrew equivalent is *chen* or *chesed*, which mean "favor and loving-kindness," respectively. God calls His people into service not based on their good works, but based on His love, His mercy, His grace and His favor for us. God called Isaiah and Jeremiah in the same way.

In Isaiah 6:1-8, we find Isaiah, after viewing the glory of the Lord of Hosts, proclaimed his own uncleanness and unworthiness. Isaiah knew that he did not deserve to be face to face with the Lord in the vision. But God had other plans for him. In verse 6, the angel touched his lips with a burning coal from the altar and pronounced him forgiven. This is God's grace in action! Once forgiven, Isaiah was ready for his commission and God simply said to go and speak the message to the people.

In Jer. 1:5-10, Jeremiah is called in much the same manner as Isaiah. God came to Jeremiah and informed him that He knew Jeremiah before his consummation. God proclaimed to Jeremiah that He had already consecrated him before he was born. Once again, this is God's grace and mercy in action. He had called Jeremiah to be a prophet to the Southern Kingdom and proclaim His word. The Lord showed Jeremiah His calling by touching his mouth and declaring that His words were now in Jeremiah's mouth.

God's election was precisely revealed through His grace to Abraham, Moses, Isaiah, Jeremiah and Sha'ul. The encouragement here is that God has called all believers to salvation and commissioned us to do a job for him. It is our duty to find out that calling and fulfill it in the power of the Ruach Kodesh.

1:16-17 God was pleased to elect, commission and transform the evil persecutor of believers into a loving, good news preaching apostle. As Sha'ul relates this message of God's election, he turns to defending God's calling him to ministry. Sha'ul reveals his lack of consulting with the Jerusalem leadership concerning his revelation with the Lord.

F.F. Bruce explains the possible reason why Sha'ul needed to defend this lack of connection with the Jerusalem apostles. He states,

> *But here he [Sha'ul] is rebutting the account which had evidently won wide circulation, that the Jerusalem leaders instructed him soon after his conversion in the principles of the gospel (including, it may have been said, the continuing requirement of circumcision), but that he broke loose from their tutelage and pursued a line of his own with his circumcision-free gospel—a line which lacked any recognizable authority.* 4

In any event, Sha'ul defends this position because the Legalizers were using some angle to get the Galatians off course. Sha'ul reveals to the Galatians that it was not man but God who called and commissioned him to preach the good news message of His grace. The implication is that they should stay the course that he laid out for them.

1:18-20 How influential were the Legalizers? Very! Sha'ul had to assure the Galatians that he was not lying in these verses. He makes certain that there were three years between his salvation experience and the first time he fellowshipped with the Jewish Apostles in Jerusalem. In his defense of his ministry, he makes clear that he did not receive the good news as tradition from the Jerusalem Apostles but from the Lord Himself. The contrast here is between the Legalizers claiming their authority from the Jerusalem Council and Sha'ul's claim that his authority comes from Yeshua.

1:21-22 Sha'ul's defense continues to the point in relating to the Galatians that none of the congregations of Judea even knew what he looked like. Dr. Stern reveals why this is important for his defense. He declares, "As further evidence that Sha'ul's version of the good news was not taught to him by others (verses 11-12), he writes that in Y'hudah [Judea], where the greatest concentration of believers was, the Messianic congregations didn't even know what he looked like, much less had they instructed him in their version of the Gospel." [5] Therefore, if these congregations had never even seen Sha'ul, then it would have been impossible for them to commission him as their ambassador for the good news.

Verse 22 reveals an interesting fact not readily known. "Churches" (ekklesiais) is found to be in the plural. There was not just one Messianic Jewish congregation found in Jerusalem but many congregations found throughout the Land. The MJM of the first century was a force to be reckoned with and yet there were many Messianic Jewish congregations scattered throughout Israel. Although Sha'ul is unknown by sight, these congregations had certainly heard about him.

1:23-24 Sha'ul's transformation from persecutor to preacher had a great effect on the Messianic Jewish community in Israel. They praised and glorified God because only He could perform such a transformation. And it does not seem in Jewish history there were many of these occurrences. Craig Keener states, "The few Jewish stories that culminated in the conversion of a persecutor always emphasized the greatness and power of God. Paul's genuine repentance would naturally produce the same response among Jewish Christians." [6] This is exactly what the Jewish and Gentile believers in Galatia were doing – praising God for His transformation of Sha'ul.

Why praise God for the good news transformation? Simply stated, it brings God the glory that He so deserves. Should not all believers give God the glory for our salvation? Should not all believers give God the glory when we live a victorious life in Yeshua? Should not all believers give God the glory when we can prove to a dying world that Yeshua changed us from wretched evil people to joyful holy believers of the Lord! Yes, the good news message of Yeshua transforms!

Chapter 4

The Truth of The Good News
(2:1-10)

2:1 Then fourteen years after I went up again to Jerusalem with Barnabas, and took Titus with me also.
2:2 And I went up by revelation, and communicated unto them that gospel which I preach among the Gentiles, but privately to them which were of reputation, lest by any means I should run, or had run, in vain.
2:3 But neither Titus, who was with me, being a Greek, was compelled to be circumcised:
2:4 And that because of false brethren unawares brought in, who came in privily to spy out our liberty which we have in Christ Jesus, that they might bring us into bondage:
2:5 To whom we gave place by subjection, no, not for an hour; that the truth of the gospel might continue with you.
2:6 But of these who seemed to be somewhat, (whatsoever they were, it maketh no matter to me: God accepteth no man's person:) for they who seemed to be somewhat in conference added nothing to me:
2:7 But contrariwise, when they saw that the gospel of the un-circumcision was committed unto me, as the gospel of the circumcision was unto Peter;

2:8 *(For he that wrought effectually in Peter to the apostleship of the circumcision, the same was mighty in me toward the Gentiles:)*
2:9 *And when James, Cephas, and John, who seemed to be pillars, perceived the grace that was given unto me, they gave to me and Barnabas the right hands of fellowship; that we should go unto the heathen, and they unto the circumcision.*
2:10 *Only they would that we should remember the poor; the same which I also was forward to do.*

Patrick Henry, one of the founding fathers of the United States of America, had a very distinctive message for Congress in one of his speeches. He famously stated, "Give me liberty or give me death!" Everyone knows that statement he made. Patrick Henry and many other Americans were willing to fight to the death for freedom. Sha'ul has a similar, distinctive message for not only first century Jewish and Gentile believers of Yeshua, but for us as well. Stern writes concerning this distinction,

> *What does make Sha'ul's message distinctive is his insistence that Gentiles do not have to become Jews in order to believe in Jesus. (Today the shoe is on the other foot: Messianic Jews are having to insist that a Jew need not become a goy [Gentile] in order to put his trust in Yeshua, the Jewish Messiah). This point, irrelevant for Jews and therefore not part of the Gospel as it was presented to them, is essential for the Gentiles; because it removes a major barrier, namely, the requirement... that Gentiles should leave one culture and join*

another. Sha'ul saw... that insistence on it was a grave danger to the truth of the Good News. [1]

In the last chapter, Sha'ul defended his ministry and apostleship by proclaiming that he was a super-Jew, the Jew of all Jews. And yet, he was willing to give up being Torah-observant and Talmud-minded for Messiah. He had given up all things including all Jewish things for Yeshua the Messiah. I believe Sha'ul was additionally comparing himself with the Legalizers. He knew exactly what the Legalizers were all about because he himself used to be one of them. They were false brethren teaching a false doctrine. Their false teaching included the need for Gentiles to become circumcised and Torah observant to be saved. Belief in Yeshua's death and resurrection was not enough. For these false teachers to become believers, they would have to give it all up for Messiah just like Sha'ul did.

The message today with the modern-day Legalizers is similar. Some Legalizers teach that believers need to be Torah-observant for salvation and many Legalizers teach that believers need to be Torah-observant for sanctification. Although this is the message heard today within the MJM; the Scriptures are very clear that the works of the Law do not bring sanctification to anyone! This is the truth of the good news message that Sha'ul shares with the Galatians.

2:1 These years are known as the 14 silent years of Sha'ul's life. The biblical accounts do not reveal much of what happened in Sha'ul's life. But we do know that he was sharing the good news message of Yeshua. In 1:21, he traveled to Syria and Cilicia, where his hometown of Tarsus was. Therefore, he went home and preached the good news message.

Then, toward the end of these silent years, Bar-Nabba (Barnabbas) called on Sha'ul to come to Antioch. The Legalizers had received a similar call to Antioch and preached their message that the new believers had to follow Torah and be circumcised to be saved (Acts 15). Sha'ul fought against them and it was decided to bring this major argument over theology to the founding fathers in Jerusalem for a presiding judgment.

2:2 Sha'ul, Bar-Nabba, Titus and the Legalizers all went up to Jerusalem to bring this major issue to the founding fathers. At first, Sha'ul met with the pillars only – Yacov (James), Cephas (Peter), and Yochanan (John). Was Sha'ul fearful that he had the wrong good news, or that the revelation that he received from Yeshua was incorrect? Absolutely not! I believe Sha'ul was concerned for how this attack against the good news message (given to him by Yeshua) would affect his own ministry to the Gentiles. Warren Wiersbe explains,

> *What he [Sha'ul] was concerned about was the future of the Gospel among the Gentiles, because this was his specific ministry from Christ. If the "pillars" sided with the Judaizers, or tried to compromise, then Paul's ministry would be in jeopardy. He wanted to get their approval before he faced the whole assembly; otherwise a three-way division could result.* 2

F.F. Bruce concurs with Wiersbe:

> *What Paul was concerned about was not the validity of his gospel (of which he had divine*

> *assurance) but its practicability. His commission was not derived from Jerusalem, but it could not be executed effectively except in fellowship with Jerusalem. A cleavage between his Gentile mission and the mother-church would be disastrous: Christ would be divided, and all the energy which Paul had devoted, and hoped to devote, to the evangelizing of the Gentile world would be frustrated. 3*

It was therefore in Sha'ul's best interests to bring the matter before the Jerusalem Council and receive their blessing of his ministry.

I believe Sha'ul had another motive in referring this matter to the Jerusalem Leaders. He was looking for the prevailing Jewish majority vote that should end the accusations against his ministry and his good news message. Craig Keener writes, "When views were disputed in the later rabbinic academies, the majority view always prevailed..." 4 Typically within Judaism, the rabbis in the academies disputed views. Many theologies were discussed, re-discussed, argued over and the majority view always won out. For example, when Rashi (1040-1105 A.D.) came out with his new idea that the suffering servant of Isaiah 53 was Israel and not the *Meshiach* (Messiah), after much discussion and argumentation he was viewed by the rabbinic at large as being *"meshugenah"* (crazy). The rabbinical majority view declared the suffering servant to be the Jewish Messiah. However, a thousand years later, Rashi's viewpoint has become the rabbi's majority viewpoint. Most of today's rabbis believe that the suffering servant is Israel and Rashi is considered one of the greatest rabbis in Judaism. Majority rule is very important in Judaism not only today but in the first century as well and Sha'ul needed this majority rule to bless his ministry.

2:3 Titus, a Gentile believer of Yeshua, filled with the Ruach Kodesh, was the perfect evidence to prove that Gentiles did not need circumcision for salvation. The Ruach had not compelled him to be circumcised. If circumcision was necessary for salvation, then the Ruach would most certainly have instructed Titus to get one. Neither did the Legalizers arguments compel Titus to receive circumcision either.

In today's body of Messiah it is very simple to understand that Gentile believers do not need to follow Torah to be saved. However, for the first century Jewish person this situation was an enigma. For the most part since Moses' days Gentiles had to join themselves with the God of Israel and become Jewish to be saved (I am speaking of the processes of salvation here). For 1,500 years, these Gentiles learned the Torah and lived by Jewish customs and lifestyle. Then along comes the Jewish Messiah and suddenly their whole world turns upside down. The very foundation of their life had been ripped out from underneath them. I can only imagine the possible statements made: "What do you mean the Gentiles do not have to be Jews anymore? How can this be, all because this Yeshua died on the tree?" Yes, it is not such a simple thing to comprehend for the Jewish people. This was a major shift in Jewish theology and practice.

However, the Jerusalem Council (in Acts 15) correctly judged the situation that Gentile believers did not need to follow the Torah for salvation. If they would abstain from certain things in their lives then they would do well in their new walk with the Lord and stay in fellowship with their Jewish brethren. This judgment as noted by Keener was revolutionary in that the Council significantly deviated on this issue from the majority views of their culture. [5] Instead of following their traditions and Torah on this issue they followed the Ruach Kodesh's leading toward freedom. The Council had a lot of *chutzpah* (fortitude, nerve) to follow through with their decision. There must have been quite an aftershock reverberating through the Jewish community at large.

2:4 The false brethren are the Legalizers. These are the wolves in sheep clothing that Yeshua warns all believers to stay away from (Matt. 7:15). They snuck into the fellowship to spy on their liberty and tried to bring them all into bondage to the Torah. In Sha'ul's plural use of "our" and "us," he thus includes himself, all the Jewish believers and Gentile believers as those being attacked by the Legalizers. Circumcision was only one of many commandments and traditions the Legalizers were using to put the Gentile and Jewish believers under bondage.

"Liberty" (*eleutheria*) means freedom. The question that begs an answer is, "Freedom from what?" Spiros Zodhiates supplies the answer: "Freedom is presented as a signal blessing of the economy of grace, which, in contrast with the OT [Old Testament] economy, is represented as including independence from religious regulations and legal restrictions. [6] In other words, Jews and Gentiles who become born again by believing in Yeshua have been made free from the bondage of the Law. The Torah Observant branch of the MJM would not believe this statement and yet the immediate context and the context of the whole book of Galatians show this to be true. Sha'ul writes in Gal. 2:19, *"For I through the law am dead to the law, that I might live unto God."* If believers want to live for God we must recognize that the Law brings us into bondage and we must die to the Law and become free in Messiah Yeshua. This is the truth of the gospel and it must remain as truth!

2:5 Sha'ul did not yield into subjection to the Legalizers at all because he already knew the truth of the good news. He wanted the Jerusalem Council's decision on the matter so that this truth would not only remain with the Galatians but be delivered to the world without the Legalizers' intrusion. The truth of the good news Sha'ul is speaking of is the fact that Jewish and Gentile believers are not required to follow Torah to be saved. J. B. Lightfoot asserts, "This expression in St. Paul's language denotes the doctrine of grace, the maintenance of Christian liberty, as opposed to the false teaching of the Judaizers." [7] Sha'ul is saying that all believers of Yeshua have freedom from the Law and can worship God as the Ruach Kodesh instructs.

The question often asked by Messianic Jews is, "Can we still follow the Law?" The answer is a resounding "Yes!" Although Sha'ul confidently states that all believers are free from the Law, this freedom that God gave us allows us to follow the Law as well. Dr. Arnold Frutchenbaum explains,

> *The biblical basis for this freedom to keep the law can be seen in the actions of Paul, the greatest exponent of freedom from the law. His vow in Acts 18:18 is based on Numbers 6:2, 5, 9 and 18. His desire to be in Jerusalem for Pentecost in Acts 20:16 is based on Deuteronomy 16:16. The strongest passage is Acts 21:17-26, where we see Paul himself, the apostle of freedom from the law, keeping the law. The believer is free from the law, but he is also free to keep parts of it.* [8]

The problem with following the Law in freedom is that the Torah Observant movement within the

MJM has lost sight of this freedom and replaced it with bondage. It truly is a matter of the heart. Is a believer following aspects of the Law being led by the Ruach or are they keeping Torah for Torah's sake? There is a fine line between these two aspects of Messianic Jewish life and living the Torah observant lifestyle can be very dangerous to one's sanctification process. Now this Torah observant idea states that all Messianic Jews and Gentiles should obey the Torah and yet Sha'ul emphatically states that this is not the truth of the good news. He strongly fought against this bondage two thousand years ago just as we should be fighting against this bondage today.

2:6 Those who are of "somewhat" (meaning 'of high reputation') are the Apostles of the Jerusalem Council. Sha'ul's statements concerning the Apostles are not trying to destroy these leaders' reputation but reveal one more time to the Galatians that God views these Apostles as equal with Sha'ul even though they are called to different peoples.

"Added nothing to me" does not mean that these leaders of high reputation from Jerusalem did not give Sha'ul money for support of his ministry. The context gives no indication that monetary support is in question. However, the context reveals Sha'ul's discussion of the good news message given to the Gentiles and the Legalizers insistence of adding obedience to the Law for salvation. After hearing Sha'ul's explanation, the Apostles confirmed Sha'ul's understanding of the good news and thus they contributed nothing in addition to that good news message.

Acts 15:19-20 reveals an interesting ending to the Jerusalem Council's meeting:

> *Wherefore my sentence is, that we trouble not them, which from among the Gentiles are turned to God: But that we write unto them,*

that they abstain from pollutions of idols, and from fornication, and from things strangled, and from blood.

Yacov took over the meeting and concluded that the new Gentile believers were not required to follow the Torah for either salvation or sanctification. However, if they could abstain from four essentials then they would do well (15:28-29). Why only these four essentials and not the whole Law? If the Gentile believers were able to follow these four rules then the Jewish believers would typically see them as being ritually clean. Henceforth, the two groups would be able to have table fellowship and even worship together as one body of Messiah (Eph. 2:13-16).

Acts 15:21 is a verse that the Torah Observant branch of the MJM uses to support their position of the need for Torah observance within the Messianic Community. It states, *"For Moses of old time hath in every city them that preach him, being read in the synagogues every sabbath day."* The problem with this position is that it contradicts the context of the whole section (15:1-20) leading up to verse 21! This context states that all people are saved through God's grace and not by the following of Torah. It is not necessary for believers to even follow Torah for sanctification. Then why mention that Moses is read on every Sabbath in every city? I believe that Yacov is saying that outside of the four essentials, the Gentile believers have liberty in their sanctification process as they listen to the Scriptures read in the synagogues. In other words, Yacov is directing the Gentile believers to be led by the Ruach in their walk with the Lord by listening to Scriptures read each week in the synagogues.

At this early stage of the development of the *ekklesia* (the body of Messiah) from 45-58 A.D., the only Scriptures available were the Tenach (the Old Covenant Scriptures). It therefore makes sense that Yacov and the Council would want the new Gentile believers to listen to God's Word read every week in the synagogues. This was the best way to hear God's Word and grow in His Word at that time in history.

2:7 As Sha'ul continues his summary statement of the Jerusalem Council's decision, he brings forth a profound statement that combats a rapidly advancing anti-Semitic teaching within today's Christian and religious communities. This teaching is called Two Covenant Theology (a.k.a. Dual Covenant Theology). The preamble of "The Willowbank Declaration on the Christian Gospel and the Jewish People" explains what this theology believes and what the dramatic effects are. It declares,

> *Some church leaders have retreated from embracing the task of evangelizing Jews as a responsibility of Christian mission. Rather, a new theology [Two Covenant Theology] is being embraced which holds that God's covenant with Israel through Abraham establishes all Jews in God's favor for all times, and so makes faith in Jesus Christ for salvation needless so far as they are concerned.* [2]

In other words, Two Covenant Theology believes that the Gentiles are under the New Covenant and have the need to believe in the good news message of Yeshua for salvation. However, Jewish people are saved under the Abrahamic and Mosaic Covenants regardless of their belief in Yeshua. The resultant effect of this theology is the belief that it is unnecessary to evangelize the Jewish people.

Sha'ul destroys any arguments that try to

support the Two Covenant Theology with just this one verse. God entrusted Sha'ul to share the good news of Yeshua with the uncircumcision (meaning the Gentiles) just as He entrusted Kefa to share the same good news of Yeshua to the circumcision (meaning the Jewish people). If Two Covenant Theology is correct then God would have made a mistake in calling Kefa to preach the good news to the Jews. If there is no good reason to preach the good news to Jewish people in this age then why would God call Kefa to do just that! Obviously, God did not make a mistake, it is the Two Covenant Theologians who made the mistake.

2:8 Sha'ul makes it clear that his apostleship is equal to Kefa's since the same Lord called them both. He reminds the Galatians that God is the One at work here and they should not believe the attacking Legalizers. This Scripture does not mean that Sha'ul should not bring the good news to the Jews or Kefa should not share the good news with the Gentiles. They are both allowed to bring the good news to everyone. But God called them to a specific people. Sha'ul, even though he was the Apostle to the Gentiles, would first go to the synagogue and the Jewish people in every city he visited (Acts 17:1-2, 10, 17).

Not only was this Sha'ul's custom to go to the Jew first then the Gentile but it was his theology as well. Rom. 1:16 states, *"For I am not ashamed of the gospel of Christ: for it is the power of God unto salvation to every one that believeth; to the Jew first, and also to the Greek."* For the Lord as well as Sha'ul, this was a priority issue and not an historical one. God effectively worked the same for Sha'ul and Kefa in their respective ministries since the good news message was the same for Jews and Gentiles (as this section of Scripture proclaims).

2:9 Keener suggests that receiving one another's right hand usually connotes a greeting or a welcome, but here it indicates an agreement or even a treaty. [10] The leaders of the movement are making an agreement believing God called Yacov, Kefa and Yochanan to the Jews and Sha'ul to the Gentiles with the exact same message of the good news. These pillars of the Jerusalem congregation heard the arguments from the Legalizers and the discussion of the Council and decided by the Ruach Kodesh that the good news message given by God to Sha'ul was equal to their own and there was absolutely nothing to add to it. Therefore, by giving Sha'ul their right hand of fellowship they were blessing his ministry to the Gentiles. Obviously, the contrast here is that the pillars did not bless the Legalizers ministry to anyone because it was clearly not the truth.

Sha'ul additionally paid the leaders of the Jerusalem congregation a compliment by calling them "pillars." J. B. Lightfoot explains "pillars" was, "A natural metaphor occurring now and then in classical writers, but commonly used by the Jews in speaking of the great teachers of the law." [11] Sha'ul regarded Yacov, Kefa and Yochanan to be the great teachers of the Scriptures to the Jewish believers in Jerusalem.

Sha'ul may have had a dual understanding to his metaphor of "pillars." In 1 Kings 7:15-22, Solomon had two pillars set up on the outside of the Temple. They were named Yachin (meaning "he shall establish") and Boaz (meaning "in it is strength"). The metaphor is obvious. The Lord was using Yacov, Kefa and Yochanan to establish and strengthen His new assembly in Jerusalem. In addition, Sha'ul called Kefa in this verse by his Aramaic name, Cephas.

2:10 The only request the pillars asked of Sha'ul was to remember the poor. Sha'ul was just as eager as Yacov, Kefa and Yochanan to help the poor Messianic Jews of the Jerusalem Congregation. In this great desire to help, Sha'ul was simply making application of the Torah. God's heart was to care for the poor. Therefore, He commands the Jewish people: *"...Thou shalt open thine hand wide unto thy brother, to thy poor, and to thy needy, in thy land"* (Deut. 15:11). Deut. 14:28-29 state that every third year the Jewish people were to bring in the tithes of their produce for the poor: the Levite, the alien, the orphan and the widow. As Sha'ul traveled to each city he would ask the congregations for their gifts for the poor believers in Jerusalem.

    The truth of the good news message is liberty. Sha'ul encourages the Galatians to stay with this truth and not be swayed to "another" good news that would put them in bondage. Specifically, he warns them of the false brethren who are the Legalizers. They are the ones who added to the good news message and tried to put Jewish and Gentile believers into bondage to the Law. Sha'ul tells the Galatians that their current situation had already been dealt with at the first Jerusalem Council. Yacov, Kefa and Yochanan did not side with the Legalizers but even recognized Sha'ul's calling and blessed his ministry of sharing the good news to the Gentiles. The obvious encouragement in this section then would be to walk in the truth of this good news and not to walk in the false teaching of bondage.

Chapter 5

The Good News Confronted
(2:11-21)

2:11 *But when Peter was come to Antioch, I withstood him to the face, because he was to be blamed.*
2:12 *For before that certain came from James, he did eat with the Gentiles: but when they were come, he withdrew and separated himself, fearing them which were of the circumcision.*
2:13 *And the other Jews dissembled likewise with him; insomuch that Barnabas also was carried away with their dissimulation.*
2:14 *But when I saw that they walked not uprightly according to the truth of the gospel, I said unto Peter before them all, If thou, being a Jew, livest after the manner of Gentiles, and not as do the Jews, why compellest thou the Gentiles to live as do the Jews?*
2:15 *We who are Jews by nature, and not sinners of the Gentiles,*
2:16 *Knowing that a man is not justified by the works of the law, but by the faith of Jesus Christ, even we have believed in Jesus Christ, that we might be justified by the faith of Christ, and not by the works of the law: for by the works of the law shall no flesh be justified.*

2:17 *But if, while we seek to be justified by Christ, we ourselves also are found sinners, is therefore Christ the minister of sin? God forbid.*
2:18 *For if I build again the things which I destroyed, I make myself a transgressor.*
2:19 *For I through the law am dead to the law, that I might live unto God.*
2:20 *I am crucified with Christ: nevertheless I live; yet not I, but Christ liveth in me: and the life which I now live in the flesh I live by the faith of the Son of God, who loved me, and gave himself for me.*
2:21 *I do not frustrate the grace of God: for if righteousness come by the law, then Christ is dead in vain.*

It is one thing to gather all the leaders and congregation of Jerusalem and have a council meeting with everyone agreed that the truth of the good news does not include being Torah observant, but it is totally another thing to place this newly approved theological position into practice. As Sha'ul continues his defense of his Apostleship, he shares a wonderful example of how false brethren (the Legalizers) confront the truth of the good news and how easy it is for believers (even elders) to fall prey to their fears.

Kefa attended the Jerusalem Council and even contributed to the resulting decision that Gentile believers did not have to convert to Judaism to be saved; that is, they did not have to follow the Law and be circumcised for salvation or sanctification. Although he knew the dictate from the Jerusalem Council, he was not able to put it into action in this instance at Antioch. He fell prey to the teachings of these Legalizers and caused others to stumble as well. Yochanan wrote the answer on how to deal with false brethren when they sneak into our congregations and try to woo the sheep away from the truth of the good news. He wrote years later in 2 John 1:9-11,

> *"Whosoever transgresseth, and abideth not in the doctrine of Christ, hath not God. He that abideth in the doctrine of Christ, he hath both the Father and the Son. If there come any unto you, and bring not this doctrine, receive him not into your house, neither bid him God speed: For he that biddeth him God speed is partaker of his evil deeds."*

With Yochanan's counsel, Kefa could have spared himself the humiliation of his hypocritical actions. Kefa did not abide by Yochanan's warning and fellowshipped with those who did not abide in the correct doctrines of Messiah. Unfortunately, once you become friends, you tend, as the Scripture says, to partake in your friends' actions which in this case were evil deeds. Kefa participated in evil actions even though he theologically knew they were not correct. Ironically, Kefa kept fellowship with the wrong group and broke fellowship with the right group.

2:11 Sha'ul's authority as an Apostle was so well founded, the he decided to publicly oppose a pillar of the Messianic Movement. [1] This confrontation, in effect, should be evidence enough that Sha'ul was equal in authority to Kefa. Sha'ul's opposition to Kefa occurred in the city of Antioch. Antioch, as Merrill Tenney reports, became the third largest city in the Roman Empire with a population, in the first century A.D., of about 500,000. A cosmopolitan city from its foundation, its inhabitants included many Jews. Antioch has an important place in the early history of Christianity. It was the center of the Jewish-Christian mission to the Gentiles (Acts 11:20; 13:1-3; 14:26-27). Sha'ul and others were sent out on missionary journeys from the congregation in Antioch. [2]

2:12 Religious Jews in the first century did not, under any circumstances, participate in table fellowship with Gentiles. Acts 10:28 goes as far as explaining that Jewish people were not even to associate with Gentiles. The reason is that the Jewish people felt they would become ritually unclean. The belief was that the Gentiles were unholy and therefore unclean. Craig Keener supports this view:

> *"Pious Jews were not supposed to engage in table fellowship with Gentiles (Acts 10:28; 11:3). The Jerusalem leaders may have agreed with with Paul on paper (in theory), but they also had to keep peace within their own Jerusalem constituency and maintain their witness to their own culture, with its rising anti-Gentile sentiments...withdrawing from table fellowship with culturally different Christians made them second class citizens, violated the unity of the church and hence insulted the cross of Christ. Although Peter and others undoubtedly claimed to oppose racism, they accommodated it on what they saw as minor points to keep peace, whereas Paul felt that any degree of racial separatism or segregation challenged the very heart of the gospel."* [3]

What Kefa did by pulling away and making himself aloof from the Gentile believers caused division within the body of Messiah. Sha'ul, on the other hand, felt that any action of racial separatism directly attacked the truth and the outworking of the good news. Wiersbe concurs that it is one thing for the Messianic Jews in the first century to defend doctrines in a council meeting, but something entirely different to put those doctrines into practice. Kefa's freedom in regard to the truth of the good news was threatened and confronted by his fear of the circumcision. 4

Why did Kefa fear the circumcision, especially since the time of Acts 15 and the action of the Jerusalem Council had put this issue to rest? Scripture does not tell us why Kefa feared the Legalizers, however, I believe their relentless attack against living by faith and grace may have had something to do with it. The Legalizers continued to teach Jewish traditions even when these traditions contradicted the Scriptures or contradicted the Jerusalem Council mandates. This is the same problem we have today in the MJM. Those who prescribe Torah observance for salvation and/or sanctification continue to do so even when it contradicts the Scriptures.

One major issue within the MJM with this verse is the phrase *"eat with the Gentiles."* The issue is whether or not Kefa kept *kosher* while he ate with the Gentile believers of the Antioch congregation. *Kosher* (or *kashrut*) means being clean or fit to eat according to biblical laws (today, *kosher* also means being clean to eat according to rabbinical laws). The MJM would say that these Gentile believers were pious God fearers and would have been already keeping *kosher* and therefore Kefa would not have eaten the dreaded *treif* (or unclean foods, i.e. pork, shrimp, lobster, etc.).

However, Acts 16:4-6 tells us that the Gentile population in these Galatian congregations was growing daily. Not all the Gentile believers would have been keeping *kosher*. Furthermore, Sha'ul was additionally sharing the decrees from the Jerusalem Council (of Acts 15) to the congregations in Galatia and asking them to observe these decrees. Stated again, the Council decided that the Gentile believers did not necessarily need to observe the Law of Moses but to preserve fellowship with Jewish believers they should abstain from four certain things. The key issue here is not the keeping of *Torah* and therefore keeping *kosher* laws, but the preservation of fellowship between Gentile and Jewish believers.

What the apostles and elders of Jerusalem were doing was creating new *halachah* as new circumstances were coming up for the universal Body of Messiah. *Halachah* means "the way to walk." Within Judaism, Rabbis developed laws to help the Jewish people live a Godly lifestyle and walk with the Lord and His commandments. The Jerusalem Council did exactly the same thing for the new Gentile believers in Antioch. They created new rules for the Gentile believers so that they could have intimate fellowship with Jewish believers and fulfill the new understanding that the two groups had become one in Messiah.

The MJM of the first century did not completely ignore the *kosher* laws. Acts 21:20-21, reveal that these Messianic Jews in Jerusalem were zealous for the Law and were observing it because of their love for Yeshua. This additionally shows that Torah observance can be properly performed if the heart behind the observance is one that follows the Ruach. However, the inclusion of Gentile believers to the Body of Messiah had a great impact on Jewish and Gentile believers' *halachah*. Preserving fellowship between Jewish and Gentile believers became more important than keeping *kosher*. Stern agrees: "The Messianic Community has not ignored them [the laws of keeping *kosher*] (see Acts 21:20-21) but rather has determined that Jewish-Gentile fellowship takes precedence over *kashrut* – just as circumcision of a boy on the eighth day takes precedence over not working on the *Shabbat* (John 7:22-23)." [5]

The outworking of this new rule would have required both groups of people to make adjustments in their lives. The Gentile believers would have to change their eating and social habits, while the Jewish believers might have to set aside their *kashrut* laws while fellowshipping with Gentile believers. This great determination gave the whole believing community freedom from the Law and freedom in God's grace for living in unity.

Defending this position that Jewish believers do not have to keep kosher is not the scope of this book. However, let us analyze one set of Scripture in which Yeshua Himself clearly reveals that eating treif (unclean foods) would not make any person (let alone a Jewish person) unclean. Mark 7:18-19 states, *"And he saith unto them, are ye so without understanding also? Do ye not perceive, that whatsoever thing from without entereth into the man, it cannot defile him; Because it entereth not into his heart, but into the belly, and goeth out into the draught, purging all meats?"* "Purging all meats" is re-written in the NASB as "declared all foods clean." The MJM believes that the "foods" spoken of here were only kosher foods. The problem with this belief is that it makes no sense within the context of the passage.

The context of Mark 7:14-23 is concerned with what causes the defilement of man. Yeshua first makes a general statement in that nothing outside the man can defile him. Then He specifically states that no foods eaten can defile a man. What truly defiles a man is all the evil that comes out of his heart. If Yeshua meant to say that "no kosher foods can defile a man" then this would be a redundant statement and would make no sense at all to the Jewish people who already know kosher foods do not defile anyone. The new revelation Yeshua is teaching here is that "no unclean foods can truly defile a man." Yeshua is saying that all foods are now considered to be ritually clean and will not cause a person to be defiled if they eat them. This declaration truly opened the door for the Jerusalem Council of Acts 15 decisions and then Sha'ul's determination here in Gal. 2:12 that it is okay for Jewish believers to eat *treif* with the Gentiles in order to preserve fellowship. This is truly what freedom in Messiah is all about. The opposite is quite okay as well. If a Jewish believer does not wish to eat *treif* with their Gentile brethren then they certainly do not have to as long as they do not cause them to stumble. For example, my family and I keep biblical kosher. However, when we are invited to eat at a Gentiles' house we politely accept their invitation with a qualification that we do not eat foods that are not biblically kosher. This usually leads to questions and explanations whereby our hosts are perfectly happy with abiding by our wishes. In this way, therefore, no one is caused to stumble and everyone is happy with our table fellowship.

2:13 Hypocrisy was frowned upon even in ancient times. Keener reports, "'Hypocrisy' or pretense was universally regarded negatively; philosophers and Jewish wisdom writers alike attacked it." [6] Since Kefa became aloof, then all the Jewish believers became aloof and joined him in his sin. Bar-nabba was one of the spiritual leaders of the congregation in Antioch (Acts 11:19-26) and even he was influenced by Kefa's hypocrisy. If the great fathers of the faith can easily slip into deception, then all believers can easily follow suit as well. We all need to keep our eyes fixed upon Yeshua and be careful in how we react to life's situations. We need to be mindful of this truth because each one of us has a great influence over people in some way. Although Bar-nabba was influenced by Kefa's sin, Sha'ul was not.

2:14 The truth of the good news is that all believers have been freed from the confines of the Law. The Law has no jurisdiction over our lives anymore and yet Kefa, Bar-nabba and the rest of the Jews allowed it to come back in their lives and judge them. Sha'ul was not going to allow this to happen for the consequences were too great.

Keener notes that, "Jewish piety demanded that reproof be given in private; for Paul to reprove Peter publicly suggests that he regarded the offense as quite serious and urgent." [7] Sha'ul went right to the hypocrisy in a quick and offensive fashion. If Kefa's goal was to convert the Gentile believers to Judaism then he was doing a poor job, that is until the Legalizers showed up. Warren Wiersbe paraphrases Sha'ul's rebuke: "You are a Jew, yet you have been living like a Gentile. Now you want the Gentiles to live like Jews. What kind of inconsistency is that?" [8]

The Greek here makes this understanding very clear. The word "livest" (zao) means "to live in any way, to pass one's life in any manner." [9] This indicates that Kefa who is Jewish was living like a Gentile and not like a Jew. If he was passing over his life like a Gentile, then he was most certainly engaged in a Gentile lifestyle such as eating treif (i.e. pork)! Actually, these actions are quite biblical. Sha'ul spoke of this same style of living in 1 Corinthians 9:19-23:

> *"For though I be free from all men, yet have I made myself servant unto all, that I might gain the more. And unto the Jews I became as a Jew, that I might gain the Jews; to them that are under the law, as under the law, that I might gain them that are under the law; to them that are without law, as without law, (being not without law to God,*

but under the law to Christ,) that I might gain them that are without law. To the weak became I as weak, that I might gain the weak: I am made all things to all men, that I might by all means save some. And this I do for the gospel's sake, that I might be partaker thereof with you."

Sha'ul tells all of us that we need to become all things to all men so that some would be saved. Sha'ul did this for the sake of the good news message that he may become a fellow partaker of it. This means that it is okay for Jewish believers to set aside their Judaism and Jewish lifestyle for the purpose of winning unsaved Gentiles to the Lord and lifting up their Gentile brethren in their sanctification walk. Under the New Covenant and Messiah's Law it is okay for a Jewish believer to eat *treif* while they are with Gentile believers. Why? So they would not cause anyone in this life to stumble.

Kefa unfortunately caused the whole Messianic Community to stumble. Not only did he stumble and sin by listening to the Legalizers, he caused the whole community to stumble, started a rift between the Gentile and Jewish believers and even proselytized for the Legalizers. David Stern boldly proclaims: "The implication is that not only had Kefa hypocritically altered his own eating habits to conform with the wishes of the Judaizers, but he was now himself proselytizing on their behalf." [10] Can you imagine that? A Jewish believer was proselytizing on behalf of the Legalizers against his own brethren.

It is amazing what some Jewish believers would do and to what lengths they would go just to be approved by Judaism. The current MJM has a great desire to become the fourth branch of Judaism. Basically, this means they desire to be accepted and approved by unsaved Jewish rabbis and leaders as a viable option to Orthodox, Conservative and Reform Judaism. Hence, they go to great lengths to accomplish their goal even if it means compromise-ing the truth concerning Yeshua. For example, Rich Robinson and Ruth Rosen reported this news in their article entitled, "The Challenge of Our Messianic Movement Part 2":

> *"Recently, a delegation from the Union of Messianic Jewish Congregations (UMJC) held a conference in Israel. In the course of their visit, they gave a generous donation to a secular Jewish organization, which caught the attention of the media. Two delegates were asked by (an admittedly hostile) reporter for the Jerusalem Post newspaper, 'So, are Jews who don't believe in Jesus doomed to hell?' The delegates responded, 'No, absolutely not,' and as a result, the article reported, 'He [Rich Nichol] said that the UMJC...does not believe that Jews who have not accepted Jesus as the Messiah are doomed to hell.' That quote touched off a furor among Israeli believers."*
> [11]

The article goes on to say that these two delegates were trying to prevent the hostile reporter from casting a bad light on Messianic Judaism. However the point here is that we as believers of Yeshua have an obligation to share the good news of Yeshua whether it is going to be received warmly or rudely rejected by our adversaries. Furthermore, we as believers of Yeshua are commanded to bring this good news to our brethren without compromising the truth. This quote clearly shows a compromise of truth.

2:15 Jewish people definitely regarded Gentiles as sinners and second class citizens. Keener explains the Jewish position: "Jewish people regarded Gentiles as different by nature because they believed that Gentiles' ancestors were not freed from the evil impulse at Sinai as Israel was." [12] Jewish people believed this falsehood in the first century and still do today. Many Jewish people today believe they are "better" than the rest of the world based on the fact that God began a covenant relationship with them at Mt. Sinai by giving them the Law. Unfortunately for most Jews, they do not realize that the Law was primarily given to show them that they were sinners and needed the Messiah to save them.

What is fascinating about Sha'ul's opening statement of verse 15 "we who are Jews by nature" reveals a confident understanding of who Jewish people really are. Today's Judaism begs to answer the age-old question, "Who is a Jew?" The answer lies within an age-old joke concerning this issue. When you have two Rabbis discussing an important issue you will always have three opinions! And so to get an answer to the question depends on the Jewish person that you ask. Books have been written, opinions have been served and yet Sha'ul and his audience clearly know "Who is a Jew?"

Sha'ul revealed these truths to the Messianic Jewish believers at Antioch to show them how treacherous their sinful acts of hypocrisy truly were. Erich Kiehl states,

> *"Paul reminded Peter (and also all the Jewish Christians present) that by nature they were*

ethnically Jewish. By birth they were true descendants of Abraham, and a part of God's covenant people (Genesis 12:1-3), and, as such, they were ethnically members of God's covenant people. The Gentiles were exactly the opposite. Because of their ethnic origins, not being descended from Abraham, they were considered by the Jews to be habitual, chronic sinners. They were completely outside the covenant relationship with God. Therefore, they could not help but live in gross sin." [13]

And yet since the time of Yeshua's death, these two groups of people had become spiritually equal before God. The Gentiles were no longer to be considered second-class citizens.

2:16 After revealing to the Messianic Jews that their separation from the Gentile believers at Antioch was a dramatic sin of hypocrisy, Sha'ul then made his strongest declaration concerning the Law that should send fear into the hearts of the MJM and anyone who is trying to be Torah observant. He declares that no man is justified by the works of the Law. Anyone who tries to be justified by their good works is only fooling themselves because in God's eyes these efforts are fruitless. Sha'ul is so emphatic about this theology that he repeats the statement three times. Why does he say the same thing three times? The answer lies in the understanding of the Greek grammar of the verb "justified" (*dikaioo*).

"Justified" (*dikaioo*) means "to declare to be just… and in relation to God and the divine Law, it means to declare righteousness, to regard as pious." [14] Sha'ul is obviously stating that anyone who wants to be declared righteous by God has to approach Him though faith in Yeshua Hameshiach (Jesus the Messiah). "Justified" is used three times in this verse and the Greek grammar shows that it is used in three different ways.

The first "justified" is in the indicative mood, present tense and middle voice. The indicative mood indicates a positive and clear-cut statement is made. Sha'ul is absolutely sure that no one can be justified by the Law. The present tense shows a continuous action in progress. Therefore, a believer in the present is continuously not justified by the works of the Law. In other words, no matter how many good works the believer performs in the present, God will not justify them. The middle voice specifies that the subject is acting in reference to himself. Here, "a man" is trying to show he is justified by his own workings of the Law. Sha'ul states this is impossible because we can only do this by faith in Yeshua. Later on in Gal. 3:6, Sha'ul even quotes Gen. 15:6 which states, *"And he [Abraham] believed in the LORD; and he counted it to him for righteousness."* Abraham did not perform the works of the Law to be declared righteous before God. He simply believed God and then was justified. If Abraham did not have to work for his righteousness then why should we have to work for ours?

The second "justified" is in the subjunctive mood, aorist tense and passive voice. The subjunctive mood indicates a doubtful or hesitant statement. Sha'ul has doubt that everyone included in the "we" are truly believers. Some of the "we" may not be believers revealed by their current action of separation from the Gentile believers. He may also be including the group of unsaved Legalizers who instigated the separation. The aorist tense reveals an action as a point in past time. Sha'ul is saying that the true believers were justified by their one past action of faith in Yeshua. In other words, Sha'ul is saying the believers were justified in the past when they acted on their faith in Yeshua for salvation. The passive voice shows the subject is the receiver of the action. These believers did not work for their justification but received their justification from God through their faith in Yeshua.

The third "justified" is in the indicative mood, future tense and passive voice. The indicative mood reveals a positive and clear-cut statement. Sha'ul is sure that no man will be justified by the works of the Law. The future tense indicates an action as a point in future time. Sha'ul is saying no man will be justified in the future by the works of the Law. The passive voice shows the subject is the receiver of the action. Here, God performs the justification upon the believer through faith and not by works of the Law.

Taken collectively, the Greek grammar in this verse emphatically reveals Sha'ul's theology on how a man can or cannot be justified. No man can be justified in the past, present or future by the works of the Law. No man can even perform good works of the Law to earn justification from God. However, a man can be justified in the past, present or future through faith in Yeshua. A man can be justified by God if he receives it from God through faith.

My question to the Torah Observant of the MJM is, "Why are you trying to become justified in God's eyes through your Torah observance when Gal. 2:16 is so clear that to be justified by God it is necessary to only have faith in Yeshua and to live by this faith and not by the works of the Law?" Heb. 11:6 encourages all believers but especially Messianic Jews to live by faith: *"And without faith it is impossible to please Him..."*

2:17   Sha'ul's question refutes the Legalizers' assumptions that Messiah is a minister of sin and that He caused many Jewish people to walk away from the Law. Kenneth Wuest reveals a logical understanding of this verse:

> *"Paul repudiates the false assumption of the Judaizers who charged that Christ is the promoter and encourager of sin in that He causes the Jew to abandon the law as a justifying agency, and in doing so, puts himself on the common plane of a Gentile whom he calls a sinner and a dog. The Judaizers argued that in view of the fact that violation of the law is sin, therefore, abandonment of the law in an effort to be justified in Christ is also sin. Thus Christ is the promoter of sin."* [15]

The Legalizers confronted the good news message of Yeshua head on. They attacked Messiah in any way they could and even attacked His followers on an emotional level. How could they give up the very Law our forefathers personally received from Hashem (means "the name" and is typically used by Jewish people instead of Yahweh) and have followed for centuries? I believe Kefa and the others were dazed and confused on how to react to the Legalizers accusations. Their actions reveal an emotional compromise of the truth of the good news based on fear. Sha'ul keeps everyone in line stating that Messiah can never be a minister of sin. His Law supersedes the Mosaic Law. Justification comes through faith in Him and not by the observing of the Law. It is that simple.

2:18 "Build again" (*oikodomeo*) means "to render or declare valid." [16] Sha'ul states in this instance that a person who tries to revalidate something that was already destroyed is sinning. "Destroyed" (*kataluo*) means "abolish, annul, and bring to an end." [17] This verb is found to be in the indicative mood, aorist tense and active voice. The Greek grammar tells us this statement is positive and clear-cut whereby the "I" is the doer of the action in the past. Whatever was destroyed was destroyed in a past event and presently is trying to be rebuilt or revived. The glaring question is, "What was brought to an end and is now trying to be rebuilt?" The context, which is quite clear, suggests that the Law and the idea (which seems to be prevalent in first century Jewish life) that justification can come through the workings of the Law was destroyed! How was the Law destroyed? By having faith in Yeshua! Wuest makes a nice application of this truth to the present example of Kefa's abandonment of his Gentile brethren. Wuest writes,

"Peter, by withdrawing from fellowship with the Gentiles, was obeying the letter of a law he knew had been set aside by God, and was ignoring its significance... Peter became a transgressor in that he, declaring by his conduct that the law was null and void, now declares valid again that which he destroyed, thus admitting his guilt in that destruction." [18]

Sha'ul's concern is for the truth of the good news. Anything that confronts and contains the good news from saving people is declared as sin. Trying to rebuild the Law and return believers to following the Law for justification purposes is a sin. The Law has been destroyed in this respect and no man should try to bring it back to life for sanctification reasons. In actuality, the Law has caused all believers to become dead to the Law and alive to God. The very opposite of what the Torah Observant of the MJM believe.

2:19 When Sha'ul writes "For I through the Law" he means "for I through trying to keep the Law." All pious Jews who are Torah observant are trying to keep or follow the Law. Sha'ul, who claimed to be the Jew of all Jews in his time, was most definitely a pious Jew trying to keep the Law and actually believed that he was obeying the Law. However, he finally recognized through a personal encounter with Yeshua what Yacov wrote years later, *"For whosoever shall keep the whole law, and yet offend in one point, he is guilty of all."* (James 2:10). Sha'ul realized that he broke the commandments and therefore broke the whole Law which caused him to not only break the Mosaic Covenant but to die to the Law.

When Sha'ul says that he is "dead to the law," he means that he ceased to have any connection to the Law. Wuest explains further, "... it [the Law] has no further claim upon or control over him. It is a law as conceived of as a body of legalistic statutes, that he has died to." [19] The idea he is conveying here is that the Law was his master but then Yeshua came into his life and became his master so that he could live a life for God. The Law is not his master anymore and he is no longer under its authority. Faith in Messiah Yeshua was the cause of Sha'ul's full and permanent fracture with the Law. Sha'ul develops this concept more in Gal. 3.

The last part of this verse makes spiritual life interesting for those who are Torah observant. Sha'ul makes it very clear that he had to die to the Law to be able to live for God. Therefore, the obvious conclusion here is that when he was living for the Law, he was not living for God! Most Torah observant believers are living for the Law believing their actions will bring salvation or sanctification. Neither belief is true nor are any of these actions the true way to live for God and please Him. The way to please Him is to die to the Law and live in faith. The decisive word that helps us to fully understand this theology is the word "that" (*hena*). *Hena* denotes purpose and generally answers the questions "Why?" Why did Sha'ul die to the Law? So that he might live to God and for God. Could he live for God following the Law? No, because it does not please God and a believer cannot be justified through keeping the Law. Sha'ul's encouragement here is for the Galatians to stop listening to the Legalizers preaching about keeping the Law and start hearing his teaching on living for God by the power of the Ruach (Spirit) through faith in Yeshua.

Even though Yeshua lived under the Law, we do not have to live under the Law. Why? Wuest explains, "The Lord Jesus lived under the law, assumed the guilt and the penalty which the human race incurred by having violated the law, and in dying under the law satisfied its requirements. Thus, He passed out of the realm where law in its legalistic aspect had control over Him." [20] Even for Yeshua, the law was His master and He had to obey all of its commands. However, He conquered the Law by not breaking any of the commandments and hence fulfilled the Law. Sha'ul's point here is that since all believers have sinned and broken the Law, we should not try to follow the Law any longer. We died to the Law and should not try to resurrect that death but should live our spiritual lives for the Lord. Why? When we become believers of Yeshua, we are all connected to His death and resurrection.

2:20 Sha'ul shows how he died to the Law specifically by dying with Messiah, who died under the penalty of the Law. Yeshua was crucified and when we believed in Him, we were crucified with Him. That's what the Scripture says. The Law's demands were satisfied and therefore had no more hold on Sha'ul. When he was crucified with Messiah, Sha'ul also died to self. This is great encouragement for all of us. We who have believed in Yeshua for salvation have then been crucified with Messiah and have died to self. We have been set free! We need to continue living our lives in this crucified manner and not resurrect our "old self" since we have died to it.

Sha'ul wrote of this same theme in Romans 6:2-14. He stated that once we were immersed (baptized) into Messiah we were immersed into His death and resurrection so that we could walk in the newness of life. Our "old man" was crucified with Messiah so that we should no longer be slaves to sin. Why? Because sin is not to be our master any longer for we are not under the Law but under grace. The Law is no longer our master but Yeshua is!

Sha'ul's point then reveals the fact that since we are not under Law but under grace living a new life of faith in the Son of God then we should freely and lovingly give up our lives for Yeshua and let Him live in us. This type of lifestyle has set aside the Mosaic Law for the new Law of Messiah (Gal. 6:2). This new Law is the Law of Love.

2:21 Sha'ul does not invalidate the grace of God like the Legalizers were doing. The Legalizers were stating that righteousness comes about by keeping the Law. If this is true, then Yeshua died needlessly. Once again Sha'ul states that righteousness does not come by following the Law but through faith in Yeshua. When you add anything to the good news message of Yeshua then you set aside or nullify the grace of God. The plain fact is this: the Legalizers were obeying God simply because the Law tells them they must. We as believers of Yeshua obey God simply because we love Yeshua!

In the second section of Gal. 2 we found the good news confronted by the Legalizers. They were desirous to bring believers of Yeshua into the bondage of the Law. Kefa feared the Legalizers and joined them in hypocrisy to the good news by staying aloof from and not keeping table fellowship with the Gentile believers of Antioch. Sha'ul recognized this action as a direct attack on the grace of God's good news and thus set everyone straight declaring that no man is justified by the works of the Law. We can only be justified by faith in Yeshua. Since He has set us free from our former lives of sin we should continue to live by that faith and not by the letter of the Law. We have died to the Law through faith in Messiah and therefore we should live our new lives in pleasing God.

Chapter 6

Righteousness Is By Faith Not By The Law
(3:1-9)

3:1 O foolish Galatians, who hath bewitched you, that ye should not obey the truth, before whose eyes Jesus Christ hath been evidently set forth, crucified among you?
3:2 This only would I learn of you, Received ye the Spirit by the works of the law, or by the hearing of faith?
3:3 Are ye so foolish? having begun in the Spirit, are ye now made perfect by the flesh?
3:4 Have ye suffered so many things in vain? if it be yet in vain.
3:5 He therefore that ministereth to you the Spirit, and worketh miracles among you, doeth he it by the works of the law, or by the hearing of faith?
3:6 Even as Abraham believed God, and it was accounted to him for righteousness.
3:7 Know ye therefore that they which are of faith, the same are the children of Abraham.

3:8 *And the scripture, foreseeing that God would justify the heathen through faith, preached before the gospel unto Abraham, saying, In thee shall all nations be blessed.*
3:9 *So then they which be of faith are blessed with faithful Abraham.*

It is an amazing and all too frequent event to watch Jewish and Gentile believers of Yeshua become so enthralled with Torah observance in the MJM that they are willing to dispose of God's grace and faith in Yeshua. Warren Wiersbe nicely summarizes this idea,

> *"For the Christian to abandon faith and grace for law and works is to lose everything exciting that the Christian can experience in his daily fellowship with the Lord. The law cannot justify the sinner (Gal. 2:16); neither can it give him righteousness (2:21). The law cannot give the gift of the Spirit (3:2), nor can it guarantee the spiritual inheritance that belongs to God's children (3:18). The law cannot give life (3:21), and the law cannot give liberty (4:8-10). Why, then, go back into the law?"* [1]

I would add one truth to Wiersbe's list: the Law cannot provide powerful miracles either (3:5). Wiersbe asks a great question that needs answering in the MJM. Why go back to a system of worship that does not please God and cannot provide exactly what God tells New Covenant believers they need to have for mature spiritual life. The book of Galatians is written to show that the Law cannot provide the righteousness we need to have. It is only obtainable through faith.

Sha'ul, in this section of chapter 3, uses two arguments to prove salvation and sanctification are by faith alone and not by the works of the Law. First, he argues from the Galatians' past personal spiritual experiences in verses 1-5. In this first argument, Sha'ul asks the Galatians six questions. Asking questions is a typical Jewish thing to do. This technique for teaching has been used by the rabbis for thousands of years. The second argument found in verses 6-9 is scriptural. It centers on one of the most important Jewish people in our history – the father of our people, *Avraham* (Abraham).

3:1 Sha'ul immediately changes his writing tone in the third chapter. In the first two chapters he was very defensive concerning his ministry. Now he goes on the offensive and calls the Galatians "foolish." "Foolish" (*anoetos*) means "foolish and senseless." [2] It does not point to their lack of intelligence or lack of belief in God like the "foolish" of Psalm 14:1-2. However, it does indicate their need of spiritual wisdom prompted by their distrust of Sha'ul's prior teachings. The Galatians had left behind grace in their delusional pursuit of following the Law. Sha'ul calls this foolish!

Not only were the Galatians foolish in their actions, they were "bewitched" as well. "Bewitched" (*baskaino*) means "hypnotized, fascinated, in a trance-like delusion." [3] Have you ever wondered why so many in the MJM are willing to give up grace and embrace false doctrine? One reason is because they have become so fascinated with the beauty of Judaism. For example, a Torah service usually involves an expensive Hebrew scroll of the Law marched around the sanctuary. Everyone views with great excitement and all are even encouraged to kiss the Torah. Within Judaism, the Torah service is definitely a sight to see! In addition, these believers hear (many for the first time) teachings from the Law about their need to be Torah observant for righteousness sake. They become so enthralled with this new teaching because they have never heard it taught in their own churches. Since they lack the knowledge of the Tenach (Old Testament) and the understanding of its connection to the New Covenant, they are easily swayed into believing this false doctrine. Many times I have heard statements from those in the Torah observant movement like, "I never knew that I was supposed to keep the Shabbat (Sabbath) on Saturday. My old pastor never taught me that before."

A second reason why Messianic believers lay aside grace for false teaching is answered by Kenneth Wuest in his commentary on Galatians. Wuest states concerning this "bewitching": "It is always true as it was with the Galatians that the act of a believer who embraces false doctrine is due to sin in his life." [4] This statement shows that these believers have a major stronghold in their spiritual lives that caused immaturity and the inability to discern false teachings. Therefore, these believers become easy targets for Hasatan (the adversary Satan) to confuse. Most of these believers put themselves under the Law thinking and believing they are doing it for their own good. Their teachers additionally reinforce this understanding. Sha'ul tells them they are foolish and have been bewitched. In verses 2-3, it seems as if he is asking these questions: "Have you not seen with your own eyes Yeshua hung on the tree? Did not God's grace through Yeshua's death and resurrection fascinate you enough? Did you not see the truth with your own eyes and now you turn away from Yeshua to the Law?"

3:2 Sha'ul continues to draw on the theme of senselessness and foolishness. He confronts the Galatians' thinking by asking the question of how they received the Ruach Kodesh (Holy Spirit). He wants them to remember how they were saved. He is basically telling them they need to get back to the basics of becoming mature in the Lord, a major doctrine that was previously taught them.

Whenever believers are having trouble with their walk with the Lord, I counsel them to get back to the basics. I call the four basics of a mature walk with the Lord the Messianic Mitzvot (good deeds). The Messianic Mitzvot are reading the Word, praying, witnessing and fellowshipping. If believers desire to be close to our Lord, they must minimally perform each of these good deeds by faith and love on a continuous basis in their lives. If they slack off then there will be problems. The Galatians had obviously slacked off in their walk with God and therefore we see Sha'ul bringing them back to reality with a rhetorical question. He knows the answer and he knows that the Galatians should know the answer as well. Actually, Sha'ul answers the question for them in verse 3. But the answer is obvious: they received the Spirit only by hearing with faith.

3:3 Sha'ul uses "foolish" a second time in describing the Galatians' understanding about their current actions. It's obvious that they began their walk with the Lord through faith in Yeshua. Sha'ul wants to know why they would abandon this newfound faith in Yeshua for the old system of working through the Law. Do they really believe they are being perfected in the flesh through the workings of the Law?

The meaning of "perfect" (*epiteleo*) is "to finish, complete, perfect." 5 First Sha'ul tells the Galatians that they became born again and started their walk with the Lord when they received the Ruach. So having begun in the Spirit, are they now going to complete their walk with the Lord by following Torah? The obvious answer, again, is no.

"Flesh" (*sarx*) means "flesh, human, mortal nature, physical life... Therefore, *sarx* signifies man's sinful nature, the seat of sinful desires and passions.

In this sense 'flesh' includes not only the physical body but the spiritual side as well." [6] Wiersbe, however, focuses on the spiritual meaning: "The word flesh here does not refer to the human body, but rather to the believer's old nature. Whatever the Bible says about "flesh" is usually negative (see Gen. 6:1-7; Rom. 7:18; John 6:63; Phil. 3:3). Since we were saved through the Spirit, and not the flesh, through faith and not law, then it is reasonable that we should continue that way." [7] This is what Sha'ul is saying to the Galatians, "Having begun in the Ruach, isn't it reasonable that you should continue to walk in the Ruach and not turn away from Him for the Law?"

Sha'ul makes it very clear that being Torah observant for sanctification sake is actually being fleshly and considered a sin. He encourages all the Galatians to repent and return to their original position of walking in the Spirit. What a wonderful encouragement for all of us in today's MJM – get back to following the Ruach and give up following the Law for the Law's sake!

3:4 Sha'ul then questions whether the Galatians' past suffering for the Lord was it in vain or not. Truly he is questioning whether they are saved or not. Why would he question their salvation since he was the one that led them to the Lord and planted the congregation in the first place? Because they were so quick to leave their newfound faith in Yeshua for following the Law. Please notice in this section of Scripture Sha'ul's method of asking these questions. It is in an "either or" format. The answer is either "by faith" or "by works of the Law" but both cannot be correct. The point here is to show that one can only receive the Ruach through faith and one can only grow mature by faith. So why go back to the Law if it cannot save you nor help you become mature in the Lord?

Sha'ul knows through personal experience that suffering is going to be a part of a believer's lifestyle as long as they desire to live a Godly life. 2 Tim. 3:12 states, *"Yea, and all that will live godly in Christ Jesus shall suffer persecution."* Sha'ul lived a godly life in Yeshua and underwent some tremendous suffering for the Lord. Some believers are actually called to suffer for Messiah. 1 Pet. 2:20-21 states, *"For what glory is it, if, when ye be buffeted for your faults, ye shall take it patiently? But if, when ye do well, and suffer for it, ye take it patiently, this is acceptable with God. For even here unto were ye called: because Christ also suffered for us, leaving us an example, that ye should follow his steps:"* Why are we called to suffer for Messiah? The plain and simple answer is that Yeshua was called to suffer for us! Sha'ul understood this call to suffering and even taught these concepts to all his new disciples as he went on his missionary journeys. Therefore, the Galatians should have known that some sort of suffering would emerge in their walk with the Lord if they desired to live Godly lives. Their original suffering for the Lord should not have been in vain and yet Sha'ul needed to ask the question due to the tremendous current circumstances of their lives.

3:5 Sha'ul asks another rhetorical question. The obvious answer is that God provides the Ruach (Spirit) and works miracles through hearing with faith and not the works of the Law. "Miracles" (*dunamis*) means "power, might, ability, force." [8] *Dunamis* is where we get our English word "dynamite" from. When "dunamis" is connected with God (as it is found in this verse) it speaks of tremendous supernatural power. In Acts 14:8-10, the Galatians were privy to the miraculous power of God when a man, lame from his mother's womb, was healed. In Acts 14:19-20, Sha'ul was stoned by the Jews of Antioch and Iconium, supposed to be dead and yet he arose and re-entered the city! Sha'ul is telling the Galatians that these miracles and others like them did not come about through believers keeping the Torah but through believers walking in faith.

In the first five verses of chapter 3, Sha'ul asks six very simple questions. At first glance, we may see these questions as unusual and wonder why Sha'ul even asked them. But I believe he was taking the Galatians back to the beginning of their salvation experiences to show them that God powerfully worked in their lives through faith and not by the works of the Law. The Galatians had most certainly quenched the Ruach Kodesh and possibly were bordering on blaspheming the Ruach by attributing God's miracles to their obedience to the Law! Sha'ul had to encourage them in a dramatic way.

3:6 In the second section of chapter 3 (verses 6-9), Sha'ul uses a scriptural argument to show that salvation and sanctification are given through faith and not works. Since the Legalizers are Jewish, Sha'ul appeals to one Jewish man greater than they, the father of all the Jewish people, as a perfect example of his theology taken right out of Torah. Wiersbe comments concerning this issue, "Since the Judaizers wanted to take the believers back into the law, Paul quotes the law! And, since they magnified the place of Abraham in their religion, Paul uses Abraham as one of his witnesses." [2]

Sha'ul uses Avraham (Abraham) as a perfect example of his theological point. Avraham and his actions should have some influence on the Galatian Jewish believers since he is the father of all the Jews and is highly revered in Judaism. Avraham believed in God when the Lord made a promise to him. God rewarded Avraham with righteousness because he trusted in Him. Avraham did not perform good works for this righteousness nor did he follow the Law for righteousness sake. Actually, Sha'ul's additional point in using Avraham as an example is to show that he could not keep Torah because Torah had yet to be written! It was not until hundreds of years later that God gave the Torah to Moshe (Moses) on Mt. Sinai.

The Greek word for "believed" (pisteuo) means "believe, have faith in, be convinced of, trust and rely on." [10] "Believed" is found in the aorist tense. This aorist tense shows a simple action occurring in the past. This tells us that one action of trust by Avraham caused the resulting reward of righteousness and not a series of good works involving faith. What was that one moment of trust? We find the answer in Genesis 15:1-6.

God makes a promise to Avraham in verse 1. First, He tells Avraham not to fear for He is his protector. Then God promises to make his reward great. Avraham replies with concern over this great reward. Since he has no son, whom can he give this great reward to in his inheritance? The reward just does not amount to much in Avraham's thinking if he has no heir to receive it. God then promises Avraham that he will have an heir even from his own loins. He takes Avraham outside of the tent and says in verse 5: *"...Look now toward heaven, and tell the stars, if thou be able to number them: and he said unto him, so shall thy seed be."* God not only promises Avraham a son, which is what Avraham asked for, but also promises him billions of descendants!

Showing Avraham His creation of billions of stars should remind him that God is not only omnipotent but faithful as well. If God has the power to create the universe out of nothing, then He certainly can bring Avraham one son and many descendants. Avraham believed and trusted in the Lord and it was reckoned to him as righteousness.

The Hebrew word for "believe" (*aman*) means "to be reliable, to be faithful, and to believe in." [11] Baker and Carpenter note that "*aman*" is found in Gen. 15:5 in a metaphorical sense. They state, "Metaphorically, the word conveys the notion of faithfulness and trustworthiness, such that one could fully depend on ...Therefore, the word can also signify... belief, in the sense of receiving something as true and sure." [12]

The idea behind this word "believe" reveals an action of Avraham's trust of God based on his understanding of who God is. This idea is further enhanced by the preposition attached to the personal pronoun (*"ba"*) of the Lord (ba YHVH) in verse 6. This construction indicates that Avraham believed in the Lord. It is obvious in the context of this passage that Avraham believed God was the faithful and omnipotent Creator of the universe. Therefore when God made a promise, Avraham knew God was powerful enough to keep it and faithful enough to bring it about. With this kind of trustworthy faith, Avraham received God's righteousness. Sha'ul's purpose in 3:1-9 is to prove to the Galatians that righteousness is by faith and not by works of the Law. Verse 6 is the summary verse of this theme which was started in 2:16-21. It is interesting to note that in Gal. 3:6, the Greek leaves out the preposition "in" and only quotes "Avraham believed God." Without checking the equivalent Hebrew wording, one could erroneously think that Avraham's belief was solely based on God's actions rather than on God's attributes as well.

3:7 "Know" is in an emphatic place in the Greek grammar. It means "know!" for sure that this is true. Know that only those who are of faith in Yeshua are truly sons or children of Avraham. Those who do not have faith but have their good works according to the Law are not the children of Avraham. Sha'ul knew exactly what he was up against when he made this statement.

Jewish people were and are today very proud of their connection to the father of all the Jews, Avraham. Some Jewish people are taught and believe they will receive automatic righteousness from the Lord simply because of their physical connection to Avraham. In other words, they believe they are righteous before the Lord simply because they are physically Avraham's offspring! Sha'ul destroys this reasoning by appealing to the Abrahamic Covenant that promises blessing not only to the Jews but to the Gentiles as well. However, Sha'ul qualifies this blessing is only given to those of the faith. Even Yeshua had an altercation with this type of Jewish mindset in John 8:31-40:

"Then said Jesus to those Jews which believed on him, If ye continue in my word, then are ye my disciples indeed; And ye shall know the truth, and the truth shall make you free.

They answered him, We be Abraham's seed, and were never in bondage to any man: how sayest thou, Ye shall be made free?

Jesus answered them, Verily, verily, I say unto you, Whosoever committeth sin is the servant of sin. And the servant abideth not in the house for ever: but the Son abideth ever. If the Son therefore shall make you free, ye shall be free indeed. I know that ye are Abraham's seed; but ye seek to kill me, because my word hath no place in you.

> *I speak that which I have seen with my Father: and ye do that which ye have seen with your father.*
>
> *They answered and said unto him, Abraham is our father. Jesus saith unto them, If ye were Abraham's children, ye would do the works of Abraham. But now ye seek to kill me, a man that hath told you the truth, which I have heard of God: this did not Abraham."*

Yeshua tells His Jewish listeners that they are truly bound to their sin and if they desire to follow Him they will have to abide in His Word. He then shares the good news message that He is the Son of God and can set them free from their sin. However, instead of appealing to God their Father for mercy, they appeal to their father Avraham! They are basically making the statement, "We are not slaves to sin, we are descendants of Avraham and we do not need you to make intercession on our behalf." Yeshua then challenges them to do the deeds of Avraham (which truly is believing in God and living by faith). Yeshua then clearly states that He is better than Avraham since he is now telling them the truth that Avraham never was able to do. Unfortunately, these Jewish people did not hear with their ears.

Yeshua is speaking of spiritual things and is saying sin causes people to be slaves to sin. Once they sin they no longer are considered to be "sons" but "slaves" of sin. Sha'ul, later in chapter 3, reveals one reason for the existence of the Law. It was given to the children of Israel to show them that they are sinners in need of a Savior. One purpose of the Law was to bring them to Yeshua the Messiah understanding that they needed to have faith to become righteous and that nothing else could help them – not even their obedience to the Law or their ethnic connection to Avraham. There is a big difference between being a physical descendant of Avraham and a spiritual descendant of Avraham. That's the whole idea here.

Keener reports that Jewish people normally applied the title "Abraham's offspring" to themselves and would never apply this designation to Gentiles. [13] But this is exactly what Sha'ul did in this verse. He applied the title to the Gentiles as well based on his understanding of the Abrahamic Covenant. However there is a qualification. They have to be believers in Yeshua. It is those who are of faith who are the children of Avraham. Sha'ul is combating the Legalizers with this argument. He is basically saying that Avraham believed in God and all those who follow his lead whether they are Jew or Gentile become children of Avraham. It is not by works but by faith.

3:8 God justified Avraham by faith. God justifies the Gentiles by faith as well. This teaching is a gigantic blow to Judaism. In general, Jewish people believe they are first class citizens in God's world because they are the chosen ones. Gentiles are second-class citizens because they are not a part of the commonwealth of Israel. Verse 8, contrary to this current Jewish belief, teaches God's truth that Jews and Gentiles are spiritually equal before God, both groups can become justified before God and both groups can become sons of Avraham in the same way. One needs only to have faith like Avraham had faith. What is fascinating here is that this idea of spiritual equality was first made known to the Jewish people through the father of the Jews about four thousand years ago. So then, why is this knowledge not a part of Jewish theology today?

The fact that God preached the good news to Avraham through one of His many promises found in Gen. 12:1-3 is amazing. When God makes a promise we can know for sure He will keep it because He is faithful and does not lie but only tells the truth. God spoke of five blessings given to Avraham.

In Gen. 12:1, we see God's first blessing of bringing Avraham to the land of Israel: *"Now the LORD had said unto Abram, Get thee out of thy country, and from thy kindred, and from thy father's house, unto a land that I will show thee."* After God instructs Avraham to leave Chaldea for the land of Israel, He announces His second blessing in verse 2. He states, *"And I will make of thee a great nation..."* This nation is, of course, the nation (people) of Israel living in the promised land of Israel. God's third blessing is found in the rest of verse 2: *"...and I will bless thee, and make thy name great; and thou shalt be a blessing:"* One evidence of this is found in Gen. 23:6 when Avraham was looking for a burial site for his beloved Sarah, the sons of Heth responded to Avraham and said, *"Hear us, my lord: thou art a mighty prince among us..."* This statement is a great compliment of Avraham, especially since he is a sojourner (sojourners were typically frowned upon in those days) in the land. He would have had to earn their respect and admiration. Obviously, God's promise was being fulfilled.

The fourth blessing is found in the first section of verse 3: *"And I will bless them that bless thee, and curse him that curseth thee..."* This blessing is not only for Avraham but also for his seed including all the Jewish people. History has made these statements come alive. Those individuals and even nations who have blessed the Jewish people have greatly been blessed by God. Those who have come against the Jewish people trying to destroy them have been cursed.

There are actually two different Hebrew words used for "curse" in this verse. Understanding this difference helps us to know how serious God is about people who curse Israel. When God said He would "curse" (*arar*) those who curse the Jewish people, He meant to "inflict or bind with a curse." [14] It is the same type of strong cursing He inflicted upon the serpent and Adam for their sin in the Garden of Eden (Gen. 3:14,17). Those who "curseth" the Jewish people has a different understanding. "Curseth" (*qalal*) is used "to describe speaking lightly of another or cursing another..." [15] This cursing can even include speaking lightly of the Jewish people. It is hard to believe, but God says He would bind a strong curse on those who even speak lightly of the Jewish people! And God is faithful to keep His promises.

God's fifth blessing found in verse 3 is the blessing quoted in our study of Gal. 3:8. He says, *"... and in thee shall all families of the earth be blessed."* God's blessing here is unconditional upon Avraham. Avraham cannot do anything to earn this blessing but can only receive it. God pronounced that through Avraham and his seed all the Gentiles of the earth would be blessed. Sha'ul tells us this blessing is none other than the good news message of Messiah Yeshua. Coupled with the second blessing, Sha'ul tells us that God was going to bless not only the Jews but also the Gentiles with the Messiah. The Jewish people should have been prepared for this since Scripture makes it clear. Isa. 49:5-6 states, *"And he [the LORD] said, It is a light thing that thou shouldest be my servant to raise up the tribes of Jacob, and to restore the preserved of Israel: I will also thee for a light to the Gentiles, that thou mayest be my salvation unto the end of the earth."* The Jewish Messiah was to be a light to the Gentiles also.

This is exactly what Sha'ul is saying in verse 8. God had a plan to bless, justify and make righteous not only the Jewish people but the Gentiles as well. He would justify and make righteous any person who had faith in Yeshua as Lord and Savior. This plan was brought to light when God preached this good news to Avraham through the five blessings in Gen. 12:1-3. It is interesting to note that later on in Gal. 3, Sha'ul discusses more details concerning the covenant promises that God gave to Avraham. It was through the Abrahamic Covenant that the New Covenant was born.

3:9 In concluding this section, Sha'ul pinpoints a key aspect in Jewish life. All Jewish people greatly desire God's blessings. Sha'ul is saying if anyone wants to be blessed right along with Avraham, if a person (whether Jew or Gentile) wants to be eternally connected with the believing Avraham, then they need to have faith in Yeshua as Messiah and Lord. Their works are not good enough in God's new system but faith alone in Yeshua alone will achieve it.

This teaching, stated again, is a difficult one for Jewish people to understand. For thousands of years, anyone who wanted to become righteous or justified before God had to become a Jew and convert to Judaism. From the time of Yeshua's death and resurrection, this conversion process was deemed unnecessary. Jewish people even today have a difficult time imagining that believing Gentiles of Yeshua have their names written in the Book of Life whereby non-believing Jewish people have their names blotted out. Fortunately, this theology was written about a long time ago and even spoken to Avraham so that the truthfulness of this matter does not rely upon the one who restates it but with the One who promised it – God!

Sha'ul's point in this section is to show these Galatians that the Scriptures foretold all of this. It is in the Tenach! They just need to read it and then make application. God showed the whole world how to receive righteousness from Him. It's by faith and not by works and this has been God's plan from the time that He called Avraham to be the father of all the Jewish people.

Verse 9 is actually the beginning of a contrast that extends through verse 14. The contrast is between two groups of people, those who have faith and those who have the Law. The first group is blessed because they have faith like Avraham. The second group lacks faith like Avraham but has the works of the Law. They are not blessed but cursed. The Law actually pronounces a curse upon those who put themselves under the Law or the works of the Law (i.e. verse 10). Therefore, the obvious question to ask the Torah observant of the MJM is, "Do you understand that you place yourself under God's curse by putting yourself back under the Law?" No truly born again believer following the Ruach Kodesh would ever want to place themselves under God's curse! So once again I ask the original question stated in the introduction of this chapter, "Why do the Torah observant go back to following the Law?" "What is it about the Law that fascinates Jewish and Gentile believers?" Why do so many of these believers abandon grace for the Law?

Besides the two answers in the introduction of this chapter, I, through my personal experience in the MJM, have gleaned three more answers (although there are probably more). First, following the Law appeals to the flesh. As the Scripture states the flesh loves to be religious. It loves to boast of its' religious accomplishments. For example, a Torah observant believer might make one or more of the following statements: "Look how I've been able to follow the Ten Commandments." "Look how Jewish I am." "Look at how many times I prayed today." "I can even pray in the Hebrew language."

Second, following the Law appeals to all the senses. Sha'ul says to walk by faith and not by sight. Many Torah observant believers enjoy to a tremendous degree the Shabbat (Sabbath) Torah service. The Torah is usually dressed up in beautiful array while an elder carefully and methodically travels around the sanctuary so that each person may kiss the Torah with either their Bible, *Siddur* (the prayer book used for liturgy), or the corner of a *tallit* (prayer shawl draped around the shoulders and neck). An elaborate service centered around the Torah scroll usually lasts many hours with reading of the Torah and Torah teaching. Many of the men dress up with *kippot* (plural form of the Jewish head covering, a.k.a. yarmulke) and *tallit.* Women usually have their own form of *tallit* which is used as a head covering for prayer. The beauty of the Torah service can and often does become a major stumbling block. Just as Christians can worship the cross instead of the One who died on it or Baptists can worship the baptismal instead of the One who was baptized, Messianic believers can worship the Torah instead of the One who wrote and fulfilled it!

Third, following the Law causes believers to become their own judge leaving God out of the equation. They actually can replace God as the Judge with themselves. Once there is a human system set up to measure their good works, then comparisons are sure to be made. The following statements can indicate this judgmental attitude: "Look how easy it is for me to follow the Law – but for so and so they are having so much trouble" and "I feel more spiritual since I became more Jewish."

Part of the problem here is the lack of discernment between blessings and being righteous. The idea of being blessed by God and feeling wonderful during a Torah service in and of itself is good. However, to believe that these feelings prove a believer is righteous before God is in error. To believe that partaking in the Torah service is helping a believer become justified before God is in error. (If in fact this believer is keeping Torah for the purpose of sanctification). Unfortunately, many in the Torah Observant group within the MJM have made this mistake and continue to live in it.

I need to make this following statement very clear. The issue here is not the actual following of the Law. Later in Gal. 3:19, this book tackles the topic of the purpose and reason for the Law and even how a New Covenant believer can fulfill it. Suffice to say that the issue is the believers' heart behind the keeping of the Law! Believers have freedom in Messiah and can follow the Law; but we had better be sure that the Ruach Kodesh is guiding us in that direction. Is the Holy Spirit the One who motivates and empowers the believer to follow the Law or is it the flesh? Much of the time there is a very fine line in determining this. So we have to be very careful. As stated earlier, it is very dangerous to try to keep the Law. Many Messianic believers have become shipwrecked in their faith because they came up short in their efforts.

Galatians is an awesome book written for Jewish and Gentile believers alike. Sha'ul wrote it to warn both Jewish and Gentile believers not to fall into the trappings of the Law or the works of the Law. The Galatians were bewitched by the Legalizers and had already started veering off the straight and narrow path of Messiah. The Greek grammar in this section (3:1-9) proves beyond a doubt that they had turned away from Yeshua and began to follow the Law for righteousness sake. Sha'ul's language use in this section is very stern. He challenges them to rely on their God given knowledge through the power of the Ruach rather than their own fleshly foolishness. Additionally, he reminds them that the only way to receive righteousness from the Father is by faith and not by the Law.

Chapter 7

Avraham's Blessing And The Law's Cursing
(3:10-18)

3:10 For as many as are of the works of the law are under the curse: for it is written, Cursed is every one that continueth not in all things which are written in the book of the law to do them.
3:11 But that no man is justified by the law in the sight of God, it is evident: for, The just shall live by faith.
3:12 And the law is not of faith: but, The man that doeth them shall live in them.
3:13 Christ hath redeemed us from the curse of the law, being made a curse for us: for it is written, Cursed is every one that hangeth on a tree:
3:14 That the blessing of Abraham might come on the Gentiles through Jesus Christ; that we might receive the promise of the Spirit through faith.
3:15 Brethren, I speak after the manner of men; Though it be but a man's covenant, yet if it be confirmed, no man disannulleth, or addeth thereto.
3:16 Now to Abraham and his seed were the promises made. He saith not, And to seeds, as of many; but as of one, And to thy seed, which is Christ.

3:17 *And this I say, that the covenant, that was confirmed before of God in Christ, the law, which was four hundred and thirty years after, cannot disannul, that it should make the promise of none effect.*
3:18 *For if the inheritance be of the law, it is no more of promise: but God gave it to Abraham by promise.*

In Gal. 3:1-9 we found the Lord appropriated righteousness to Avraham because he believed and trusted in God. All believers have become righteous because we have faith in Abraham's seed, who is Yeshua. Righteousness was, is and always will be given freely by God to those who are of faith and not to those who are of the works of the Law. Additionally, those who are of faith are blessed right along with Avraham. Gal. 3:10-18 is a continuing contrast between Avraham's blessing and the Law's cursing. The contrasting cursing is upon anyone who believes they can receive righteousness by being of the works of the Law.

3:10 There are two very important words found in the first phrase of this verse: "For as many as are of the works of the law are under the curse..." The first is the word "of" (ek). "Of" is a preposition meaning "of the source, i.e., the person or thing, out of or from which anything proceeds, is derived, or to which it pertains." 1 The Legalizers, who are Torah observant, believe they must follow the Law and be "of" the Law for salvation or sanctification sake. The Legalizers are definitely "of the works of the Law." Why? Their source for righteousness is the Law rather than Yeshua. Their faith is in following the Law instead of following Yeshua. This was Israel's sin in the first century and it continues to be Israel's sin today. It also seems that much of the MJM has followed Israel's leading. Sha'ul explained how this happened in Rom. 10:1-5.

In Rom.10:1-2, Sha'ul tells the Roman believers that his heart's desire is for the salvation of

Jewish people. Unfortunately, they lack knowledge: *"...they have a zeal of God, but not according to knowledge."* The understanding here is that although the Jewish people had a great zeal for worshipping God, they approached Him in an inappropriate way. They lacked the proper biblical understanding on how to gain righteousness. God says, *"My people are destroyed for lack of knowledge..."* (Hosea 4:6). Rom. 10:3 tells us how this occurred, *"For they being ignorant of God's righteousness, and going about to establish their own righteousness, have not submitted themselves unto the righteousness of God."* They approached God trying to establish their own righteousness through the works of the Law and not through faith like Avraham. Sha'ul says this is plain ignorance. Therefore, Israel was and still is zealously searching after God through their own power of Torah observance while lacking understanding of the true purpose of the Law. Verse 4 brings us this purpose, *"For Christ is the end [or goal] of the law for righteousness to every one that believeth."* The goal of the Law was to show that all people break the Law, are declared sinners and lack the righteousness necessary for salvation. The Law was the agent or the helper to show that all people need to have faith in the Messiah to achieve this righteousness. Verse 5 shows that the pursuit of righteousness based on Law requires complete obedience to the Law: *"For Moses describeth the righteousness which is of the law, That the man which doeth those things shall live by them."* Following the Law is based on complete obedience and not on faith. It is obviously impossible for men to accomplish such a feat. This is the point that Sha'ul argues, so why do so many try? Gal. 3:1-18 has duplicated this same truth.

    The second important word found in the first phrase of verse 10 is "under." Those who are of the works of the Law are *"under the curse."* "Under" (*hupo*) has a variety of meanings: "under, by, by means of, about, subject to." However, with the accusative case (*"curse"* is found in the accusative case) *hupo* is used both literally and figuratively. The figurative sense found in verse 10 indicates subordination. 2 The Legalizers, whose source of power is the Law, created their own righteousness through the works of the Law. Truly anyone who follows the Legalizers' teaching is of the works of the Law too. Anyone who is working to earn their righteousness by following the Law has not only placed themselves in subordination to the Law but has subjected themselves to the Law's cursing! The Torah Observant of the MJM who try to gain righteousness by the works of the Law place themselves under the curse of the Law! Once a person thinks they can really obey all the Law and desires to try then they come under the curse of the Law.

Sha'ul then quotes Scripture from the Torah to not only reveal this truth but to show the purpose of the Law. Sha'ul quotes Deut. 27:26 which is the last cursing the Levites pronounced over the Israelites after they finally entered the Land. He argues his point from the Torah because the Legalizers are trying to convince everyone to follow Torah for righteousness sake. In Deut. 27:11-26, Moshe (Moses) instructed the children of Israel, after they entered the Land, to have six of the tribes stand on Mount Gerizim to bless the people and six of the tribes stand on Mount Ebal to curse the people. If the people of Israel would listen, obey and follow the commandments of the Lord then they would be blessed. If they did not keep the Law and perform all that was in the Law then they would be cursed. The Levites pronounced the twelve curses in verses 14-26. The last curse is what Sha'ul quoted in Gal. 3:10. It says that God curses everyone who does not perform all the commandments found in the Torah. There are a total of 613!

That's a whole lot of commandments to keep perfectly!

This statement reveals God's perfect standard for mankind derived from the Law. Once a person does not obey one of the commandments they are placed under the curse whether they make atonement for their disobedience or not! Performing an animal sacrifice did not result in the lifting of the curse. Only Yeshua's sacrifice could do that. The purpose of the Law is to reveal to the Jewish people that once a person breaks a commandment that person is a sinner and is placed under the curse. The point being that each and every person will eventually break one of God's commandments and thus put themselves under the curse of the Law revealing that there truly is no hope in this system! They then needed to realize that their righteousness was not based on the works of the Law since this brought cursing instead of blessing. This, in turn, should have brought them to the point of having faith in Messiah for righteousness and therefore receive the blessing right along with Avraham.

Wiersbe reports that salvation could never come by obedience to the Law because trying to follow the Law brings a cursing. The Law demands strict obedience and this means obedience in all the commandments. The Law is not a 'religious cafeteria', where Jewish and Gentile believers can pick and choose what they want to follow in the Law. [3] When people put themselves under the Law, they have to follow all the commandments. If they break one commandment, then as Yacov said, they have broken them all (Yacov 2:10-11).

3:11 After Sha'ul uses Torah to show that there is a cursing if believers place themselves under the Law or under the works of the Law, he plainly states his theological position: *"Now that no one is justified by the Law before God is evident..."* Coupled with verse

10, this should be evidence enough that no believer should try to keep the Law for they will ultimately and permanently fail. They will not be justified by God nor receive righteousness from God through the Law. Kenneth Wuest profoundly states the reason: "The reason why obedience to the law cannot justify a sinner is that his obedience cannot pay for his sin." [4] Only faith in Yeshua can do that and once a person has it they need to never let it go.

Sha'ul continues his argument in verse 11 by using a typical Jewish technique whereby Jewish interpreters regularly linked Scriptures on the basis of key words that they shared. [5] The key words that he connects are 'righteousness' and 'faith'. Both are found in verse 6, here in verse 11 and in Habakkuk 2:4, *"...for, the just shall live by faith."*

However, Sha'ul's version is slightly different than Habakkuk's version. Hab. 2:4 states, *"...but the just will live by his faith."* The context of Habakkuk's statement is centered on the contrast of the righteous versus the proud. The proud are never satisfied, their souls are not right within them and undoubtedly they are living by sight. But the righteous are content, their souls are right within them and they live by their faith in the Lord. "Faith" (*emunah*) means "steadiness, faithfulness." [6] The righteous will live by their steadfast faithfulness in the Lord. I believe the focus should not be on the person's faith but on whom the person's faith is in! Obviously this is the Lord. If believers desire to be righteous before God then we need not be so concerned with following the letter of the Law, but be concerned that we are pleasing God through our faith which was a gift that He gave us in the first place.

In an obvious contrast to the Law, Sha'ul shows in verse 11 the way to receive righteousness and continue in righteousness is to "live by faith" and not by obedience to the Law. "Live" (*zao*) means, "to live, physically live, or a spiritual existence." [7] If believers wish to spiritually live before God in righteousness then they need to do it by faith.

3:12 Sha'ul takes his argument in a new direction as he continues to contrast faith and the Law. The word "of" (ek) is the same word found in verse 10. It was already defined as "of the source." The Law is not of the source of faith. This means that observing or keeping the Law is not based on faith. Believers do not have to have faith to follow the Law. Wuest explains it another way, "The two principles of law and of faith as a means of justification are mutually exclusive of one another. In other words, they are diametrically opposed to one another." [8] So what is the Law based upon if it is not of faith? The answer is complete obedience!

"Doeth" (*poieo*) means "to do, to perform." [9] This verb is also found in verse 10 as "to do." The Law, then, is based on doing, practicing and performing. Warren Wiersbe compares the Law with grace, "Law says, 'Do and live!' but grace says, 'Believe and live!' [10] There is a dramatic difference between these two statements. One says if a believer can keep all the Law all of the time then they will have life. However, we learned this is impossible according to verse 10. Believers who try to keep the Law are only fooling themselves and placing themselves under God's curse. The second statement shows the only way to please God is through faith. If believers live by faith, then they will have life. The word "but" reveals this contrast. Sha'ul, once again, ironically quotes from the Torah to show those who are Torah observant that God's truth is living by faith and not by the works of the Law.

Sha'ul quotes Lev. 18:5 whereby the Lord spoke to Moses and commanded him to speak to the sons of Israel these words,

"...*I am the LORD your God. After the doings*

> *of the land of Egypt, wherein ye dwelt, shall ye not do: and after the doings of the land of Canaan, whither I bring you, shall ye not do: neither shall ye walk in their ordinances. Ye shall do my judgments, and keep mine ordinances, to walk therein: I am the LORD your God. Ye shall therefore **keep** my statutes, and my judgments: which if a man **do**, he shall **live** in them: I am the LORD. (Lev. 18:2-5) [Bold emphasis is mine]*

The context reveals God's great desire for the Jewish people to be separate and different from the nations in lifestyle and worship. God tells the Jewish people to listen and obey and they will have life. "Keep" (*shamar*) means "to watch carefully over, to keep, and to observe something for a purpose." "Do" (*asah*) means "to do, to make, to accomplish, and to complete." "Live" (*chayah*) means "to be alive, to live, to keep alive." [11]

God's command was for Israel to carefully observe His commandments for the purpose of continued blessed life. However, God knew that Israel would not be able to completely keep His commands. Thus each and every Jewish person broke His commands, sinned against Him and thus broke the Mosaic Covenant. Hence they fell under the curse of the Law which has the severe penalty of spiritual death and having their names blotted out of the Book of Life. God had a dilemma: all of His beloved chosen people were cursed and their sin was ever before them. How could He solve this dilemma? Though His Son Yeshua!

3:13 Yeshua Hameshiach is the answer of course! He redeemed us from the curse of the Law. "Redeemed" (*exagorazo*) means "to redeem, deliver, buy back, rescue." It denotes "to release by paying a ransom price." While *exagorazo* refers to redemption, its meaning focuses on the price paid. [12] Since everyone sins against God by breaking one of the 613 commandments, God sees them as sinners with a broken relationship with Him and thereby incurring the curse of the Law. Yeshua, knowing all this, suffered and died so that He could redeem all believers of Him from this curse. The curse has to fall upon someone since it is written in God's Word that justice needs to be served. However, Yeshua became our substitution on the tree so that the curse upon us could be lifted and then we could live a life of freedom for Him.

It is interesting to note the classical Greek usage of *exagorazo*. The term became widely used of "buying slaves" or of "redeeming slaves" in the marketplace. [13] All people who sin are slaves to sin (Rom. 6:17). Yeshua's death on the tree redeemed us out of slavery to sin (He bought us out of slavery to sin with His broken body) and broke the curse of the Law so that we would live a glorified life of freedom from sin and the Law. He took the curse of the Law upon Himself that was to be perpetuated against us because of this substitutionary death, He became a curse for us.

Sha'ul then proves his point further by quoting from Deut. 21:22-23,

> *"And if a man has committed a sin worthy of death, and he is put to death, and you hang him on a tree, his corpse shall not hang all night on the tree, but you shall surely bury him on the same day (for he who is hanged is accused of God), so that you do not defile your land which the Lord your God gives you as an inheritance."*

Yeshua became the curse God had in store for those who committed a sin worthy of death by hanging on the tree (i.e. through crucifixion). People of the first century understood that anyone who was executed by crucifixion was under God's curse. Erich Kiehl concurs from his research, "From two of the Dead Sea Scrolls.... we know that by the Second Century B.C., anyone executed for certain religious crimes by crucifixion was understood to be under God's curse as found in Deut. 21:22,23. Paul's words reflected this understanding." [14] This is quite evident from the railing accusations of the Jewish people's understanding of the horrible death of Yeshua found in Isa. 53:4, "... *Yet we ourselves esteemed Him stricken, smitten of God, and afflicted.*" It was obviously believed that Yeshua was afflicted and struck down by God for His own grievous sins and hence came under the curse of God. Although He did come under the curse of God, His death was not for His own sins but ours.

"Tree" *(xulon)* means "wood, timber, and tree." He who "hangs on a tree" should be understood in light of the shame associated with having a guilty sinner put to death and then hung on a tree for all to see (Deut. 21:22-23 quoted above). Yeshua, although not guilty of sin and full of joy, despised this shameful way to die. Heb. 12:2 states, "... *Jesus, the author and perfecter of faith, who for the joy set before Him endured the cross,* **despising the shame**, *and has sat down at the right hand of the throne of God."*
[Bold emphasis is mine].

3:14 This verse connects Sha'ul's argument back to Avraham's blessing in verse 9. "That" *(hina)* is a conjunction that directs the meaning of this verse. *Hina* is a word that shows purpose. [15] The purpose of Messiah redeeming us from the curse of the Law was to bring the blessing of Avraham to the Gentiles (Gen. 12:3). Part of Messiah's calling was not only to bless

Jewish people but also to be a covenant and a light to the nations (Gentiles). Isa. 42:5-6 states,

> *"Thus saith God the LORD, he that created the heavens, and stretched them out; he that spread forth the earth, and that which cometh out of it; he that giveth breath unto the people upon it, and spirit to them that walk therein: I the LORD have called thee in righteousness, and will hold thine hand, and will keep thee, and give thee for a covenant of the people, for a light of the Gentiles..."*

God prophesied that the good news of the Messiah would bring light to a dying Jewish and Gentile world. Therefore, it should not have been such a big mystery when Sha'ul penned Col. 1:27, *"to whom God willed to make known what is the riches of the glory of this mystery among the Gentiles, which is Christ in you, the hope of glory."* In any event, this mystery that Gentiles too could receive the Jewish Messiah and be saved was connected to God's promise and the blessing of Avraham.

In Jewish expectation, the "blessing of Abraham" included the whole world to come. Sha'ul states that Jewish and Gentile believers have the down payment of that future world. [16] The down payment is the pledge of our inheritance, the Ruach Kodesh, who indwells us once we believe in Yeshua Hameshiach (Eph 1:13-14).

3:15 Sha'ul shifts the focus of his argument to ordinary covenant relationships made in those days. Sha'ul follows Yeshua's leading in using common real life examples to explain important theological truths. When men make a covenant between themselves they bind themselves to the terms of the covenant. After negotiating the terms and conditions of the agreement and the covenant was already enacted, there was no way to re-open the covenant to make any changes. A promise made is a promise kept. When someone makes an agreement they are bound to keep it. Yeshua said in Matt. 5:37 concerning taking an oath, *"But let your statement be, 'Yes, yes' or 'No, no'; and anything beyond these is of evil."*

A great example of men making and keeping a covenant is when Laban pursued the runaway Yacov in Gen. 31. Yacov had secretly left Laban's household with all his wives, children and livestock. After Laban catches up with Yacov, they settle their differences and begin to negotiate terms of the agreement (Gen. 31:1-42). In verses 43-55, they set up a covenant of peace between them with certain conditions placed on both men. They set up a stone pillar as witness for them and even invoked the God of Abraham to judge between them. Each man made a promise to keep the covenant before God and he did! Sha'ul uses the lessons learned through man's covenants and applies them to God. In the same way, God cannot change His mind by adding or subtracting conditions from an already ratified covenant. God made promises to Avraham and the Jewish people and He is faithful to keep them. If God were able to break His promises to the Jewish people, then what would stop Him from breaking His promises to the Body of Messiah in this age?

3:16 Sha'ul tied this section of Scripture with the prior section 3:1-8 that spoke of God bringing salvation and the Ruach to the Gentiles through faith in Yeshua and the blessing promised to Avraham. This was God's main promise (although there are many promises) of the Abrahamic Covenant that through Avraham's line the Messiah would come to bless the Gentiles, as well as the Jews, with salvation and the Ruach. God would do this through

Avraham and his seed.

"Seed" in the Greek is "sperma" and the corresponding Hebrew (found throughout the book of Genesis) is "zera." Both mean "seed" literally and "descendent" metaphorically. It is interesting to note that both words are found to be in the singular. However, many times this singular is taken to mean a collective singular such as posterity. [17] Sha'ul's point in bringing out the singular nature of "sperma" was to show that the blessing of Avraham would flow through only one of his descendants. Obviously that seed was Yeshua Hameshiach. Sha'ul's intention here was not to negate Avraham's posterity or Yeshua's spiritual posterity. For in 3:29, "seed" is definitely used of a collective singular describing all of Yeshua's Jewish and Gentile followers.

When most believers talk about the promises of God made to Avraham, the foremost promise usually discussed is that of Isaac, God's promise of a son. It is interesting to note that Avraham was an immature uncircumcised Gentile living in the flesh when Ishmael was conceived (see Gen. 16). However, Avraham was a mature circumcised Hebrew living by faith when Isaac was conceived (see Gen. 17, 21). God's promise of blessing through Avraham's seed would not be through Ishmael the son of the bondwoman, but through Isaac the son of the free woman. This understanding plays a significant factor as we study Gal. 4:21-31 where Sha'ul contrasts Sarah the free woman with Hagar the bondwoman.

3:17 Sha'ul's main point stated here is that the institution of the Law by God for the Jewish people did not negate His promises given earlier to Avraham. The Law had no effect on the fulfillment of God's promises through the Abrahamic Covenant. Nothing can cause God to change His mind about a previous promise; not even the Mosaic Covenant.

God is immutable. Sha'ul brings this point to the forefront because the Legalizers were teaching that the Gentiles needed to keep the Law for salvation and/or sanctification. They elevated the importance of the Law so that following it took precedence over God's promises of blessing to Avraham and his seed. Therefore, the Legalizers instructed the believers of Galatia (who were recipients of God's promise to Avraham) to follow the Law rather than live by faith like Avraham.

Sha'ul here clearly states that the Law came 430 years later. The question to ask is "Later than what?" The context dictates the answer must be the Avrahamic Covenant. Therefore, the Law was enacted 430 years later than the Avrahamic Covenant. However, there is a problem when we add up the numbers of years. The amount of years between the Avrahamic Covenant and the Mosaic Covenant is more than 600 years! F.F. Bruce states, "In the MT [Masoretic Text] the interval between the promise and the law was more like 645 years; in Seder 'Olam 3 the 430 years are reckoned from the covenant of Gn. 15 to the exodus." [18] In his calculations, Sha'ul may have been using Exo. 12:40-41 which states that the Jewish people lived in Egypt for exactly 430 years. However, this would set the beginning of the counting of the years at Jacob's arrival in Egypt and not with Avraham. Warren Wiersbe explains his belief, "Paul is counting from the time Jacob went into Egypt, when God appeared to him and reaffirmed the covenant (Gen. 46:1-4). The 430 years is the time from God's confirmation of His promise to Jacob until the giving of the law at Sinai." [19] Although I would note that we should not be dogmatic about any of these answers, the last one seems to be the best.

3:18 The Legalizers were teaching salvation by the promise and observance of the Law. Sha'ul countered this erroneous teaching with the truth that salvation was based solely on God's promise and not the Law. Once again we see Sha'ul's either/or argument. Salvation is either by promise or Law, but it cannot be both. In addition, the Greek grammar proves this point as Wuest proclaimed, "The words, law and promise are without the definite article, indicating that Paul is speaking of them here in their character of two opposing principles." [20]

Sha'ul introduces a new Greek word "inheritance" (*kleronomia*) in which Jewish people would be very familiar with. *Kleronomia* means, "inheritance, possession, or portion." [21] The Jewish people's long-awaited inheritance is the Land of Israel being ruled by the Messiah in the Messianic Age. This is the ultimate conclusion of God's promise to Avraham concerning the Land. However, Sha'ul's usage of "inheritance" is a metaphor for salvation and all the rewards that come with it. His point is that our salvation and future rewards are based on God's promise to bless the world through Avraham and his seed, Yeshua the Messiah. God's intention from the beginning was never to bless the world with salvation through the Law.

This section of Galatians is very clear. If believers put themselves under the Law or the works of the Law, they have put themselves under God's curse. However, if believers live by faith in Messiah then they receive the blessing of God promised to Avraham. The MJM needs to understand and make application of this truth: God brings justification to those who live by faith and not to those who obey the Law. The reason for Yeshua redeeming us from the curse of the Law was for the blessing of Avraham to pour out on believers so that we could live not under the Law but "above" the Law in the Ruach through faith. It is important for the MJM to know the Law has no effect on God's prior promises. It does not invalidate nor nullify these promises. It cannot because our redemption is not based on the Law but based on the promise.

The logical question one may ask is, "Why the Law then?" "What is the purpose of the Law?" The answer to this question is very important to our understanding of God and how He is working in this age, especially in the MJM. Our theological position concerning the Law carries great weight on many issues of our Messianic Jewish life. Therefore, we must have a proper theological position when it comes to the Law. This is the topic of the next chapter.

Chapter 8

Why The Law Then?
(3:19-29)

3:19 *Wherefore then serveth the law? It was added because of transgressions, till the seed should come to whom the promise was made; and it was ordained by angels in the hand of a mediator.*
3:20 *Now a mediator is not a mediator of one, but God is one.*
3:21 *Is the law then against the promises of God? God forbid: for if there had been a law given which could have given life, verily righteousness should have been by the law.*
3:22 *But the scripture hath concluded all under sin, that the promise by faith of Jesus Christ might be given to them that believe.*
3:23 *But before faith came, we were kept under the law, shut up unto the faith which should afterwards be revealed.*
3:24 *Wherefore the law was our schoolmaster to bring us unto Christ, that we might be justified by faith.*
3:25 *But after that faith is come, we are no longer under a schoolmaster.*

3:26 *For ye are all the children of God by faith in Christ Jesus.*
3:27 *For as many of you as have been baptized into Christ have put on Christ.*
3:28 *There is neither Jew nor Greek, there is neither bond nor free, there is neither male nor female: for ye are all one in Christ Jesus.*
3:29 *And if ye be Christ's, then are ye Abraham's seed, and heirs according to the promise.*

Thus far in chapter 3 of Galatians we have learned that the Jewish and Gentile Galatians believers were foolishly deceived by the Legalizers into believing that following the Law was justifying them before God. God's plan for salvation and sanctification was and always is through faith as Sha'ul showed us through Avraham's example. Avraham believed God and it was accounted to him as righteousness! This occurred over 600 years before the Law was ever given to the Jewish people. Sha'ul proved the blessing of Avraham was brought through Messiah Yeshua's death and resurrection. Yeshua redeemed us from the curse of the Law. Our redemption and thus, our inheritance, was never based on following the Law, but based on the promise of God given to Avraham.

Sha'ul, then, posed one of most important questions concerning the Torah observant of the MJM, "Why the Law then?" In other words this question could be rephrased, "If the Law could not bring salvation or sanctification to the Jewish people then what is the purpose of the Law?" In this section, Sha'ul gives two reasons for the purpose of the Law.
3:19 Sha'ul answers his question with a obvious statement that "it was added." What was the Law added to? The prior section 3:10-18 already gave us this answer. It was added to the promises that God gave to Avraham. Why was it added? It was added "because of transgressions." "Because of" (*karin*)

means "for, on account of, and for the sake of." [1] Therefore, the Law was added for the sake of defining and revealing sin in the Jewish people's lives. Rom. 3:19-20 concurs with this statement: *"Now we know that what things soever the law saith, it saith to them who are under the law: that every mouth may be stopped, and all the world may become guilty before God. Therefore by the deeds of the law there shall no flesh be justified in his sight: for by the law is the* **knowledge of sin***."* [Bold emphasis is mine]. The "knowledge of sin" has the same meaning as "for the sake of defining sin." The Law brought about the knowledge and the definition of sin.

Not only did the Law define and reveal sin in the Jewish people's lives but it also showed them how utterly sinful their sin truly was. Kenneth Wuest explains this additional understanding,

> *"... when the law was given, sin was seen to be, not merely the following of evil impulses, but the violation of explicit law. Thus, the exceeding sinfulness of sin was recognized by the human race, which otherwise might not have been evident. The law therefore was not given because of the existence of transgressions, but to show sin in its true light, an overstepping of what is right into the realm of what is wrong."* [2]

Rom. 7:12-13 confirms this assertion, *"Wherefore the law is holy, and the commandment holy, and just, and good. Was then that which is good made death unto me? God forbid. But sin, that it might appear sin, working death in me by that which is good; that* **sin by the**

commandment might become exceeding sinful." [Bold emphasis is mine]. The Law is holy, just and good because it is God's Word. The Law did not cause Sha'ul's death but sin caused Sha'ul's death. The Law was developed to show how evil sin is and to show that sin causes death.

Sha'ul even reveals a personal account of how the Law acted to define and reveal sin in his life and to show him how great his sin was. Rom 7:7-8 states, *"What shall we say then? Is the law sin? God forbid. Nay, I had not known sin, but by the law: for I had not known lust, except the law had said, Thou shalt not covet. But sin, taking occasion by the commandment, wrought in me all manner of concupiscence. For without the law sin was dead."* Sha'ul states that without the Law telling him he was a coveter, he would not have seen the light that he was coveting. He was the Pharisee of Pharisees, a teacher of Israel, the Jew of all Jews and yet he realized through the Law that he was just as grievous a sinner as the common folk who did not know the Torah or Tenach. Therefore, the purpose of the Law was to show Jews (and Gentiles as well) that they were sinners in need of a Savior.

Sha'ul states that the Law "...*was ordained through angels*..." was fact and yet the biblical account written in Exo. 19 does not plainly speak of angels in attendance at Mt. Sinai. Rather it speaks of "clouds" and "smoke" (Exo. 19:16, 18). How did he know that the Law was given or ordained through angels? Deut. 33:2-3 gives us the answer and indicates God was among many of His angels as He gave the Law to the Jewish people: *"And he said, The LORD came from Sinai, and rose up from Seir unto them; he shined forth from mount Paran, and he came with ten thousands of saints: from his right hand went a fiery law for them."* The phrase "with ten thousands of saints" (*merivvot kodesh*) means "with some of the holy myriads." Rashi stated, *"... God came to give the*

Torah with an escort of only some of, but not all, His myriads of holy angels." 3 Even today's Rabbis quote from Rashi who believed this verse spoke of angels assisting God.

In any event, the New Covenant clearly states the belief that angels ordained the Law to the Jewish people. Acts 7:53 states, *"Who have received the law by the disposition of angels, and have not kept it."* Heb. 2:2 asserts, *"For if the word spoken by angels was steadfast, and every transgression and disobedience received a just recompense of reward..."* So the Law was ordained through angels ... by the hand of a mediator.

"In the hand of a mediator" is an obvious reference to Moshe as he mediated the covenant between God and the Jewish people. There are too many Jewish people today, when presented with the good news message, claim they do not need a mediator between them and God. They claim they can go directly to God and hence dismiss Yeshua with the swipe of the hand. Unfortunately for them Scripture says otherwise. In the Old Covenant writings we find many mediators for the Jewish people: Moses, Joshua, Samuel, the kings, the judges, the prophets, the Levites and the *Cohen* (priests). These were all mediators in one way or another for the Jewish people. So throughout the history of the Jewish people there were mediators for the people. Why do they think today would be any different?

Verse 19 actually refutes any assertion that states there is no need for a mediator. Why? Because the Law was given by God to the Jewish people through Moshe the mediator chosen by God. Even the New Covenant was given by God to the Jewish people through Yeshua the Seed, another mediator chosen by God. The New Covenant Scriptures state that if you deny the Son then you cannot have the Father but if you acknowledge the Son then you will have the

Father as well (1 John 2:23). In John 14:6, Yeshua Himself encouraged the Jewish people of His day when He proclaimed, *"... I am the way, the truth, and the life: no man cometh unto the Father, but by me."* Therefore, it is paramount for the Jewish people to recognize they need a mediator.

The Law was added to God's promise to Avraham through the mediator Moshe *"till the seed should come."* "Till" (*achri*) when followed by the word "which" (*hou*), which is the case here in the Greek, always is used of time to mean "as long as" or "until." [4] Spiros Zodhiates also concurs that *achri hou* is a time sensitive conjunction. [5] This tiny phrase is monumental in understanding this verse! The main purpose of the Law, to reveal sin to sinners, would actually cease to exist. The seed, Yeshua, took that role when He came in His first advent. Once Yeshua came, it was not necessary to use the Law to reveal sin to sinners (although the Law can still be used in this age to reveal sin to sinners). Why? There is a more powerful influence on people to recognize their sin in the New Covenant. He is the Ruach Kodesh! In John 16:8, Yeshua tells His *talmidim* (disciples) what the Ruach will do when He comes, *"And when he is come, he will reprove the world of sin, and of righteousness, and of judgment..."*

The Ruach Kodesh sent by Yeshua and the Father took the job of the Law to convict the world of sin, righteousness and judgment. The Ruach, obviously, can do this job much better than the Law can. Is the following statement then not a biblically logical conclusion to make? Since the Mosaic Covenant was superseded by the New Covenant and the mediator changed from Moshe to Yeshua, would it not follow that the Mosaic Law was superseded by Messiah's Law? This verse alone, taken at its face value, should have a tremendous impact on the Torah Observant position within the MJM.

In summary, the Law was added to God's promises to Avraham to reveal sin and how wickedly evil sin truly is. It was given through angels at Mt. Sinai through Moshe the mediator until God's promise of Messiah Yeshua should come. The main purpose of the Law was then transferred over to the Ruach simply because He would do a better job at convicting the world of their sin and eternal position before God. Can the Ruach Kodesh use the Law to convict people of their sin? Most certainly yes! However, the idea of the Ruach's intercession is on a more personal spiritual level with the world than the Law could ever reach. However, this does not mean that the Law is dead! God forbid, since the Law is God's Word and some of it has yet to be fulfilled, it is still alive and active (Matt. 5:18).

3:20 In the Mosaic Covenant, Moshe was the mediator not of one party but two parties: God and the Jewish people. However, in the Avrahamic Covenant, God who is one did not use a mediator and gave promises to Avraham. God had no need for a mediator because He was the only one who made any promises in the covenant. Hence, at the ratification of the Avrahamic Covenant, Avraham was found to be asleep. J.B. Lightfoot agrees with this assessment: "Unlike the law, the promise is absolute and unconditional. It depends on the sole decree of God. There are not two contracting parties. There is nothing of the nature of a *stipulation*. The giver is everything, the recipient nothing. Thus the primary sense of 'one' here is numerical." [6]

So what is Sha'ul's purpose in making this comparison between these two covenants? David Stern summarized it the best, "Sha'ul's point seems to be that because the promises of the Torah are unconditional and came directly from God without a mediator, they are superior to the legal portions of the Torah, which the legalists seize on." z In other words, God's promises of the Avrahamic Covenant that were made without a mediator are superior to the legal commands of the Mosaic Covenant with Moses as the mediator. The Galatian believers needed to know and understand this truth because the Legalizers were teaching them the false gospel from the Mosaic Covenant.

The New Covenant is also introduced here since it fulfilled one of the promises of the Avrahamic Covenant. Yeshua the Seed was promised by God to come. In the New Covenant, Yeshua the Messiah is the mediator between God the Father and the Jewish people. However, Israel as a nation did not enter into an agreement with God nor did they make any promises or conditions in the covenant because they did not receive the Messianic mediator of the covenant. Therefore, God began the New Covenant without the nation of Israel and opened up the covenant to individual Jewish and Gentile people of the world. For Israel as a nation, the New Covenant will begin when Yeshua comes back and sets up the Messianic Millennial Kingdom.

3:21 Similar is 2:16 where Sha'ul states that a man is not justified by the works of the Law but through faith in Yeshua. Since the Law cannot justify anyone it cannot impart eternal life to anyone either. That is not the job of the Law. It was not designed to bring righteousness, but rather condemnation. Even though the Law brings condemnation to all who try to keep the commandments, it is important to note that the Law does not work contrary to the promises of God but in conjunction with His promises.

3:22 "The scripture" has to be talking about the Torah. The context of this section dictates this understanding. The Law here is working in conjunction with the promise in that it reveals to all people we are under sin (similar is 3:19 *"it was added because of transgressions..."*). First, all people need to realize they cannot keep all the commandments of the Law, have therefore sinned and fallen short of the glory of God (Rom. 3:23). Since we have all sinned we should therefore realize we would be harshly judged for our sin. This then should lead us to the need for a Savior. This is exactly what the promise is for – to fulfill the need for a Savior. Comparable is Rom. 3:19-20 where everyone who is under the Law has become accountable to the Lord because of their sin.

3:23 If there is any doubt that "faith" here is speaking of the Seed to come, the Greek should put that to rest. It reads *"ten pistin"* which means "the faith." Our English version interpreters tend to exclude the word "the" from this phrase. However, I believe the word "the" makes the interpretation clear in that "the faith" is talking about the one and only faith in Yeshua Hameshiach, the promised seed of Avraham.

"Kept" (*phroureo*) means to "guard and keep watch over." [8] Literally, it means a guard keeping watch over prisoners and figuratively someone or something becoming imprisoned. Before we came to faith in Yeshua, we were prisoners of our own sin with the Law guarding over us and making sure we stayed prisoners. This is why Sha'ul can say that the Law is not evil (many believers think the opposite) but holy, righteous and good (Rom. 7:12). The Law is not bad in that it causes us to sin. No! The Law is God's Word and therefore good! Our sin nature causes us to sin. The Law is our guardian to keep us prisoners to sin so that we will ultimately see the light that we cannot keep all the commandments of the Torah, that we are sinners headed to Sheol and have need for the Lord our Savior to come into our lives.

Phroureo is found to be in the indicative mood, imperfect tense and passive voice. This means that it is a positive and clear-cut statement with continuous action in the past where we are the receivers of the action. The Greek grammar is very clear in that we had no choice in the matter: the Law performed the action in that it continuously was our master and guarded over us making sure we stayed prisoners to our sin. The Law did nothing to help us escape our sin but in fact helped us to stay prisoner to our sin. This is the very reason God promised that the Seed would come. Yeshua had to come to set us free and escape from our imprisonment to sin and our guardian the Law. Not only were we kept in imprisonment under the Law, but we were "shut up" to the faith as well.

"Shut up" (*sunkleio*) means to "enclose, imprison, consign." 9 *Sunkleio* is found to be in the perfect tense which shows completed action in the past with lingering results found in the present. Prior to our salvation experience, sin caused us to be enclosed or shut up to the faith in Yeshua in the past and affected our present state of being as well. This all happened until the faith in Yeshua was finally revealed to us so that we could believe. My point of verses 21-23 is nicely summarized in the following statements:

> *"Here Paul pointed out that though the Law is in itself unable to create life in people (3:21), this does not mean that the Law acts against God's purposes. The purpose of the Law is restraint (3:23) until the revelation of faith. In this sense the Law "imprisons" us in an awareness of sin without deliverance from sin,*

until the message of faith in Jesus Christ is received and understood (3:22)." [10]

Therefore, when we came to faith in Yeshua, He broke us out of the prison of sin right past the prison guard of the Law so that we could live a life of freedom not under the Law again but above the Law and under Messiah Yeshua with the Ruach Kodesh as our guard! Going back under the Law only puts us in a position of being imprisoned by sin and condemned by the curse of the Law. Moving forward under the Messiah puts us in a position of freedom being justified by the Ruach.

3:24 This verse finishes the train of thought started in verse 21. The question of concern was whether the Law was contrary to the promises of God. The answer was and always will be "no." In addition, the Law could not impart eternal life like the promise did. However, the Law could lead us to Messiah, which is the second purpose of the Law found in chapter 3 that answers the question in verse 19, "Why the Law then?"

"Schoolmaster" (*paidagogos*) means "tutor, guide." Kenneth Wuest declares,

"The word designated a slave employed in Greek and Roman families who had general charge over a boy in the years from about 6-16. He watched over his outward behavior, and took charge over him whenever he went from home, as for instance, to school. This slave was entrusted with the moral supervision of the child. Thus the word refers to a guardian of a child in its minority rather

than to a teacher or schoolmaster." [11]

J.B. Lightfoot concurs with Wuest's analysis: "The paidagogos had the whole moral direction of the child, so that paidagogia [verb form of paidgogos] became equivalent to 'moral training,' and the idea conveyed by the term need not be restricted to any one function... thus the main idea is that of strict supervision." [12] The comparison of the Law with the "paidagogos" is obvious. The second purpose of the Law was to be our strict supervisor or guide to bring us to the saving grace of Messiah through faith. The Law showed us that we could not keep the commandments of God and therefore declared us as sinners in need of God our Savior. The Legalizers taught that the Law was necessary for life and righteousness. But Sha'ul's argument here reveals they were wrong. Only faith brings life and only faith brings righteousness.

3:25 Once again, it is unfortunate that our English translators did not see the need to include the article "the" (*tes*) which appears right before "faith." Wuest reports that "The faith" refers to the faith in the historical Messiah of the Bible. [13] Now that we have faith in Yeshua, we are no longer under the guidance of the Law. "Under" is the key to understanding this phrase. "Under" (*hupo*) has many meanings: "under, by, by means of, about, subject to." When *hupo* is employed with an accusative noun (which is the case here), it is understood to mean "subject to." Thus, *hupo* indicates subordination. [14] The idea here is that once we become believers of Yeshua we are no longer to be subjected to the Law.

Sha'ul has made it very simple to understand. Once we have become believers of Yeshua, we are no longer under the Law as our guide. Yeshua replaced this purpose of the Law. He is to be our one and only guide. The Greek grammar is quite clear and strongly indicates that the Law is no longer our guide and we should never again make it our guide. Why go back to being under the Law when we are under Yeshua and His grace? Rom. 6:14 states, *"For sin shall not have dominion over you: for ye are not under the law, but under grace."* If you put yourself back under Law then sin becomes your master again because the Law was added to reveal transgressions (3:19). If you put yourself under Yeshua and His grace, then sin and the law will not be your master but the Ruach Kodesh will be. Unfortunately there are many in the MJM all over the world who put the Law back as their guide or master after receiving Yeshua as their Messiah. Sha'ul's message must be heard and applied to our lives.

3:26 Wuest documented a writing-style variation of Sha'ul in this verse. He states, "By the change from the first person we, with its reference to the Jews, to the second person ye with its reference to his readers, both Jew and Gentile, Sha'ul shows that the wall of separation between Jew and Gentile had been broken down at the Cross, and that both Jew and Gentile become children of God in Christ Jesus." [15] Sha'ul is additionally contrasting the Galatians believers with the Legalizers basically saying, "You who believe in Yeshua are the sons of God and these unbelieving Legalizers are not." So why listen to their teaching?

In the Old Covenant Scriptures, the nation of Israel was called "the children of God" and now Sha'ul is telling the Galatians believers (and truly all believers) that they are the children of God. We achieve this grand stature with the Lord solely through faith in Yeshua. However, throughout Jewish history if a Gentile desired to become a child of God (a Jew) they would have to attend conversion classes and perform *mikveh* (water immersion) with some even desiring circumcision. Today, some Gentiles who convert to Judaism have to renounce Yeshua before they are accepted into the Jewish faith. The Legalizers were obviously teaching some of these fallacies. All that is required in God's conversion is faith in Yeshua.

3:27 This immersion (or baptism) is a spiritual one. When people believe in Yeshua as Messiah, they become believers baptized by the Ruach Kodesh into Messiah (and into the body of Messiah). Both "baptized" and "clothed" are in the aorist tense in the Greek. This means the action of the verbs took place at a point in past time. Therefore, at the moment of salvation, believers were immersed into Messiah and were clothed with Messiah. It is a done deal.

The same word for "have put on" (*enduo*) is found in many other Scriptures. Rom. 13:14 states, *"But **put** ye on the Lord Jesus Christ, and make not provision for the flesh, to fulfill the lusts thereof."* [Bold emphasis is mine]. Sha'ul encourages believers that once we have put Yeshua on we should never take Him off. The idea here is to put Him on, continue to walk in faith with Him on and never allow room for the flesh to run our lives. Col. 3:10-12 conveys the same idea, *"And have **put** on the new man, which is renewed in knowledge after the image of him that created him: Where there is neither Greek nor Jew, circumcision nor un-circumcision, Barbarian, Scythian, bond nor free: but Christ is all, and in all. **Put** on therefore, as the elect of God, holy and beloved, bowels of mercies, kindness, humbleness of mind, meekness, longsuffering..."* [Bold emphasis is mine]. In Col. 3:1-17, Sha'ul exhorts believers to put off the old self and put on the new self. The old self died and our new life is hidden in Messiah so we need to clothe ourselves with Yeshua, put on the new man and walk with the new heart Yeshua gave us. Sha'ul continues his encouragement to walk with the Lord in Eph. 6:11, **"Put** *on the whole armor of God, that ye may be able to stand against the wiles of the devil."* [Bold emphasis is mine]. If we want to be strong in the Lord and in the power of His might we need to put on the full armor of God. Without God's armor we would not be able to stand and fight against *Hasatan* (the Satan).

Sha'ul is reminding the Galatian believers of their position in Messiah: that they were immersed into Yeshua and were clothed with Yeshua. There is no need for them to fall back under the Law as the Legalizers were teaching them to do. They need to continue walking forward in the faith they started with as honored sons of God. We, too, need to remember our position in Messiah: that we are sons of God through faith in Yeshua and all of us are spiritually equal before God. God is no respecter of people. It does not matter what race we are, our social position or our gender – we are all one universal *mishpochah* (family) of God.

3:28 Quoting this verse, many Gentile believers question whether Messianic Jews should celebrate and worship in a Jewish context. Quoting this verse, many Gentile believers wonder why Messianic Jews focus on sharing the good news message of Yeshua with the Jewish people. Quoting this verse, many Gentile believers ask why they need to learn the Jewish roots of their faith. Unfortunately, these questions are based on a poor exegesis of this verse. They believe this verse teaches there is no need for any Jewish distinctive in the believers' life since "there is neither Jew nor Greek." The idea is that we should therefore all worship, witness and celebrate in the Gentile way.

Unfortunately, this verse is one of the most misquoted and misunderstood verses with believers today. If believers take this Scripture literally, then there are no longer any differences between races or genders! God forbid! We do not lose our race or gender identification because we became believers of Yeshua. Obviously, Sha'ul did not intend for this verse to be taken literally but metaphorically. Sha'ul is teaching that all believers are one in Yeshua. In the New Covenant congregations, Gentiles should not be treated as second-class citizens but treated as spiritually equal to the Jewish believers. The same is true for females. They should not be treated as second-class citizens either but as equal to males before the Lord. We are all spiritually equal before the Lord and should be working together to be unified in the congregations and not concerned with who is a Jew or Gentile, slave or free man, or male and female.

3:29 The strength of Sha'ul's argument to prove the Law does not perfect or justify anyone is grounded in God's promises given to Avraham. Verse 29 is a restatement of verse 7's proclamation that all who are of faith are sons of Avraham and not all who follow Torah are sons of Avraham. Simply stated, if you belong to Messiah then you are Avraham's offspring. "Seed" (*sperma*) is the same word used in 3:16 and 3:19 which means "descendent, offspring, or seed." However, the seed in those verses referred to the one and only seed, Yeshua the Messiah. In verse 29, the seed refers to all who believe in Yeshua.

Many Gentile believers then ask the question, "Does this mean that I am Jewish now that I am a believer?" Their understanding is deduced logically yet it is still biblically incorrect. Their logic pursues along these lines: if you are a believer of Yeshua then you are Avraham's offspring. Since you are Avraham's offspring it follows that you would be considered Jewish. However, once again Sha'ul is not speaking of physical seed but spiritual seed. All believers of Jesus are considered to be spiritual descendants of

Avraham. Therefore, Gentile believers should not call themselves "Jews" or even "spiritual Jews." It is better to use the term "Messianic Gentiles."

But what about Jewish people who do not believe in Yeshua, are they considered Avraham's seed? Biblically speaking, Jewish people are only Avraham's seed when they believe in Yeshua. Physically speaking, Jewish people are Avraham's seed. However, the seed in Gal. 3:29 is taken as spiritual seed and not physical seed. What matters most in life for Jewish people is that God would see them as spiritual seed and not only as physical seed. Rom. 2:28-29 helps us to understand this concept: *"For he is not a Jew, which is one outwardly; neither is that circumcision, which is outward in the flesh: But he is a Jew, which is one inwardly; and circumcision is that of the heart, in the spirit, and not in the letter; whose praise is not of men, but of God."* In God's eyes, a true Jew is one who is circumcised of the heart by the Ruach to believe in Yeshua. Any other kind of Jewish person is not. I believe the meaning here indicates that Jewish people do not have automatic salvation based on their ethnicity (simply because they are born Jewish). They will not be able to reply to the Lord at the Great White Throne Judgment that they should be let into the New Jerusalem based on their Jewish ethnicity and the fact that they are God's chosen people.

Unfortunately, I have encountered many not-yet-saved Jewish people who did not receive the good news message because of the fact that they were God's chosen people. Sad to say, most unsaved Jewish people do not understand what God's chosen status really means. The Jewish people were chosen to be a holy nation and kingdom of priests to reveal the wonderful good news message of the God of Israel to a dying evil world (Exo. 19:5-6; Deut. 7:6-11). Being "chosen" does not mean the Jewish people have automatic salvation. Salvation has always been based on an individual basis of faith in God and in the current dispensation, based on individual faith in Yeshua. However, there is a growing movement within Christendom that believes Jewish people can be saved under the Avrahamic Covenant and/or the Mosaic Covenant without believing in Yeshua as Lord and Savior! This false teaching is known as Dual Covenant Theology, which was discussed earlier in this book.

So why the Law then? Sha'ul tells us it was added to the Avrahamic Covenant to reveal sin and to reveal how exceedingly evil sin truly is. It was added to show the Israelites and the world that we are all sinners until the time that the Messiah would come. The Law was then not necessary to help convict the Jewish people of their sins because the Ruach would come to convict the world of sin. It was also added to be the tutor to show us that we need to be justified by faith in Yeshua as the Messiah and not continue to try to be justified by the workings of the Law.

Chapter 9

Sons Of God And Not Slaves Under The Law
(4:1-11)

4:1 Now I say, That the heir, as long as he is a child, differeth nothing from a servant, though he be lord of all;
4:2 But is under tutors and governors until the time appointed of the father.
4:3 Even so we, when we were children, were in bondage under the elements of the world:
4:4 But when the fulness of the time was come, God sent forth his Son, made of a woman, made under the law,
4:5 To redeem them that were under the law, that we might receive the adoption of sons.
4:6 And because ye are sons, God hath sent forth the Spirit of his Son into your hearts, crying, Abba, Father.
4:7 Wherefore thou art no more a servant, but a son; and if a son, then an heir of God through Christ.
4:8 Howbeit then, when ye knew not God, ye did service unto them which by nature are no gods.

4:9 *But now, after that ye have known God, or rather are known of God, how turn ye again to the weak and beggarly elements, whereunto ye desire again to be in bondage?*
4:10 *Ye observe days, and months, and times, and years.*
4:11 *I am afraid of you, lest I have bestowed upon you labour in vain.*

In chapter 1 of the book of Galatians we learned that some Galatians had quickly deserted Yeshua for a different gospel: one that included being Torah Observant for salvation and/or sanctification. Sha'ul tells them that this is completely and utterly wrong. He even warns all those who are preaching a different good news message that they are going to be "accursed" if they continue. In chapter 2, he defends his apostleship and ministry and tells all believers that we died to the Law when we received Messiah Yeshua. In chapter 3, Sha'ul calls the Galatians foolish to think that they could be justified by the works of the Law, which is what the Legalizers were teaching them. Messiah is the only one who can justify and redeem us. Sha'ul then tells us that the main purpose of the Law was to bring us to Messiah. Now that we are Messiah's children, or the sons of God, we find in the first section of chapter 4 that we should not act like slaves to the Law but act like sons of the Lord.

4:1 The idea that the Law has become our tutor to lead us to Messiah (Gal. 3:24) is now expanded. In the first century, the tutors of children were typically slaves who were given power and authority by the master (or father) of the household. Even though the child would eventually receive the inheritance and ultimately become the master, he was still viewed as similar to the slave who was in charge of him. Both tutor and child had to listen and obey the master of the household.

4:2 The child was placed under the authority of the tutor until the date set by the master. Once the set date was reached, then the child was no longer under the tutor's authority. The Greek word for "under" (*hupo*) means "place, time or subjection to authority or subordination." When used with an accusative noun in a figurative sense (which is the case here), *hupo* indicates subordination. [1] Therefore, the child was to submit to the manager's authority even though the guardian was a slave to the master.

"Tutors" (*epitropos*) is a word that means "stewards, managers, or servants with authority." [2] The tutor was a slave of the master who had authority within the household. "Governors" (*okinomos*) were the managers or stewards of the household. They were entrusted with complete control over all of the affairs of the household. [3] This shows us the governor would have been in charge of the entire household including the master's children until the date set that would release the children from the authority of the manager. Then the children can become the master over the manager.

Similar was the situation with the Jewish people and the Law. The Lord placed them under the authority of the Law until the set date. The set date was the death and resurrection of Messiah Yeshua. Once Yeshua came, faith then replaced the Law as the authority over all those who would believe.

4:3 What was true of the child in verse 1 is also true of the Jewish people. The Jewish people from the time of Mt. Sinai were held in bondage under the Law until Messiah Yeshua came to set them free. However, the "we" spoken of here specifically includes the Galatians and Sha'ul (and generally includes all believers).

Again, we find the word "under" (*hupo*) used here but it has a little different meaning. When it is used with a genitive noun (which is the case here) it indicates, "the agent from which a fact, event or action originates." [4] The agent that held people under bondage was the elemental things of their world. What are the "elemental things?" These are the basic teachings or principles of the world. The obvious elemental things of the Jewish world were of the Law. The unchanged context of the text since 3:19 has been the Law. The Law taught the Jewish people the elemental principles of life: how to live spiritually, emotional and physically.

The Law also taught that every person is a sinner in need of God the Savior. The Law was never designed to set us free from our bondage to sin but to guard over us in our bondage to sin. Additionally, the Law was to show and teach us (as the tutor taught the masters' children) that the way of escape from under the Law's bondage was through the Messiah. Sha'ul's obvious message to the Jewish and Gentile Galatians was for them not to fall back under the power and tutelage of the Law but recognize that Yeshua redeemed them from being slaves to the Law to be sons of the Lord.

4:4 Many commentators write of the "Pax Romana" or the Roman peace when they explain that the "fullness of the time came." They write about how the world was ready to receive a Savior, old religions were dying out, citizens had individual rights, roads were built to connect all cities to Rome and the soldiers kept the peace. However, this only explains the physical historical view of the completeness of time.

I believe that the "fullness of time" means that the time was right for God to begin His fulfillment of all the prophecies concerning His Son's first coming. Keener concurs, "Jewish texts often speak of the fulfillment of appointed times in history as a way of recognizing God's perfect wisdom in and sovereignty over history." [5] However, the Jewish people realized that God was in charge of human history and the

Messiah would come at His direction.

A great example of God being in charge of time is found in Leviticus 23. Here, the Lord speaks of His perfect timing for the Jewish people's worship of Him during all seven feasts called, "God's Appointed Times." These times for the Jewish people to collectively worship at the Tabernacle or Temple were God directed and God appointed. It is the same understanding with the first coming of the Son of God, Yeshua. God directed and God appointed the time and prophecy would then be fulfilled.

It is interesting to note that Judaism, ancient or current, does not have a theology concerning God's Son. There is no Son of God in Judaism because of the belief that God is one and only one. And yet there are a few verses in the Tenach that speak of God's Son. In addition to these verses, we will look at some of the prophecies concerning God's appointed time for the Messiah to appear.

Proverbs 30:4 is a stand-alone verse that compares God and His Son. Both are identified as being equally sovereign and omnipotent. It states, *"Who hath ascended up into heaven, or descended? who hath gathered the wind in his fists? who hath bound the waters in a garment? who hath established all the ends of the earth? what is his name, and what is his son's name, if thou canst tell?"* This verse is very clear in declaring that God has a Son!

Psalm 2 is a Messianic psalm that proclaims God's Son as the Messiah. In verse 7, God's Son is speaking, *"I will declare the decree: the LORD hath said unto me, Thou art my Son; this day have I begotten thee."* This Psalm is a Messianic psalm because in verses 8-9 we find the Son of God is promised the nations as an inheritance and the earth as His possession. He will break them with a rod of iron. This promise can only pertain to the Messiah who is the Son of God who will reign as King in the Messianic Millennial Kingdom! In verse 12, we are all encouraged to *"Kiss the Son, lest he be angry, and ye perish from the way, when his wrath is kindled but a little. Blessed are all they that put their trust in him."* All who trust and take refuge in the Son will be saved.

Gen. 3:15 is the first prophecy concerning the Messiah's death on the tree that takes away Hasatan's power over sin and death. Isa. 7:14 speaks of a great miracle that a child would be born to a virgin. This child's name would be *"Immanuel"* which means *"God is with us."* Therefore, this child would take on the characteristics of God. Only the Messiah who is the Son of God could do this. Isa. 9:6-7 declares that a child would be born and He would take on the character traits of the almighty God and everlasting Father. This child who would be God is declared to be the Messiah whose Kingdom would have no end of peace, justice and righteousness. Isaiah 53 proclaims that the Suffering Servant Messiah would die for the sin of the world. Dan. 9:24-27 prophesies about the Messiah coming to Israel and dying before the Second Temple and the city of Jerusalem were destroyed in 70 A.D. What a wonderful set of Scriptures to give to your Jewish friends that reveals God's perfect timing concerning the prophecy of His Son the Messiah sent forth from heaven to come to earth to die for the sins of the world to set us free from the power and mastery of the Law, sin and death.

"God sent forth His Son" means that the Son of God was sent from God's presence in heaven to earth to live a holy, sinless life ending in a suffering death for the sin of the world but only to have victory over death in the resurrection. How many unsaved Jewish people even know about this truth? Unfortunately, the answer is very few. This most important aspect that the Father sent His Son is so sorely lacking in the MJM's presentation of the good news message to the Jewish people that it is embarrassing. I hope and pray this book will have a great affect on our wonderful MJM.

"Born of a woman" has reference to the fact that the Messiah, although declared the Son of God equal to God the Father in nature and essence, would also become a human being born of a woman. Both Isa. 7:14 and 9:6-7 reveal this wonderful truth.

The little phrase "born under the Law" in verse 4 is powerful and very important to our understanding of this verse. As was noted earlier, "under" (*hupo*) means "place, time or subjection to authority or subordination." When used with an accusative noun in a figurative sense (which is the case here), *hupo* indicates subordination. Therefore, when Yeshua was born He was subjected to the authority of the Law just like all the other Jewish people were in Old Covenant times. Why is this important for us to know? Since He was in every way of life subordinate to the Law, He would have to listen and obey all of the applicable commandments in the Law. He was required by God and the Law to keep the Law. If Yeshua broke just one of the commandments, then He would be classified as a sinner and need to confess sin and sacrifice the appropriate offerings.

However, Yeshua never sinned, perfectly kept the Law and therefore fulfilled all the aspects of the Law like no else could. Unfortunately, many Messianic Jews and Gentiles try to fulfill the requirements of the Law by keeping the letter of the Law. They believe this somehow pleases God and yet the Scriptures say quite the opposite. Why is it important that Yeshua fulfill the Law? Since He was submitted to the Law, He needed the witness of the Law to prove that He was the sinless Messiah who was to come! Once the Law proved He was the sinless Messiah, He could then perfectly (and without blemish) redeem all the Jewish people who were also subjected to the same Law and yet found to be wanting.

4:5 Yeshua is the One who has given all people the possibility of redemption. The Greek word for "redeem" (*exagorazo*) means to "deliver, buy back, rescue or ransom." [6] *Exagorazo* is found to be in the subjunctive mood which indicates a doubtful or hesitant statement meaning a "maybe yes" or "maybe no" situation. This is why the word "might" is inserted in the text before "redeem" in other English versions than the KJV. This reveals that redemption is based on faith. People can only be redeemed if they truly believe and receive Yeshua Hameshiach. Therefore, they might be redeemed or they might not be redeemed depending on whether they become believers or not. Ultimately though, Yeshua has delivered, rescued and ransomed all believers from the curse and the authority of the Law.

Although Yeshua has redeemed all believers the question remains, "Who are 'those who were under the Law'?" There are some clues in this verse that help us to know. The pronoun change from "we" to "those" reveals at least that "those" are not the Galatians. "Might redeem" shows that some of these people will be redeemed and some will not based on whether they believe or not. Once again the word "under" (*hupo*) is used with an accusative noun which means "subjection to the authority of the Law." These people who are found to be "under the Law" are in subordination to the authority of the Law. The only people who are subjected to the Law are the Jewish people (and Gentile proselytes who make themselves subjected to the Law). Therefore, "those who were under the Law" were Jewish and Gentile people living under the mastery of the Law. Some of "those" people received Yeshua and became "adopted sons."

Therefore, Yeshua was born under the Law, lived under the Law, fulfilled the Law, died under the penalty/curse of the Law so that He might redeem some of the Jewish and Gentile people found to be under the Law so that we could become adopted sons of the Lord.

Denis Vinyard, who is one of the editors of the Complete Biblical Library Greek – English Dictionary, notes that "adoption" (huiothesia) concerns the believer's relationship to God (Rom. 8:23) and is defined in terms of receiving the Ruach Kodesh which affects sonship (Rom. 8:15; Gal. 4:6). Since the believer is by nature a child of wrath, he needs adoption into sonship. [7] Once the blood of Yeshua redeems a person they receive the promise of the Ruach Kodesh and hence begin a father/child relationship. Furthermore, Yeshua died and resurrected not only for us to become adopted children of the Lord but that we could then live a life free from the bondage of the Law. The idea here is to live not like the slaves who have nothing but as sons who have a great inheritance waiting for them.

4:6 Once we become believers of Yeshua we receive the Ruach Kodesh into our hearts and He cries out to the Father, "Abba!" "Abba" is a common Aramaic word even used by Jewish Israeli children as an endearing title for their fathers. However, in Judaism, it is not a commonly used word for God. Stern reports, "Hebrew has incorporated the Aramaic word 'Abba,' which is a familiar way of addressing one's father. It is equivalent of 'Dad' or 'Daddy'... Judaism regards it as unacceptable to appear overly familiar with God." [8] Sha'ul, obviously knowing this tradition, reveals the contrast of believers who have a close personal Father/son relationship with God as opposed to the unsaved Jewish people (including the Legalizers) who find a close personal relationship with the Lord as historically and culturally unacceptable.

This type of thinking hurts the Jewish people's understanding of who God really is. Many Jewish people when asked to describe God would say He is the Judge. This is true because of the belief that either God caused the thousands of years of Jewish suffering and persecution or that God allowed it all to happen. In either case, the Jewish people suffered through persecution and wonder why God did not answer their prayers for help. Unfortunately, many Jewish people do not see God as the loving, caring and merciful God that He is.

Believers can cry out to our Father, "Abba" and thank Him for all of the blessings He has bestowed upon us because He is a loving, kind and merciful God. We can praise Him for: salvation, the Ruach Kodesh who directs us, eternal life, adoption as sons, redemption and the power to live our lives above the bondage of the Law.

4:7 This verse is the summary for this subsection. The conclusion is that believers of Yeshua are no longer slaves held in bondage to the Law but free sons of the Lord who have a great inheritance from the Father. The Galatians were now free from the tutor of the Law because the Messiah had come on the date set by the Father. Keener reiterates, "The Galatians are now freed from the slave guardian of 3:24-25, for the time has come (4:4)." [9] Messiah has set all believers free and caused us to be sons with an inheritance. Yeshua said in John 15:15-16,

> *"Henceforth I call you not servants; for the servant knoweth not what his lord doeth: but I have called you friends; for all things that I have heard of my Father I have made known unto you. Ye have not chosen me, but I have chosen you, and ordained you, that ye should*

go and bring forth fruit, and that your fruit should remain: that whatsoever ye shall ask of the Father in my name, he may give it you."

Believers are no longer slaves or servants to sin or the Law, but are chosen by God to be sons and friends of the Lord to live in freedom to bring forth good works performed by faith and love for the Lord. Therefore, we should keep our eyes fixed on Yeshua and the prize of our inheritance and give Him the glory for it all while crying out to our Father, "Abba!"

4:8 It seems that Sha'ul is quoting from Jewish theology that states there is only one God, the God of Israel and there are no other gods but Him. Keener reports, "Jewish people often said that the pagans did "not know God," and that their gods, which were creations of the true God, were "not gods at all." [10] Sha'ul reveals to the Galatians before they became true believers of Yeshua they did not know God and were therefore ultimately worshiping Hasatan and his demons. "Knew" (*oida*) means "to know fully, understand and recognize." [11] These Jewish and Gentile Galatians did not have a proper understanding or full knowledge of the Lord until they came to know Yeshua.

Romans 1 was written to inform that no person has any excuse for not knowing the Lord. Everyone in this world is able to recognize the Creator because of His creation. Once this knowledge is known the Lord would send someone to those people to share with them the wonderful good news of Yeshua just like what happened at Galatia. God sent Sha'ul to Galatia to preach the gospel and many responded by "knowing" Him. But before the Galatians heard the good news from Sha'ul they worshipped other gods who were really demons. Even the Jewish people throughout their history worshipped idols and demons: the golden calf; Baal; Moloch; etc. Today we have Messianic Jews and Gentiles that worship Torah scrolls, kippot (head coverings) and tallitot (prayer shawls) and other Judaica (Jewish gifts and items). Today we also have believers that worship crosses and baptismals. It is a given that those without the Lord would be slaves to these demons but believers who have "known" the Lord and fall away by worshiping idols and demons is considered a travesty.

4:9 "Have known" or "are known" (*ginosko*) means, "to know, become aware, perceive, understand and be conscious of... Ultimately, the one who knows God – who is known by God – demonstrates that knowledge in practical ways which bring glory and honor to the Giver of knowledge." [12] Sha'ul changed the Greek word "to know" from *oida* to *ginosko* in this verse. I believe *ginosko* was used to show a much stronger and more personal understanding of knowing God and being known by Him. It reveals a two directional personal relationship between God and man: from God to man and from man to God.

So after God dramatically saved these Galatians, Sha'ul wants to know how is it possible that they could so easily turn from the Lord and turn back to slavery under the elemental things that are the Law spoken of in verse 3. Thus far in this book we have seen time and time again how Sha'ul encourages the Galatians to get out from being under the Law! And yet here Sha'ul describes the Law as being "weak and worthless." This has to have a detrimental effect on the MJM in that if the Law was such an important part of our walk with the Lord then why is Sha'ul calling it "weak and worthless?"

"Weak" (*asthenes*) means, "weak, sick and ill... Paul, however, rarely used it in this sense... but preferred to apply *asthenes* figuratively... to the inability of the Law." [13] What is the weakness or inability of the Law? As stated throughout this commentary, the

Law cannot save or sanctify anyone. It does not have the ability to draw a person close to God which is what the MJM so desperately wants the Law to do! Instead the Law condemns and curses. The Law is not only weak but also worthless.

"Beggarly" (*ptochos*) means, "poor, oppressed, destitute, pitiful and beggarly... *Ptochos* can describe financial as well as spiritual impoverishment." [14] The Law is described as being spiritually impoverished and worthless. Remember, the Law cannot save or sanctify anyone. One purpose of the Law was to help enslave the Jewish people to their sin so that they could be tutored by the Law and led to the Messiah.

The application here is to the Galatians and their willingness to listen to the Legalizers teaching of Torah observance and place themselves back under the Law. The final phrase of verse 9 reveals this truth, "*you desire to be enslaved all over again.*" They personally desired to go back under the Law believing it was the right thing to do and yet Sha'ul even questioned in verse 12 whether he labored over them in vain. Sha'ul questioned those Galatian believers who turned back to following the letter of the Law after God had dramatically blessed them by making them sons and heirs through faith in Yeshua. I wonder how the MJM of today could do the same thing after the Lord has tremendously blessed us?

4:10 If the MJM does not believe Sha'ul is talking about the Law when he makes the statement "weak and beggarly elements," now they have to believe this because of verse 10. The Galatians were told by the Legalizers to keep the Law for salvation and/or sanctification reasons and Sha'ul confirms that this is exactly what they were doing. "Observe" (*paratereo*) means "lie in wait for, to observe carefully and watch closely... [this] verse takes this word in the sense of scrupulously observing rituals or rules..." [15] The obvious meaning here is that the Galatians were keeping the commandments of the Law for salvation and/or sanctification reasons. They were enslaved all over again by the Law even though they were believers of Yeshua who gave them the power to live above the Law in freedom.

"Days" refers to the *shabbat* or the Sabbath day where Messianics (Messianic Jews and Gentiles) and not-yet-saved Jewish people celebrate and worship God on the holy day of the week (sunset Friday to sunset Saturday). "Months" means "Rosh Chodesh" (head of the month) where the Israelites celebrated the new moon of the month. "Times" includes God's appointed times (the seven feasts of Leviticus 23), Chanukah and Purim, and probably other minor festivals and "fast" (fasting and praying) days of the year. "Years" refers to the sabbatical year (every seven years the Land was to lay fallow) and the Jubilee (every 50 years ownership of the Land reverts back to the original owners). Many commentators believe this verse is speaking of the rituals of the Law. [16]

The key in understanding exactly what Sha'ul is teaching here is the Galatians' willingness to be enslaved by the Law all over again. This is a matter of the heart. The Galatians were observing the commandments of the Law based on their desire to gain spiritual value or worth with the Lord. This was a sin which is why Sha'ul rebuked them. However, if the Galatians had kept the Law through the leading of the Ruach Kodesh, through the freedom of Messiah, through loving God and loving their neighbor and through faith not by sight, then they would not have sinned and Sha'ul would not have rebuked them! There is a fine line between living by the Ruach in learning about your Jewish Roots and even living as a Messianic Jew or Gentile as opposed to living by the

Law and trying to keep the Law believing this action pleases the Lord. It is a very difficult and almost impossible thing to live by the Ruach and keep the Law without falling into the spiritual grips of an attitude that says "I must keep the Law." Messianic believers can easily fall into sin and become shipwrecked in their faith because they believed they must keep the Law to please God.

There is however a very good reason why Messianic Jewish and Gentile believers should be involved in the MJM and explore our shared Jewish Roots found in the whole Bible. It is so that some Jewish people may be saved and have their names written in the Book of Life! 1 Corinthians 9:19-20 states, *"For though I be free from all men, yet have I made myself servant unto all, that I might gain the more. And unto the Jews I became as a Jew, that I might gain the Jews; to them that are under the law, as under the law, that I might gain them that are under the law."* We are to proclaim our Jewish heritage, which includes the Jewish good news of the Jewish Messiah who set us free from the Law, to a dying Jewish world so that some Jewish people would be saved. This is an awesome responsibility before the Lord as He has directed us to share the good news message of Yeshua to the Jewish people first (Rom. 1:16)! Should we, Messianic Jews and Gentiles, not fear the Lord in every word and action of how we reveal this good news message to the Jewish people? We need to prayerfully reconsider where the MJM is headed with its' Torah observance and look to reform. Should we not be headed in Yeshua's direction in our worship of Him so that the Jewish community would see the light of our Messiah?

4:11 The prophets of old complained of pleading with Israel to no avail and had hoped their devotion was not in vain. [17] What was the prophets' message? Repent! Repent from sins or face God's judgment.

Sha'ul's immediate fear over the Galatians is not for their future but for their present. His concern is that his work among the Galatians was already in vain because their actions were bringing God's judgment.

"Labour" *(kopiao)* means, "to labor to the point of exhaustion." [18] Sha'ul usually worked day and night to be able to share the good news message with any city, town or village. So his concern was that all of his hard work in Galatia was for naught. Truly, Sha'ul was not only concerned about his own eternal rewards for his labor but also more worried for the Galatians' spiritual welfare. Why? Their actions were not revealing that they were born again or that they had received the Ruach. They were instead attempting to do what the Legalizers taught them: to follow the letter of the Law.

If a Messianic Rabbi or teacher teaches to follow the Law for no other reason than that the Law says so, then run from this teaching! Instead, listen to the Lord, read the full Bible (Genesis through Revelation) and make up your own mind as the Lord leads you. The Galatians quickly fell back into the legalism of the Law. They left the freedom of Messiah for the bondage of the Law. Sha'ul told them to live by God's grace and the Ruach, to read the Scriptures, pray and be led by the Lord. They were no longer to live as slaves under the Law, but as sons of the living God.

Chapter 10

Maintain Your Freedom From The Law
(4:12-20)

4:12 Brethren, I beseech you, be as I am; for I am as ye are: ye have not injured me at all.
4:13 Ye know how through infirmity of the flesh I preached the gospel unto you at the first.
4:14 And my temptation which was in my flesh ye despised not, nor rejected; but received me as an angel of God, even as Christ Jesus.
4:15 Where is then the blessedness ye spake of? for I bear you record, that, if it had been possible, ye would have plucked out your own eyes, and have given them to me.
4:16 Am I therefore become your enemy, because I tell you the truth?
4:17 They zealously affect you, but not well; yea, they would exclude you, that ye might affect them.
4:18 But it is good to be zealously affected always in a good thing, and not only when I am present with you.
4:19 My little children, of whom I travail in birth again until Christ be formed in you,
4:20 I desire to be present with you now, and to change my voice; for I stand in doubt of you.

Sha'ul showed the Galatians in the last chapter that they were no longer slaves to the Law but sons of the living God. Now that they had become adopted sons of God and received a great inheritance through faith in the one and only Son Yeshua, the question remained, "Why would they then turn back and be enslaved all over again to the 'weak and worthless' Law?" In this section of Gal. 4, the conveyed message is that once believers have received our freedom from the Law, we need to maintain our freedom from the Law. Sha'ul begins his exhortation in verse 12 with this "maintaining" aspect.

4:12 Sha'ul "beseeched" the Galatians to become as he was. "Beseech" (*deomai*) means "beg, pray, beseech, request and urge." [1] There seems to be a strong urging and pleading from Sha'ul which shows his deep concern for the spiritual welfare of the Galatians. He wanted them to "become as I am." Sha'ul, by his own admission in 1:13-14, was extremely zealous for the Law and realized he was under the bondage of the Law. He perfectly empathized with what the Galatians were experiencing as they had turned back to the Law. He now was freed from the Law by the blood of Yeshua and continued to maintain that free status. He simply wanted the Galatians to repent and turn back to being free in the Ruach just like he was and just like they were at the beginning of their walk with the Lord.

In 1 Cor. 11:1, Sha'ul commanded the Corinthians to "*be ye followers of me, even as I also am of Christ.*" Not only did Sha'ul tell the Corinthians to imitate his Godly actions because he was following Yeshua, he also told the Galatians to follow his Godly deeds since he was imitating Yeshua. The point Sha'ul was making here was to tell the Galatians that if they needed to follow someone they should choose Sha'ul rather than the Legalizers because Sha'ul was following Yeshua and the Legalizers were following their own fleshly desires. He was, after all, the human agent that fathered the movement of the Lord in Galatia. They did have a close personal history with Sha'ul and yet they quickly abandoned him for the Legalizers. Therefore, Sha'ul is basically saying to the Galatians, "Follow me because I am a Messianic Jew who is not under the Law anymore but under God's grace and am able to fulfill the Law by bearing others burdens (Gal. 6:2), loving God and my neighbors (Matt. 22:36-40), walking in the Ruach (Rom. 8:1-4) and having faith in Yeshua (Rom. 3:31) instead of by following the letter of the Law."

When Sha'ul tells the Galatians "I also have become as you are" I believe he's stating that he had "become all things to all people;" he had become a Jew to the Jewish people and a Gentile to the Gentiles. He had become all things to all people just like the Galatians were in process of becoming all things to all people. The Scripture that reveals this is 1 Corinthians 9:19-22. It states,

"For though I be free from all men, yet have I made myself servant unto all, that I might gain the more. And unto the Jews I became as a Jew, that I might gain the Jews; to them that are under the law, as under the law, that I might gain them that are under the law; To them that are without law, as without law, (being not without law to God, but under the law to Christ,) that I might gain them that are without law. To the weak became I as weak, that I might gain the weak: I am made all things to all men, that I might by all means save some."

Sha'ul reveals that although he is free in Messiah he is willing to be a servant or slave to all people so that some would be saved. This means that Sha'ul although Jewish "became as a Jew" so that some Jewish people would be saved. Now this is an odd statement because Sha'ul is already Jewish; why does he need to become like a Jew? I believe Sha'ul is saying that he is willing to adjust his Jewish lifestyle to fit the variety of the Jewish people's lifestyles around the world. In today's vernacular, Sha'ul would act orthodox to the orthodox Jew, reform to the reformed Jew and conservative to the conservative Jew. He did this so that he could bridge the cultural diverse gap between himself and the Jewish people so that they would see him as equals and therefore listen to his good news message with the result of some becoming saved.

To those Jews and Gentiles who were under Law, Sha'ul would act similar to being under the Law although definitely not putting himself under the Law, so that he could help some to be saved. To those who were without the Law, he acted and sympathized like he was without the Law, so that some without the Law could be saved. Sha'ul became all things to all people so that some would be saved. After all these statements about the Law, Sha'ul made the bold statement that at all times he was "under the Law of Messiah." If the Law of Moses is still in effect like the MJM teaches and desires, then why didn't Sha'ul confess that he was still under the Law of Moses rather than the Law of Messiah? This is a question for the MJM that needs to be answered. The Law of Messiah has obviously replaced the Law of Moses since the time of the death and resurrection of Yeshua.

Sha'ul's point in this section of Scripture is to reveal that although believers become free from the Law at salvation we are still bondservants of the

Lord and need to do whatever it takes to reach Jewish and Gentile people with the love of God in Messiah Yeshua. This action reveals a great desire to love God and love your neighbor which is truly the same essence of the Law of Moses.

4:13 It seems that Sha'ul contracted a physical illness as he was passing through Galatia which caused him to stay longer than he originally intended. This sickness obviously temporarily halted Sha'ul's ability to travel. As usual, Sha'ul took full advantage of this situation and preached the good news message and many were saved. Verse 15 of chapter 4 gives us a clue as to the physical problem: *"...ye would have plucked out your own eyes, and have given them to me."* The implication here is that Sha'ul had an eye problem for the Galatians would have given him their own eyes to replace his own if that were possible.

Chapter 6:11 additionally reveals pertinent information, *"Ye see how large a letter I have written unto you with mine own hand."* It is proposed that because of an eye illness Sha'ul's eyesight became so bad that when he penned a verse or two in this letter he wrote with unusually large letters so that he could see what he was writing. Wuest further asserts, "… in the lowlands of Pamphylia, a region through which Paul had just passed on his way to Pisidian Antioch, an oriental eye disease called ophthalmia was prevalent. In addition to all this, the Greek words translated despised and rejected, indicate that the illness had caused him to have a repulsive appearance, which answers to the symptoms of ophthalmia." [2] Therefore, it is more than probable that Sha'ul suffered with an eye disease in Galatia causing him to stay longer than he planned which in turn caused him to preach the good news message more so that more Galatians were saved and more Galatian congregations were birthed.

Sha'ul caused the Galatians to remember the past history so they would cherish the close relationship they had with him and therefore listen and obey his counsel.

4:14 Keener comments that typical ancient and current Jewish belief thought personal illness/sickness was a divine retribution for sin. [3] Even in Lev.13:45-46 we see how the leper was separated from the camp of the Israelites and had to publicly warn the people of his disease. It proclaims, *"And the leper in whom the plague is, his clothes shall be rent, and his head bare, and he shall put a covering upon his upper lip, and shall cry, Unclean, unclean. All the days wherein the plague shall be in him he shall be defiled; he is unclean: he shall dwell alone; without the camp shall his habitation be."* This unclean disease and others like it caused the sick person to be a despised and rejected outcast of society. Sha'ul's disease was most certainly an unclean illness and therefore, it was very likely that the Galatians would despise and loathe Sha'ul and never get to hear his message. "Despised" (*exoutheneo*) means to "despise utterly, disdain, make of no account and treat with contempt." [4] "Rejected" (*ekptuo*) means to "despise, disdain, reject, loathe and spit out." [5]

The idea here is clear that the Galatians could have easily rejected Sha'ul and treated him with contempt because of his eye disease and yet they did not. In fact the very opposite happened; they received him as if he were an angel from heaven or Messiah himself! The Lord obviously had a plan devised and this is what Sha'ul is reminding the Galatians about. God is in control even when bad things happen to us and He can and will turn all things to good for those who love the Lord and are called according to His purpose (Rom. 8:28). So remember the blessings that come out of dire circumstances in life. The Galatians were greatly blessed through Sha'ul's personal trials.

In all reality this was an amazing reaction by the Galatians to Sha'ul's physical calamity. Instead of cowering away from Sha'ul, they embraced him and hence his message. I believe that Sha'ul saw in the Galatians a little bit of himself and his sacrificial actions. Sha'ul was always willing to sacrifice himself to share the good news message of Yeshua. He was even willing to be accursed of God! Romans 9:3 describes it this way, *"For I could wish that myself were accursed from Christ for my brethren, my kinsmen according to the flesh."* Sha'ul knew all about sacrifice in his ministry and he was blessed by the Galatians' sacrificial acceptance of him despite his ailment. Here, Sha'ul reminds the Galatians of these events so that he can admonish them to return back to this kind of loving heart they had in the past.

4:15 Sha'ul questions them concerning all of these events in the past. The Lord tremendously blessed the Galatians because they rose above the typical human response to sick people and not only received Sha'ul with great love but honorably treated him with respect like they would the Lord God. They loved him so much that he believed they would have given their own eyes to him if they could do so. So why would the Galatians not maintain their freedom, give up all those blessings, follow the Legalizers down the wrong spiritual road and then treat Sha'ul like an enemy? These are the unfortunate consequences that all believers can fall into when they fall into Torah observance for Torah sake.

4:16 Not only had the Galatians forgot their blessings, but they also flip-flopped their allegiance from Sha'ul to the Legalizers. Sha'ul even believed that he had become the Galatians' enemy. The Legalizers performed quite a disservice on the Galatians. The Galatians obviously entertained and listened to the Legalizers' statements against Sha'ul and his message. This in turn caused them to question Sha'ul's integrity. Then doubt crept in and finally they agreed with the Legalizers.

Sha'ul seems to be applying a principle found in Amos 5:10 to the Galatian situation. It states, *"They hate him that rebuketh in the gate, and they abhor him that speaketh uprightly."* "They" are the unrighteous and unjust. The elders of the city are the ones who make righteous judgments and rebuke evil at the gates of the city. It is therefore obvious that the evildoers are not going to agree with the righteous judgments (and even hate them). I believe Sha'ul is inferring that the Galatians are acting in an unrighteous manner because they have turned back to the weak and worthless Law. In addition, Sha'ul is wondering whether they hate him and think of him as an enemy because he spoke the righteous truth to them.

4:17 A comparison is made here between how the Legalizers sought out the Galatians versus how Sha'ul sought them out. The Legalizers desire was to drive a wedge between the newfound faith of the Galatians and the universal body of Messiah so that then they would seek even more feverishly the Legalizers and their false teaching. Lightfoot affirms this idea, "...Their desire is to shut you out from Christ. Thus you will be driven to pay court to them." [6]

What the Legalizers did was not at all "commendable." They tried and temporarily succeeded to move the Galatians away from Messiah and His freedom to the bondage of the Law and the Legalizers' control. Sha'ul, of course, then relayed his desire to always seek them out commendably whether he was physically present with them or not. Sha'ul's comparison reveals a truth about false teachers and their desires. False teachers want to build up their own ministries by taking advantage and using unsuspecting people. Wiersbe has penned a most intriguing and helpful statement for all believers. He asserts, "A true servant of God does not 'use people' to build himself up or his work; he ministers in love to help people know Christ better and glorify Him." [7]

As I have stated throughout this book, the whole matter about the MJM and Torah observance is a matter of the heart. If a Congregational Leader teaches congregants that the Torah says we all need to follow the Law to be sanctified and become a part of the MJM then he is not a teaching the truth of the Scriptures. He would be using his flock to build a ministry and would be considered "not commendable." However, if a Congregational Leader teaches from the full Bible incorporating Jewish culture, lifestyle and includes Torah teaching with the idea that all need to follow the leading of the Ruach Kodesh, then he is teaching the truth and would be considered a true servant of the Lord. Through this type of teaching, he reveals his love for the flock and desire for them to know Yeshua better. He would then be considered "commendable." The goal of having a God-centered Messianic Jewish Congregation and community can be accomplished without the strict adherence to Torah observance.

Wiersbe follows up that profound statement with another: "Beware of that religious worker who wants your exclusive allegiance because he is the only one that is right. He will use you as long as he can and then drop you for someone else and your fall will be a painful one. The task of the spiritual leader is to get people to love and follow Christ, not to promote himself and his ministry." [8] Congregational Leaders in the MJM far too often teach that we (the MJM) have the true understanding of Scripture while the Church does not because we have kept our Jewish Roots and the Church has mostly discarded them. The obvious inference is that churches do not have it right and the MJM does. Therefore, the logical conclusion would be that congregants should only attend Messianic Jewish Congregations and get out of the churches! To believe the MJM has exclusive rights to the Lord Yeshua is a fallacy and is an extreme belief that needs to be dramatically tamed. Again, this belief falls under the "not commendable" category and many of the MJM need to prayerfully seek the Lord for "commendable" change.

4:18 Sha'ul continues his comparison of himself and the Legalizers. In verse 17, the Legalizers eagerly sought the Galatians but not in a commendable manner. They desired to shut them out from the freedom of Messiah and put them under the bondage of their teachings. Sha'ul states that he eagerly sought them as well even though he had a gruesome physical ailment. He sought after them because of his love for the Lord, his desire to help save them and his desire for them to be free from the Law. This philosophy is diametrically opposed to the Legalizers. He wanted the Galatians to be enslaved not to the Law all over again, but to the Lord. Sha'ul's eagerness in seeking the Galatians continued even though he was not present with them. He reminds them that he is always with them in spirit as he thinks and prays for them. Sha'ul's great affection for the Galatians is continued in verses 19-20.

4:19 Sha'ul has changed his straightforward stern approach for a more appealing one by calling the Galatians "my little children." "Little children" (*teknion*) is an affectionate and endearing term used by both Jesus and the apostles as they address their spiritual children..." ⁹ Although Sha'ul begins this verse with a softened greeting, he quickly turns back to sternness.

"Travail" (*odino*) means to "suffer birth pangs... Paul described his anguish and concern for the [Galatians] believers as 'suffering birth pangs'. ¹⁰ In one sense this is encouragement because Sha'ul will continue to teach and labor over the Galatians. But in another sense, he is rebuking them because he is anguished over their immaturity that they have not maintained their freedom from the Law. He greatly suffered in his labor of love over them in his first visit and he will continue his anguish "until" Messiah is formed in them.

"Until" (*achri*) is the same Greek word used in 3:19 where we learned that the Law was added to the promise "until" the seed Yeshua should come. The Law was the main mode of defining transgressions until Yeshua replaced it. *Achri* is a time sensitive verb when paired with the genitive pronoun *hou* (as is the case here as well as in 3:19). Sha'ul is telling them that they are immature in their faith and he will continue to labor over them 'until' they become mature.

Similar is Sha'ul's encouragement to the Ephesians in 4:11-16,

> *"And he gave some, apostles; and some, prophets; and some, evangelists; and some, pastors and teachers; For the perfecting of the saints, for the work of the ministry, for the edifying of the body of Christ: Till we all come in the unity of the faith, and of the knowledge of the Son of God, unto a perfect man, unto the measure of the stature of the fullness of Christ: That we henceforth be no*

more children, tossed to and fro, and carried about with every wind of doctrine, by the sleight of men, and cunning craftiness, whereby they lie in wait to deceive; But speaking the truth in love, may grow up into him in all things, which is the head, even Christ: From whom the whole body fitly joined together and compacted by that which every joint supplieth, according to the effectual working in the measure of every part, maketh increase of the body unto the edifying of itself in love."

Spiritual gifts are given to the Body of Messiah for the spiritual building up of all believers until we all learn to be unified. Then, as we are in the process of maturing, we learn not to be easily led astray, tossed to and fro like waves or carried away by some new wind of teaching. Instead, with every victory of faith the Body continues to grow, to encourage one another, to build itself up in love and ultimately to achieve our full stature in Messiah. This is exactly what Sha'ul is telling the Galatians. Do not be fooled by the trickery or craftiness of the Legalizers, do not even listen to them for they are not commendably seeking you and have stolen your freedom, but remember how I labored over you and remember God's resultant blessings upon you.

4:20 Sha'ul has been very strong and even harsh with the Galatians. In 3:1, he called them "foolish." He expresses his wish to be there in person and to tone down his attitude. He is obviously very puzzled over the Galatians. Their desire to follow Torah for sanctification is unbiblical and Sha'ul is perplexed about it. What can he say on parchment to help change their minds? They need to repent, come out from being under the Law, be grounded in the Lord and His Word and maintain their freedom no matter what.

Chapter 11

Listen to The Law
(4:21-31)

4:21 Tell me, ye that desire to be under the law, do ye not hear the law?
4:22 For it is written, that Abraham had two sons, the one by a bondmaid, the other by a freewoman.
4:23 But he who was of the bondwoman was born after the flesh; but he of the freewoman was by promise.
4:24 Which things are an allegory: for these are the two covenants; the one from the mount Sinai, which gendereth to bondage, which is Agar.
4:25 For this Agar is mount Sinai in Arabia, and answereth to Jerusalem which now is, and is in bondage with her children.
4:26 But Jerusalem which is above is free, which is the mother of us all.
4:27 For it is written, Rejoice, thou barren that bearest not; break forth and cry, thou that travailest not: for the desolate hath many more children than she which hath an husband.
4:28 Now we, brethren, as Isaac was, are the children of promise.
4:29 But as then he that was born after the flesh persecuted him that was born after the Spirit, even so.

4:30 *Nevertheless what saith the scripture? Cast out the bondwoman and her son: for the son of the bondwoman shall not be heir with the son of the freewoman.*
4:31 *So then, brethren, we are not children of the bondwoman, but of the free.*

In Gal. 4, Sha'ul reminded the Galatians they were sons of the Lord and not slaves of the Law. Yet there was a movement within the Galatian congregations that embraced the Law beyond the allowable New Covenant limitations. In verses 12-20, Sha'ul encouraged them to hold on to their freedom from the Law of Moses. He specifically addressed those Messianic Jews and Gentiles who have put themselves back under the Law. He instructed them to listen to the Law. Why would Sha'ul want them to listen to the Law? Because the Law proves beyond a shadow of any doubt that New Covenant believers of Yeshua are not under the authority of the Law. Sha'ul takes great lengths in this section of Scripture to prove this point through an allegorical example of Avraham.

4:21 Sha'ul appeals with a straightforward argument to those who want to be under the Law. He questions whether they have listened to the same Law they desire to be under. "Under" (*hupo*) is used throughout the book of Galatians mostly occurring in chapter 3 and 4. As discussed in earlier chapters of this commentary, *hupo* figuratively used with an accusative noun (as is the case here) indicates an implied state or condition under something. The Greek grammar is very clear here. Those "who want to be under the Law" are those who voluntarily subject themselves under the authority of the Law. Sha'ul emphatically states that these believers make the Law their master when they put themselves under its authority.

Sha'ul then asks "Do ye not hear the law?" The obvious reasoning to the question is simple. The Law condemns disobedience to its commandments. People are cursed if they do not perfectly follow everything in the Law (3:10). So why try to keep the Law when as believers we should know that we cannot perfectly keep all of the commandments? Even Kefa proclaimed this thought in Acts 15:10 to the first Jerusalem Council concerning the idea that the new Gentile believers needed to keep Torah for salvation: *"Now therefore why tempt ye God, to put a yoke upon the neck of the disciples,* **which neither our fathers nor we were able to bear***?"* [Bold emphasis is mine] Kefa proclaimed to the Council that neither the Jewish forefathers nor the Jewish people could completely obey the Torah so how could the Gentiles do it then? Why should the Council put the new Gentile believers under the Law when the Jewish believers could not follow it fully? Obviously, their answer was not to put the Gentiles under the Law.

"Hear" (*akuo*) means to "hear, heed, listen, understand, learn and give a hearing." [1] Sha'ul's immediate response to those who want to be under Law is whether they actually "listen" to the Law. Do they hear what the Law says? Do they heed and understand that the Law curses them? Have they learned that the Law points them to Yeshua for salvation and sanctification?

The Hebrew word for "hear" (*shema*) should invoke an automatic respectful Jewish response. The *shema* is one Jewish prayer that is the backbone of the Jewish faith. The Rabbi's concur on the importance of the *shema* to the Jewish people,

> *"The role of this passage in Judaism is perhaps best exemplified by where Rambam places it*

in Sefer HaMitzvos, where he lists the commandments in logical order, beginning with those that are most central to Jewish belief and observance. Primary on his list is the commandment to believe in God...because without a God Who commands, there are no commandments. The second and third of Rambam's commandments are contained in the first two verses of the Shema, namely to acknowledge the Oneness of God and to love Him... It is indicative of the importance of the Shema that it must be recited every day, morning and night (v. 7). Indeed, it is at the very essence of Judaism. Rambam comments that its importance is indicated by the fact that the Torah places it immediately after the Ten Commandments." [2]

"Hear" (*shema*) is the first word to the *Shema* prayer that is recited by Jewish people all over the world in Shabbat services and personal daily prayers. The *Shema* prayer is taken from Deut. 6:4, "*Hear, O Israel: The LORD our God is one LORD.*" So when Jewish people hear the spoken word "*Shema*" they listen! Therefore, it is reasonable to assume, the Jewish and Gentile Galatian believers Sha'ul was writing to would perk up and listen to Sha'ul when they read the Greek word *akuo*! And they must have been perplexed because they had thought they were already listening to the Law, that's why they put themselves under it.

In summary, verse 21 reveals that if people put themselves under Law then they place themselves under the authority of the Law. When people place themselves under the authority of the Law they are acknowledging that the Law is their master and they are obeying their master. Sha'ul wrote to the Romans revealing a similar idea. Rom. 6:14 states, *"For sin shall not have dominion over you: for ye are not under the law, but under grace."* If a person is under Law then the Law has dominion over that person and is their master. If the Law is that person's master, then sin is their master as well. This is true because one purpose of the Law is to constantly remind its' followers that they are sinning (because they break the Law) and are condemned by that sin. When a person falls under grace and not Law, then their master is Yeshua and not sin! Therefore, they are not condemned by sin but forgiven through mercy.

4:22-23 Sha'ul now takes a great example from the Torah to prove his point that all believers need to be under grace and not under Law. Avraham, the father of all the Jewish people, and his life situations are analyzed. Avraham had two sons: Ishmael and Isaac. Ishmael was born by Hagar the bond-servant/slave and Isaac was born by Sarah the free woman. Ishmael was born by the slave woman according to the flesh and Isaac was born by the free woman according to God's promise. The whole point of this section of Scripture is to show the believers of Galatia are children of promise like Isaac and should thus live in freedom from the Law. How did Avraham come to have two sons by two different women?

God made some wonderful promises to Avram. (Avram is his name prior to the change to Avraham). In Gen. 12:2, the Lord said, *"And I will make of thee a great nation..."* The implication here is that God would work it out that Avram would have descendants come from his seed to create a great nation. In Gen. 12:7, the Lord additionally promised, *"...Unto thy seed will I give this land..."*

Therefore, Avram's seed or descendants would inherit the Land of Israel from the Lord. God also told Avram in Gen. 13:15-16 that his descendants would be too many to count and they would have the Land forever. By Gen. 15, the Lord and Avram are conversing about the fact that Avram does not have a son and his heir is Eliezer of Damascus. In verse 4, the Lord tells Avram, *"...This shall not be thine heir; but he that shall come forth out of thine own bowels shall be thine heir."* The Lord has now revealed some new information concerning His promise to Avram. His heir will come from his own body or seed and not an appointed heir. His son will not be adopted but one shall come from his own loins. Again, in verse 5, God reiterates His promise that Avram's descendants will be like the number of stars and this time we see Avram's response of belief whereby the Lord blesses him with righteousness.

In Gen. 16:1-4, we find Avram and Sarai waited 10 years for God to fulfill His promise and nothing happened. So Sarai finally decided to act on what she thought was the inaction of God and gave her slave Hagar into Avram's arms. She probably believed Hagar would produce children for her so that God's promise would then be fulfilled. This is similar to the surrogate mother situation currently practiced in the world. It was acceptable practice then as it is now. It is interesting to note that Avram listened to the voice of Sarai and yet the Scripture does not say that he prayed to the Lord about her request.

I believe that Sarai and Avram, although acted in the flesh, thought they were performing God's will based on their circumstances. Sarai was past the age of childbearing and believed the Lord was preventing her from conceiving so she logically deduced that someone else should take her place. They waited for 10 years; who could fault them for taking action after such a long time period? In hindsight, the problem with these actions was that they were not God's will for their lives. From that time to the present, they and the Jewish people have greatly suffered for their mistakes.

It was not until Gen. 17:16 that God revealed His will to Avraham that Sarah was to become pregnant and give birth to his son. This did, of course, occur after Hagar was given over to Avraham and gave birth to Ishmael. Gen. 17:16 states, *"And I will bless her, and give thee a son also of her: yea, I will bless her, and she shall be a mother of nations; kings of people shall be of her."* Not only is Sarah the chosen one for Avraham's son but she is also chosen to be the mother of nations. God's promise for her descendants would be just like His promise given to Avraham's seed: too many to count!

Up until this revelation, Avraham believed that Ishmael was the promised son who would receive the inheritance. His response to the Lord's prophetic statements in Gen. 17:17-18 reveal this: *"Then Abraham fell upon his face, and laughed, and said in his heart, Shall a child be born unto him that is an hundred years old? and shall Sarah, that is ninety years old, bear? And Abraham said unto God, O that Ishmael might live before thee!"* Not only did Avraham believe Ishmael was the promised one but he even pleaded with the Lord for it to be true! However, Isaac was the promised one and his seed after him. God said He would establish His everlasting covenant with Isaac (and not Ishmael for he had no part in this covenant) and his seed which is obviously Israel.

In summary, all this background is necessary to see that those who choose to put themselves under the authority of the Law will lead fleshly lifestyles just like when Avraham and Sarah chose a fleshly response to their circumstances rather than be patient and wait on the Lord. They chose the wrong response and suffered the consequences just like these Galatian believers who have chosen the wrong path in putting themselves under the Law. Very simply reiterated: Ishmael was born of the flesh, born in slavery and was never involved with God's promise or covenant plan. Isaac on the other hand, was born of the promise, born in freedom and was greatly involved with God's covenant plan.

4:24 Sha'ul went to great lengths to reveal this most important truth to the Galatians. "Allegory" (*allegoreo*) means to "speak figuratively or allegorically. *Allegoreo* was especially employed in antiquity to denote a particular type of interpretation." [3] Here Sha'ul begins to illustrate and contrast the two women of Avraham's life. The two women, figuratively speaking, represent two covenants. Hagar represents the Mosaic Covenant from Mt. Sinai and Sarah represents the New Covenant from Golgotha. When Hagar, being a slave, gives birth to children, they become slaves. Slavery begets slavery. When Sarah begets children they are free. Why? Because Sarah is free! Why is this important to know? Verse 25 gives us the answer.

4:25 Sha'ul now takes the allegory a step further. Hagar, who represents the Mosaic Covenant (which is the Law) from Mount Sinai also represents present day Jerusalem (which was Judaism in Sha'ul's day). Sha'ul was referring to the unsaved Jewish people (and their Jewish religious practices) of the day who are represented by the leaders of Judaism. Although this group would definitely include the Legalizers, Sha'ul is emphatically stating that this group includes all Jewish people who are not a part of the Messianic Community. Dr. Stern writes, "The present Yerushalayim [Jerusalem], that is, the non-Messianic Jewish community of the first century, both its establishment and the people loyal to that establishment." [4]

Stern goes on to say that although these people can claim physical descent from Abraham and Sarah, Sha'ul calls them spiritual descendants of Hagar. [5] This is somewhat of a shocking statement. Sha'ul is actually saying that all of these non-believing Jewish people are spiritual slaves of their religious system which is the Mosaic Law. He said it another way in Rom. 2:28-29: *"For he is not a Jew, which is one outwardly... But he is a Jew, which is one inwardly..."* In other words, Sha'ul is saying that a true Jew is one who is a spiritual Jew believing in Yeshua. All other Jews who are outwardly following Torah are not true Jews. I can only imagine the uproar these statements caused in the Jewish community, who quite frankly believed they were the true remnant of God and were zealously serving the Lord God much like Sha'ul himself believed before he met Yeshua on the road to Damascus.

Sha'ul not only calls the unsaved Jewish community of his day slaves of the Law, but also claims that their children are slaves as well. Just as Hagar, a slave, bore children into slavery, so the followers of Torah Observance and their children are in bondage to the Law and therefore slaves of the Law. "Children" is metaphorically speaking of *talmidim* (disciples). Again, slavery begets slavery. Sha'ul says listen to the Law as it curses you; so come out from under the Law and your slavery, and be free in Messiah.

4:26 Most commentators believe the "Jerusalem above" is speaking of the heavenly city of Jerusalem. F.F. Bruce stated, "The idea of two Jerusalem's, the lower and the upper, the earthly and the heavenly, is not peculiar to Paul. Two other NT writers make use of it (cf. Heb. 12:22, with 11:10, 16; Rev. 3:12; 21:2, 9ff.)." [5] In Sha'ul's day, Judaism believed in a future New Jerusalem. Wuest reports, "The phrase 'Jerusalem which is above,' was familiar to the rabbinical teachers who thought of the heavenly Jerusalem as the archetype of the earthly. The heavenly Jerusalem which is free, therefore represents Sarah: and finally, grace." [6] Keener concurs with Wuest, "Many Jewish texts in Paul's day reinforced the Old Testament hope of a new Jerusalem, often speaking of a heavenly Jerusalem that would come down to earth. These texts also sometimes spoke of Jerusalem (present or future) as 'our mother." [7]

Although the "Jerusalem above" is speaking of the heavenly Jerusalem that will come down from heaven in the future, within this context it also represents Sarah. If Hagar is Mount Sinai which represents Jerusalem and its religious system of slavery, then Sarah represents the heavenly Jerusalem, which represents the present believers of the New Covenant in freedom. God even promised Avraham that Sarah would be a mother of nations (Gen.17:16). This means that she would be the mother of many offspring referring to her spiritual children who are Jewish and Gentile believers in Yeshua. If Sarah was free, then all her children would be free. If this is true, then should not all of her children live in freedom and not slavery? The rest of the chapter builds on this truth.

4:27 This is a fascinating quote from Sha'ul because he told his readers to listen to the Law and yet he quotes from the prophet Isaiah. Many times the Law spoken of in the New Covenant Scriptures is talking about the whole Bible and not just the first five books of the Bible. For example, Sha'ul states in 1Cor.14:21 that, *"In the Law it is written..."* and then quotes from Isa. 28:11! Therefore, "the Law" has a broad range of meaning. It can mean the *Torah* (the first five books of the Bible), the Tenach (the Old Covenant scriptures), the *Brit Chadashah* (the New Covenant scriptures) or the whole Bible. This is an important distinction because most of the MJM emphatically believes the Law equals the Torah and vice versa and all Messianic believers should follow the Law. And yet ironically we find in the New Covenant Scriptures that the Law is truly seen as the whole word of God!

Why does Sha'ul go to great lengths to quote from Isa. 54:1? The "barren woman" spoken of in Isa. 54:1 is Sarah. Sarah is told to rejoice even though her descendants will be fewer than Hagar's. At least she will have descendants. The rest of chapter 54 is wonderful encouragement because those descendants (Israel) are reminded of God's promises given to the forefathers. Ultimately, the Jewish people will be living in peace, righteousness and justice in the Messianic Kingdom. However, we do need to remember Isaiah wrote at a time when the Assyrians took the Northern Kingdom into captivity. And yet even though they were under God's judgment at that time they could look forward to the future when God's compassion and loving-kindness would fall upon them.

Throughout her history, Israel has counted on her chosen relationship with God through Avraham as their father. Even today many Jewish people claim automatic salvation just because of their lineage through the blood of Avraham. But this is not the truth. Yeshua admonished the Jewish people as they claimed Avraham was their father. John 8:39 states, *"They answered and said unto him, Abraham is our father. Jesus saith unto them, If ye were Abraham's children, ye would do the works of Abraham."* The deeds of Avraham were done by faith in the Lord. Avraham's faith was accounted to him for righteousness. Yeshua told these Jewish people that they needed to have faith like Avraham and live by faith like Avraham if they wanted to be true children of God and engage in the promises restated in Isa. 54. Here in Gal. 4:27, the barren Jerusalem will finally become the spiritual Jerusalem in the end by faith in Yeshua.

4:28 Sha'ul makes application of Isa. 54 here. The Jewish and Gentile believers of Galatia (and of course all believers of Yeshua) are the true children of promise! They are part of the New Covenant given to the Jewish people whereby they could rest from their works and be free from the curse of the Law.

Romans 9:6-9 is similar where Sha'ul wrote to the Roman believers making it very clear that not all who are Israelites are descendants of Israel. The children of the promise (Messianic Jews and Gentiles) are the true descendants of Avraham and Sarah. Romans 9:6-9 states,

> *"Not as though the word of God hath taken none effect. For they are not all Israel, which are of Israel: Neither, because they are the seed of Abraham, are they all children: but, In Isaac shall thy seed be called. That is, they which are the children of the flesh, these are not the children of God: but the children of the promise are counted for the seed. For this is the word of promise, at this time will I come, and Sarah shall have a son."*

In verses 6-7, Sha'ul says that not all the children of the flesh of Avraham are true descendants. For example, any unsaved Muslim people living in Israel that claim lineage through Ishmael and Avraham cannot claim they are the children of the promise. Verses 8-9 identify that those who are descendants according to the promise are true Israel because it is God's promise found in Gen. 18:10. In Gen. 18:10, the Lord Himself was speaking with Avraham and promised that within a year's time Sarah would have a son. For God, a promise made is a promise kept. This promise coupled with God's promise in Gen. 12:3 where all the families of the earth would be blessed through Avraham led Sha'ul to rightly believe that all true believers of Yeshua despite their race or culture are the fulfillment of these promises. Hence, we see Sha'ul telling the Jewish and Gentile Galatians that they are the "children of promise."

4:29 Looking at this verse by itself one could suppose Sha'ul is taking a short rabbit trail to report that Ishmael, the one born according to the flesh, persecuted Isaac, the one born according to the promise and the Spirit. Not only did this persecution occur at the beginning of their relationship but it also lasted throughout the centuries through their descendants. The persecution even continues to this day and will continue right to the Second Coming of Yeshua! However, this verse cannot be taken by itself in that it is a continuation of the allegorical example Sha'ul is using to prove his point that the Messianic believers should not put themselves under the Law. Sha'ul says that even the Law agrees with this statement, so why not listen to the very same Law that they have put themselves under?

Remember, Hagar and her seed represent the Mosaic Covenant and first century Jerusalem (including the leaders of Judaism) that make most of the Jewish people slaves to the Law. Sarah and her seed represent the New Covenant and the Messianic believers who are free from the Law and under God's grace. In making application to verse 29, the Jewish leadership and their disciples who are slaves to the Law persecuted the Messianic believers who are freed from the Law according to the Spirit. Sha'ul had firsthand experience in knowing what it was like being a slave to the Law and performing evil acts of persecution against the Messianic believers of Yeshua. But he also experienced the persecution by the Jewish leadership after he became a believer. Sha'ul is also referring to the Legalizers who continuously followed his ministry and tried to destroy his work. The Legalizers put themselves under the Law and tried to put the Galatian believers under the Law and even used persecution as a method of inducement.

4:30 Sha'ul now quotes from the Torah (Gen. 21:10) as the answer to the Galatians' problem. God told Avraham to listen to Sarah and cast out the bondwoman Hagar and Ishmael because Ishmael is not an heir with Isaac. Isaac, born of the free woman Sarah, is Avraham's heir of God's promise.

In continuing Sha'ul's allegorical example, the Galatians were to cast out "the bondwoman and her son." Therefore, the Galatians were to cast out the Mosaic Covenant, the Law and those Legalizers who tried to make them bond slaves to the Law! Remember, the Legalizers include the Pharisees, Sadducees, Rabbis, scribes and any Jewish person who proclaimed the need to listen and obey Torah for salvation and/or sanctification. Those who believe and proclaim this false doctrine are not heirs to the Lord's promises of salvation, redemption and glorification. Unfortunately for them, they are the ones who Sha'ul placed under a curse (in 1:8-9) because they were teaching a false good news message. Finally, Sha'ul encouraged the Galatian believers once again that as sons of Sarah they were heirs! This is actually a re-statement of Gal. 4:7, *"Wherefore thou art no more a servant, but a son; and if a son, then an heir of God through Christ."*

4:31 We, who are believers of Yeshua, have been born according to the Spirit and not the flesh are considered to be sons of the living God who are not children of the slave woman but children of the free woman. Since we have this high position with the Lord and the inheritance that comes with it, shouldn't we listen to the Law and not put ourselves under the authority and curse of the Law? Since we are of the free woman, should we not start to act like freed people? We who are in the MJM must fight to keep ourselves in the freedom of Messiah and not subject ourselves again to the Law.

I believe Sha'ul implies the following question at the end of chapter 4, "So what covenant are you going to follow?" The Mosaic Covenant makes sin and the Law to be the master. The Law or the works of the Law cannot justify those who are under the Law. Those who put themselves under the Law are in spiritual slavery to the Law and actually are denying the fact that Yeshua's death on the tree redeemed them from being under the Law to freedom from the Law. The New Covenant makes grace and the Lord to be the master. Those who were under the Law are now freed from the curse and power of the Law to live for the Lord in the power of the Ruach Kodesh. They are not confined to the rules and regulations of the Torah but are released from them to truly love the Lord their God and their neighbor. I choose the New Covenant! What covenant do you chose?

Chapter 12

Messiah Has Set Us Free
(5:1-12)

5:1 Stand fast therefore in the liberty wherewith Christ hath made us free, and be not entangled again with the yoke of bondage.
5:2 Behold, I Paul say unto you, that if ye be circumcised, Christ shall profit you nothing.
5:3 For I testify again to every man that is circumcised, that he is a debtor to do the whole law.
5:4 Christ is become of no effect unto you, whosoever of you are justified by the law; ye are fallen from grace.
5:5 For we through the Spirit wait for the hope of righteousness by faith.
5:6 For in Jesus Christ neither circumcision availeth any thing, nor un-circumcision; but faith which worketh by love.
5:7 Ye did run well; who did hinder you that ye should not obey the truth?
5:8 This persuasion cometh not of him that calleth you.
5:9 A little leaven leaveneth the whole lump.
5:10 I have confidence in you through the Lord, that ye will be none otherwise minded: but he that troubleth you shall bear his judgment, whosoever he be.

5:11 *And I, brethren, if I yet preach circumcision, why do I yet suffer persecution? then is the offence of the cross ceased.*
5:12 *I would they were even cut off which trouble you.*

In chapter 1 of Galatians, we saw Sha'ul defend the purity of the good news message and his own apostleship. In chapter 2, Sha'ul protected his apostolic authority so that the truth of the good news would remain with the Galatians. This truth is that a person is justified not by the Law or the works of the Law, but through faith in Yeshua. Chapter 3 brought a stinging rebuke: anyone placing themselves under the Law was considered to be under the curse of God. The purpose of the Law and the promise of God were detailed in our study. Chapter 4 showed us that we are sons of the living God and not slaves of the Law. In chapter 5, practical exhortation is shared so that we can live Godly lives free from the grips of the Law because Messiah has set us free.

5:1 Chapter 5 begins with the dramatic proclamation that Messiah set us free so that we could have "liberty." "Liberty" (*eleutheria*) means "liberty, freedom." [1] The New Covenant Scriptures present freedom as a great blessing from God in the age of grace. But what did Messiah set us free from? The context dictates that He set us free from the Law! If the Law is such a wonderful thing to be religiously obeyed as the MJM would proclaim, then why did Yeshua set us free from it?! This is a great question that the MJM needs to answer.

"Made free" (eleutheroo; is the verb form of the noun *eleutheria*) means "set free, deliver and liberate." [2] This word is found in the indicative mood, aorist tense and active voice. The indicative mood indicates the statement made in this verse is positive and clear-cut. The meaning is quite obvious and straight forward to the reader. The aorist tense reveals the action of being set free was an action performed in the past. The active voice shows that Messiah is the doer of the action and that the "us" are the receivers of the action. All of this Greek grammar demonstrates that Messiah absolutely, positively set us free from the Law at a point in past time. How did this being "set free" from the Law occur? We were set free by believing and receiving Yeshua as our Messiah, Lord and Savior.

There are two responses that believers should continuously perform because Messiah gave us freedom. The first one is to "keep standing firm." The Greek word for "stand fast" (*steko*) means to "stand still, stand fast or persevere." 3 "*Steko*" is found to be in the present tense. This means that we are encouraged to continuously in the present stand fast and persevere in the freedom of Messiah.

This is exactly what Sha'ul is teaching in chapter 5 and throughout the whole book. The theme of this epistle is: Messiah has set us free and we must continuously stand firm in this freedom! We should not allow anything, especially the Law, to get in the way of our persevering in this freedom. Remember, one purpose of the Law was to identify the sin in our lives and to reveal how evil our sin truly is. Yet, Yeshua gives us freedom from the Law and from our sin.

The second response that believers should continuously perform because Yeshua set us free is to "be not entangled again with the yoke of bondage." "Be entangled" (*enecho*) has a few different meanings: be angry, hold a grudge or be ensnared. However, the context in this verse reveals *enecho* to mean "to be subject to" or "to let someone become entangled with." *Enecho* is found to be in the present tense. This means we should continuously in the present not allow ourselves to be subject or entangled in slavery. What is the slavery or the "yoke of bondage" that the Galatians and all believers are not to be entangled in again?

The obvious answer to the question is "the Law." The MJM is not going to like this answer, however, the context dictates that it is the correct one. Again, this is the theme of chapter 5 and also the whole book. Warren Wiersbe writes concerning the "yoke of bondage":

> *"The image of the yoke is not difficult to understand. It usually represents slavery, service, and control by someone else over your life; it may also represent willing service and submission to someone else. When God delivered Israel from Egyptian servitude, it was the breaking of a yoke (Lev. 26:13). The farmer uses the yoke to control and guide his oxen, because they would not willingly serve if they were free."* [5]

Here, Wiersbe explains that the yoke is the Law and it will control and enslave someone if they submit and put themselves under it. Wuest compares "the Law" (the yoke of bondage) with living in a straight-jacket:

> *"Here were these Galatian Christians, free from the law, having been placed in the family of God as adult sons, indwelt by the Holy Spirit who would enable them to act out in their experience that maturity of Christian life in which they were placed, now putting on the straight-jacket of the law, cramping*

their experience, stultifying their actions, depriving themselves of the power of the Holy Spirit. They were like adults putting themselves under rules made for children." 6

Sha'ul is definitely using the phrase "yoke of bondage" as representing the Law. Actually, this is Sha'ul's third example of the Law written about in Galatians. His first example was the "tutor" in 3:24. The second example was the "bondwoman" found in 4:22. The third example is the "yoke of slavery." We know about this yoke of slavery because almost 2,000 years ago the MJM went through the same deliberations that we are presently going through with those who are Torah Observant. Remember the definition of Torah Observant: those who require following the Law for salvation and/or sanctification reasons.

In Acts 15 we find the Jerusalem Council consisting of apostles and elders gathered to deliberate this issue concerning the Law: whether the new Gentile believers should observe it or not for salvation. Verse 1 states, *"And certain men which came down from Judaea taught the brethren, and said, Except ye be circumcised after the manner of Moses, ye cannot be saved."* At the Jerusalem Council, the Legalizers' theology was made public. They believed circumcising the Gentile believers was necessary for their salvation in addition to believing in Yeshua. Not only did they believe circumcision played a part in salvation but following the Law was equally important. Verse 5 proclaims, *"But there rose up certain of the sect of the Pharisees which believed, saying, That it was needful to circumcise them, and to command them to keep the law of Moses."* It is fair to say that the "certain men" of verse 1 were of the same mindset as the Pharisees and yet these specific Pharisees were believers of Yeshua. However, even though they believed in Yeshua they thought it was necessary to circumcise and keep the Law to be saved!

Before I carry this argument to its conclusion, it must be understood why this belief was so predominant in the first century. The reader has to understand, for almost 1,500 years, since the beginning of the Law of Moses, Judaism's theology and practice stayed the same. The Law was the primary driving force for Jewish living and society. If and when any Gentile desired to follow the God of Israel, they would have to convert to Judaism. There was and still continues to the present time to be a process for that conversion. This conversion process included brit milah (circumcision), mikveh (water immersion or baptism) and halachah (the desire to learn and live by the Torah). Basically, we see these converted Gentiles becoming Jews. Some biblical examples are Rahab and Ruth. Both converted to Judaism and worshipped the God of Israel and lived their lives as Jews (and were accepted as Jewish people by the community at large). In Exodus 12:49, the same Law of Moses applied to the Jews as well as the strangers who joined themselves to Israel.

Now 2,000 years ago, you have this Jesus and His disciples who have turned the whole Jewish world upside down. The very fiber of the Law that held Jewish life together is now on the proverbial chopping block in Acts 15. You could almost hear the Pharisees at this council cry out, "What do you mean Yeshua's death and resurrection has changed our Jewish lifestyle?!"

Kefa's response is the point of this short argument. Acts 15:10 states, *"Now therefore why tempt ye God, to put a yoke upon the neck of the disciples, which neither our fathers nor we were able to bear?"* Kefa profoundly questions the Legalizers why they would want to put the yoke of slavery of the Law upon the new believers when the Jews and their forefathers (who have been the caretakers of the Law for 1,500 years) were unable to observe such a yoke of slavery themselves! Kefa basically says, "Why try to put the Gentiles under the Law when we Jews cannot even follow the Law?" Kefa's yoke in Acts 15:10 is the very same yoke of slavery Sha'ul wrote about in Gal. 5:1. Once again, we see the yoke of slavery is the desire to observe the Law of Moses for salvation or sanctification purposes. Sha'ul in his usual way points all believers to freedom from the Law through grace rather than to slavery under the Law through obedience. Whether 2,000 years ago or today, we see this same issue plagues the MJM. We need a return to the simplicity of the Scripture which resolved this problem for Jewish and Gentile believers a long time ago!

5:2 Keener makes an astute point concerning Jewish tradition and Gentile salvation.
He proclaims,

> *"Most Jewish teachers allowed that righteous Gentiles could be saved by keeping merely the seven laws believed to have been given to Noah; but any Gentile who converted to Judaism was responsible to keep all 613 commandments given to Israel at Mount Sinai (according to rabbinic count). Rabbis said that the law was a whole, and one had to keep all of it; rejecting any part of it was tantamount to rejecting the whole thing."* z

Sha'ul's theological statements directly contradict typical Jewish tradition with Gentile conversion. He tells the Galatian believers if they listen to the Legalizers and receive circumcision then Yeshua will be of no benefit to them. This is a serious statement. So why is Sha'ul so strong against circumcision when it is a major Jewish rite of passage given to Avraham by God and completes a Gentile in their conversion process to becoming a Jew?! Verse 4 reveals that their hearts were not right before the Lord in that they were seeking to be justified by the Law through their desired obedience to receive circumcision. Sha'ul's point here is to show the Galatians they were not living by faith through love but were living by obedience to the Law to gain justification from God. Sha'ul says that this is wrong!

5:3 Being a "debtor" (*opheiletes*) means "one who is indebted or obligated, one who is bound or committed to a task, idea or person." [8] If a believer receives circumcision for the reason of keeping the Law, then they are indebted and bound to a commitment of keeping the whole Law. Sha'ul is simply saying here that believers do not want to be under obligation or indebted to the Law because they would then be under Law, fall prey to their sin and ultimately become cursed by the Law! Sha'ul said many times to not be under Law.

Warren Wiersbe writes of a wonderful definition of "being under the Law" that strongly compliments Sha'ul's statements in verses 1-3. He declares, "It [being under the Law] simply means that we no longer need the external force of Law to keep us in God's will, because we have the internal leading of the Holy Spirit of God (Rom. 8:1-4) ... To go back to law is to become entangled in a maze of 'do's and don'ts' and to abandon spiritual adulthood for a 'second childhood." [9]

Wiersbe's definition is very provocative and one greatly needed to be understood by the MJM. The Law was the external force that kept the Jewish people following God's will. But now we do not need the external force because believers have the internal guidance of the Ruach Kodesh. He directs and guides us as to God's will for our lives. This internal guidance of the Ruach was prophesied in Jeremiah 31:31-34. This Scripture spoke of a day in the future that God would make a New Covenant with Israel.

This New Covenant would be a covenant not like the Mosaic Covenant which was already broken by the Israelites at the time of Jeremiah's writing. Instead of writing the Law on stone tablets, God would write the Law on their hearts through the power of the indwelling Ruach Kodesh. He would direct the believer through faith, love, joy and the power of God would see them through. So the New Covenant believer would not be under the Law but under God's grace living by faith in the power of the Ruach. How ironic it is that New Covenant believers can fulfill the requirements of the Law, not by trying to strictly obey the commandments of the Law, but by walking in faith through the power of the Ruach!

The second issue in verse 3 is concerned with the Law as a unity. If a believer begins to keep part of the Law then they are under obligation to keep all of the Law. In Keener's quote from 5:2, the Rabbis concur that the Law is a whole and one had to keep all of the Law. Rejecting any portion of the Law was rejecting the whole Law. Yacov (James) certainly agreed with the Rabbis as he stated in 2:10, *"For whosoever shall keep the whole law, and yet offend in one point, he is guilty of all."* The Law is a unified whole and if anyone breaks one commandment then it is like breaking all of the commandments. God obviously designed it this way to show mankind that we cannot keep the whole Law and therefore cannot rely upon our own strength to try to please God. We must rely upon God's strength given to us through the Ruach Kodesh. This is most definitely Sha'ul's point in chapter 5 as we shall continue to see.

5:4 If the Galatians (or today's MJM) had not understood the seriousness of this theological situation as yet, then verse 4 should have caused some great fear. The NASB puts it this way, *"You have been severed from Messiah, you who are seeking to be justified by law; you have fallen from grace."* It is obvious that Sha'ul connects those who try to keep the Law in verse 3 with those who are seeking to be justified by the Law in verse 4. "Justified" was earlier defined as being declared just or righteous before God. If believers desire to become righteous before God by keeping the Law then Sha'ul says that Messiah has "become of no effect" unto them. This is one of Sha'ul's many profound stinging rebukes toward believers in this epistle.

"Become of no effect unto you" (*katargeo*) has many meanings: "to render inactive, idle, useless, ineffective... make to cease... to abrogate, make void... to destroy, cause to cease, do away with and put an end to." [10] *Katargeo* is found in the indicative mood, aorist tense and passive voice of the Greek grammar. The indicative mood reveals that this statement is a positive and clear cut statement of fact. The aorist tense shows that the action has occurred in the past. The passive voice shows the subject is the receiver of the action. When found in the passive voice *katargeo* means "to cease from, i.e., to cease being under or connected with any person... In Gal. 5:4...[it means] 'ye have withdrawn from Christ' (a.t.), you do not have any fellowship with Him." [11]

The Greek grammar here does not show a destruction of relationship between the believer and

God. But it does show that if any believer tries to be justified before God by keeping the Law they will cease to be in fellowship with Yeshua. This is a straight forward statement of fact that occurs at the moment of trying to be justified and Yeshua does the actual work of ceasing the fellowship (presumably until the believer confesses their sin and repents). The context of Gal. 5 additionally agrees that the topic discussed is one of sanctification and fellowship with the Lord and nothing else. In summary, Sha'ul is saying that believers who seek to be justified by the Law have become useless and ineffective. As a result, Messiah caused them to be withdrawn and disfellowshipped from Himself, thus revealing that their way of becoming just is fleshly and ungodly and there should be some sort of conviction for repentance. This truth puts the MJM at great odds with the straight-forwardness of this Scripture! The MJM believes the very opposite of what this Scripture is saying and there needs to be repentance.

The Galatian situation reminds me of the Laodicean church's predicament found in Rev. 3:14-22. The Laodiceans needed to repent from their prideful attitude of not needing anything including Yeshua. The result of their sin was a disfellowship from Yeshua. The picture in Rev. 3 is one of Yeshua knocking on the door of the congregation to get back inside to fellowship with the believers. He even pleads with them to just open the door so He can dine with them. Similar is this situation with the Galatians who are Torah observant for the purpose of being righteous before God. Through their desire to follow Torah to gain righteousness, they have pushed Yeshua out of their lives. Yeshua simply is saying for them to repent and He will dine with them once again. They must stop trying to follow the Law and put themselves under God's grace. The problem, of course, is that they who have been rendered inactive and useless have "fallen from grace."

"Fallen from grace" (*ekpipto charis*) means to "fall from, drop away or a losing of grace." [12] Those who try to justify themselves before God by following Torah are not only useless and ineffective for the Messiah because they are no longer in fellowship with Him but have also fallen from His grace. There are some that say "fallen from grace" means to either lose or forfeit their salvation. However, the context shows Sha'ul is encouraging believers to enter back into God's truth and fellowship with Yeshua (verses 4-7). He even predicts this will happen in verse 10 and says they are "in the Lord." Therefore, "fallen from grace" means just that: they have fallen from God's grace in fellowship.

The ones who put themselves under the Law have fallen from God's loving hands of grace and have put themselves into the Law's tight grip of judgment. There are only two places a believer can be under: the Law or God's grace. If a believer is Torah Observant for the purpose of sanctification then they have put themselves under the Law and are no longer under grace but have fallen from God's grace to the Law. If a believer is under grace then they are no longer under the Law and have put themselves under grace. Sha'ul is once again plainly telling us that we should not be under Law but under grace!

5:5 Trying to please the Lord by keeping Torah for sanctification reasons keeps the believer focused on the present circumstances of their life. God, instead, wants believers to fix their eyes upon Yeshua and the future hope of righteousness He will bring. As this Scripture shows, living by faith in the Ruach causes the believer to be concerned for the future hope that we have in Yeshua! That future hope is the return of Yeshua to set up His Messianic Millennial Kingdom. This kingdom will be set up in His righteousness, justice and peace.

The first five verses of chapter 5 thus far have revealed to us that we must stand firm in the freedom that Messiah gave us. We are not to put ourselves under the Law and try to keep Torah because that makes us useless and powerless in Messiah and causes us to fall from His grace. How are we to live by God's standards? How can we even fulfill the Law? The same way that Yeshua did it. We are to walk in faith and by the power of the Ruach Kodesh. Hebrews 11:6 states, *"But without faith it is impossible to please him [God]..."* Living by faith and living by the works of the Law are diabolically opposed to one another. Believers must choose one or the other; they cannot choose to live by both. One cannot please God by following the works of the Law but one can please God by living in faith. When we live by faith, our focus in life is on eternity and not on our current circumstances.

5:6 This Scripture proves beyond a shadow of any doubt that trying to keep Torah is not for the New Covenant believer of today. This verse makes circumcision a non-issue for all believers! If Torah Observance is supposed to be so important to the Lord in the theology of the MJM, then why is circumcision a non-issue? This is just another question the MJM needs to answer.

The major problem the MJM would have here is that circumcision is of great importance to Jewish people worldwide! The Torah says that all male Jewish babies should be circumcised on the eighth day to enter into the Avrahamic Covenant and become Jews! It is not only God's command but a rite of passage for all Jewish males to be circumcised (Gen. 17:9-12). The Rabbis of the Chumash commentary proclaim:

> *"Circumcision is literally a sign, a mark, on the body, stamping its bearer as a servant of God; just as their souls are different than those of other nations, so their bodies must be different. God ordained that this sign be placed on the reproductive organ to symbolize that circumcision is essential to Jewish eternity (Chinuch)... An adult who intentionally remains uncircumcised suffers karayt, spiritual excision. Excision means that the soul loses its share in the World to Come, and the violator may die childless and prematurely."* [13]

Although this rabbinical quote does not speak God's truth in that circumcision is essential to Jewish eternity, the point is made of the great importance circumcision plays in the lifestyle of Jewish people and yet the Lord says in 5:6 that circumcision has no meaning and is a non-issue in the New Covenant believer's life. How can this be if Torah is for today and Messianic believers are supposed to be following it? The obvious answer is that the New Covenant supersedes the Old Covenant. Whether believers are circumcised or not in this age is a topic that is indifferent to our God.

What then is important to our Lord in this age? That our faith is working through love. This is the truth that we in the MJM need to understand if we are going to fulfill God's calling for our movement: faith working through love is much more important than keeping Torah! Sha'ul encourages all believers to live by three character traits in 1 Cor. 13:13: faith, hope and love. It is interesting that Sha'ul discussed all three of these traits in Gal. 5:5-6. In verse 5, Sha'ul said we are waiting for the hope of righteousness to come. In verse 6, he proclaims that faith working in love means a great deal to Yeshua. Which is the greatest of these three? Love! Yeshua commanded us to love God and love our neighbor. On these two commandments hang all the Law and the Prophets.

5:7 "Ye did run well" means that the Galatians were living by God's grace. They were not working for their salvation or sanctification trying to please the Lord through their obedience to the Torah but they were living by faith working through love. Sha'ul wanted to know who sidetracked them from following the truth. Obviously, Sha'ul knew it was the Legalizers.

This group of Torah Observers followed Sha'ul from city to city to try and destroy his ministry. What is interesting is that Sha'ul here claims that Torah Observance is not God's truth. The Galatians were already following the truth of grace and the Legalizers came into town and convinced them that following the Law would please God. Sha'ul had already declared in verse 1 that the Galatians should keep standing firm in the freedom of Messiah and not be subjected again to the yoke of the Law. And yet, they fell from God's grace into the masterful grips of the Law.

5:8 Not only did the Legalizers teach wrong doctrines but they were not even called by God. "Calleth" (*kaleo*) means to "call, name, summons, invite... But more importantly, in a theological sense, God invites men and women to participate in fellowship with Him and in His salvation." [14] Therefore, this verse indicates that the Legalizers were not called by God to participate in the good news message ministry which involves teaching and discipling. If the Legalizers were not teaching the truth and were not called by God then they were teaching false doctrine which was contrary to Sha'ul's preaching. This is why he strongly encouraged the Galatians to stand firm in the truth and rebuke the false. This is profound since the Legalizers of the first century taught the very same doctrines the Torah Observant of the MJM teach today!

5:9 Pesach (Passover) is a feast of the Lord where the Jewish people were commanded to clean all the leaven out of their homes. The mother of the household would find and clean out all the leaven from the home just prior to the beginning of Passover. However, she would leave a few pieces of bread crumbs for the father of the household to find while performing his inspection. Once the house was fully clean of all leaven, he would pray unto the Lord that his home was null and void of all leaven and that the family was now ready to celebrate the Passover.

The parents of the household could not mistakenly leave some leaven lying around the house during Passover because "a little leaven leavens the whole lump." Leaven in the Bible is a sign for sin. Therefore, the symbolic meaning of the cleansing of leaven is to clean out all the sin from the household. The application then is for the Galatians to make sure that the sin of the Legalizers' teachings would not become a cancer within the Galatian congregations.

Sha'ul additionally encouraged the Corinth congregation in the same way. 1 Corinthians 5:6-8 states,

> *"Your glorying is not good. Know ye not that a little leaven leaveneth the whole lump? Purge out therefore the old leaven, that ye may be a new lump, as ye are unleavened. For even*

Christ our Passover is sacrificed for us: Therefore let us keep the feast, not with old leaven, neither with the leaven of malice and wickedness; but with the unleavened bread of sincerity and truth."

The Galatians, just like the Corinthians, were to protect their congregations from the leaven (false teaching) of the Legalizers and continue to teach the good news message of freedom from the Law by living in God's grace of sincerity and truth.

5:10 Sha'ul now believes he has won the hearts of the erring Galatians. He hopes they will adopt no other view than his own which he has documented thus far in his letter. His belief is so strong that he used the word "confidence." "Confidence" (*peitho*) means to "convince, persuade, appease, and satisfy... 'To put one's confidence in God,' then, is tantamount to 'believe and be obedient' (Gal. 5:7 [where *peitho* is used for *obeying* the truth])." [15] Here, Sha'ul tried to persuade or convince the Galatians to follow his teaching on walking with the Lord rather than keeping the false teaching of the Legalizers. *Peitho* is found in the perfect tense which means a completed action in the past with lingering results in the present. Sha'ul is not only fully persuaded the Galatians will follow his view on the false teaching but that they will continue in the present to enjoy the blessed rewards of their obedience.

Another learned lesson for the Galatians is nicely summarized by Wuest: "The words 'through the Lord,' speak of the Lord Jesus, not primarily as the object of trust, but as the One who is the basis or ground of Paul's confidence." [16] In other words,

Sha'ul's confidence in the Galatians is based solely on Yeshua knowing He has started a good work in them and will finish it! The Galatians need to learn how to grow in this type of confidence. Then they would not be so easily disturbed by any new wind of false teaching.

Kefa (Peter) completely agrees with Sha'ul concerning God's dealings with the false teachers. He proclaims in 2 Peter 2:1, *"But there were false prophets also among the people, even as there shall be false teachers among you, who privily shall bring in damnable heresies, even denying the Lord that bought them, and bring upon themselves swift destruction."* False teachers, who do not come from God and even deny the Lord Yeshua, will bear His judgment for their evil. This is God's promise for evil. Therefore believers should not be influenced by evil but have confidence in the Lord.

5:11 Keener comments on this verse: "If Paul were simply converting Gentiles to Judaism in the ordinary manner (circumcision for the men, baptism for both men and women), he would not be experiencing Jewish opposition..." [17] However, Sha'ul was not performing the typical job of a Jewish missionary converting Gentiles to Judaism. He was preaching the truth about freedom found in Messiah so that believers do not need to be circumcised or keep the Law.

It seems that the Legalizers who followed Sha'ul's ministry from city to city lied about Sha'ul's preaching of the need for circumcision. If he was preaching the need for circumcision for salvation or sanctification, then he would be abolishing or nullifying "the offence of the cross." "Offence" (*skandalon*) means "offense, snare, something that causes revulsion or anger... Stahlin states, 'the *skandalon* is an obstacle in coming to faith and a cause of going astray in it.'" [18] The very idea of Messiah dying on the cross for our sins can not only cause revulsion and anger in unsaved Jewish people but Messianic Jewish believers as well.

It is difficult for Jewish people to believe that Yeshua's death on the cross was for them because many *meshugenah* (crazy) world leaders (the most prominent was Hitler) have used the label "Christian" and the sign of the cross in their persecution of the Jewish people. I personally know Messianic Jewish believers who still cringe at the spoken word "cross" or even "Christ." This is true because anti-Semites continuously accused them of being "Christ-killers" while publicly beating and abusing them. These Jewish believers have unfortunately carried these burdens all their lives.

Messiah's death on the cross for our sins is a stumbling block to Jew and to Gentile alike. 1 Cor.1:22-23 states: *"For the Jews require a sign, and the Greeks seek after wisdom: But we preach Christ crucified, unto the Jews a stumbling block, and unto the Greeks foolishness..."* The world sees the death of Messiah for our sins as something that makes no sense at all and the Jewish people stumble over it and even get repulsed. This idea is nothing new to the Lord. Isa. 8:14 states, *"And he shall be for a sanctuary; but for a stone of stumbling and for a rock of offence to both the houses of Israel, for a gin and for a snare to the inhabitants of Jerusalem."* The context here reveals that "he" is the Lord of hosts and the children of Israel need to fear the Lord and make Him their sanctuary rather than stumbling over and being offended at the Lord.

Not only is Messiah's death a stumbling block to the Jewish people but His dying on the "cross" is an offense to them. The very word "cross" is typically not used in Jewish missions because there is an automatic understanding of hatred for this sign. We typically like to use the word "tree" instead because many Jewish people were persecuted under the sign of the cross.

Deuteronomy 21:22-23 proclaims, *"And if a man have committed a sin worthy of death, and he be to be put to death, and thou hang him on a tree: His body shall not remain all night upon the tree, but thou shalt in any wise bury him that day; (for he that is hanged is accursed of God;) that thy land be not defiled, which the LORD thy God giveth thee for an inheritance."* The Lord instructed Israel to hang the grievous sinner on a tree for all to see. This form of punishment was meant to keep the Jewish people in order. No one would want to die this kind of death because anyone who did was thought to be accursed by God. Therefore, Jewish people make an application to Yeshua in that since He died on a tree He must be accursed of God. If He was accursed of God then how could He be the Messiah?!

5:12 This is a very strongly worded ending to a section of Scripture that has been full of powerful language. Sha'ul was obviously very angry at the Legalizers who were causing trouble for his good news ministry and the Galatians' lives. "Trouble" (*anastatoo*) means to "disturb, upset, unsettle... the Judaizers were 'troubling' the Church with their errant doctrine, but who can deny that Paul saw their heresy as destructive to true faith." [19] So we see Sha'ul's dramatic statement wishing the Legalizers would even mutilate themselves!

It is hard to believe Sha'ul actually means this. However, I believe Sha'ul is making an exaggerated point to show his displeasure with the Legalizers. Instead of these Legalizers cutting off the foreskin of the Galatians in circumcision they should cut themselves completely off. "Cut off" (*apokopto*) means to "cut off, cut loose, castrate." [20] So, there is no doubt here that Sha'ul meant these Legalizers should castrate themselves!

Sha'ul does seem to be protective over the Galatians and why not?! If one seemingly little thing is added to his message of salvation and sanctification through faith, the good news that Messiah has set us free from our sins is completely destroyed. This message is sorely lacking in the MJM. We must be careful not to be ensnared by the Torah Observant message of keeping Torah for salvation and/or sanctification. Messiah has set us free from our sins and He has set us free from the "yoke of bondage" (the Law) so we can live the abundant life in the Ruach. Messiah has set us free, so we are free indeed!

Chapter 13

Messiah Called Us To Freedom
(5:13-18)

5:13 *For, brethren, ye have been called unto liberty; only use not liberty for an occasion to the flesh, but by love serve one another.*
5:14 *For all the law is fulfilled in one word, even in this; Thou shalt love thy neighbor as thyself.*
5:15 *But if ye bite and devour one another, take heed that ye be not consumed one of another.*
5:16 *This I say then, Walk in the Spirit, and ye shall not fulfill the lust of the flesh.*
5:17 *For the flesh lusteth against the Spirit, and the Spirit against the flesh: and these are contrary the one to the other: so that ye cannot do the things that ye would.*
5:18 *But if ye be led of the Spirit, ye are not under the law.*

In 5:1-12, we found that Messiah set us free from the Law at the moment of our salvation experience. Sha'ul encouraged us to stand strong in our freedom and not allow ourselves to be caught up in the yoke of slavery of the Law. Our forefathers could not master the Law so how can we be expected to do it today? Sha'ul even had harsh words against anyone trying to be justified by the Law: you have been severed from Messiah and fallen from grace. Instead of keeping Torah, we should instead continue to live by our faith in Yeshua working through love. In this section of Scripture, we find that Messiah not only set us free, but He *called* us to freedom. Therefore, we should walk in this freedom and not in slavery.

5:13 "Called" (*kaleo*) was already defined in 5:8 of this book. It means "to call, name, summon, or invite. But more importantly, in a theological sense, God invites men and women to participate in fellowship with Him and in His salvation." [1] *Kaleo* is found to be in the indicative mood, aorist tense and passive voice. The indicative mood indicates a positive and clear cut statement. The aorist tense shows the verb is a completed action in the past. The passive voice reveals the subject is the receiver of the action. Therefore, the phrase "ye have been called unto liberty" has no hidden meaning but is a straight forward statement. Our calling was in the past and hence we see the words "have been" added to the English versions. Finally, no one but God performed the action of the calling. We received the calling to be free in our walk with Messiah when we received Yeshua. God did all the work in this calling with our part as only a reaction to the calling.

It is interesting to note that this calling of God is through His grace (Gal. 1:6, 15) and never through the Law. This grace versus law dichotomy is one of the themes of Galatians in that we need to be under grace and not under Law. Sha'ul is obviously readdressing this theme in this section of Scripture. However, the question remains, "So what were we called to?" The obvious answer is we were called to freedom!

"Liberty" *(eleutheria)* has previously been defined as having liberty or freedom. In 5:1, we found out that Messiah set us free from the Law. Now, we see that Messiah has additionally set us free from sin. Since we have freedom from the Law, this does not give us a license to sin. Sha'ul encouraged the Romans with this same message in 6:1-2, *"What shall we say then? Shall we continue in sin, that grace may abound? God forbid. How shall we, that are dead to sin, live any longer therein?"* Just because we are no longer under Law but are under grace, we should not take lightly our responsibility before the Lord to walk the straight and narrow path with Yeshua and not sin. Sinning was considered bad and evil under the Law and continues to be bad and evil under grace. We are not allowed to take for granted that everything is fine when we sin under grace. It is not okay as Sha'ul points out in the rest of Gal. 5. Here in verse 13, we are encouraged to prohibit opportunities or temptations for the flesh to sin and to live in freedom through love.

Some of the Galatians received the challenge of the calling of God and some did not. Those who accepted the calling were instructed to control the flesh. "Flesh" *(sarx)* has already been defined in 3:3. It is the "flesh, human, mortal nature, physical life. *Sarx* signifies man's sinful nature, the seat of sinful desires and passions. In this sense "flesh" includes not only the physical body but the spiritual side as well." [2] The flesh sets its desires against the Ruach and is in constant battle with Him (verse 17). In the rest of the chapter the deeds of the flesh are contrasted with the fruit of the Spirit and the deeds of the flesh are found wanting. There is no life in the flesh and thus Sha'ul's command to not allow any opportunities for the flesh to open the door of freedom to the enemy of sin. Instead, Sha'ul says the Galatians should serve one another through love.

5:14 Since we were called to freedom from the Law and sin, we should serve one another in love. It is through love believers can fulfill the Law. Instead of trying to fulfill the Law through "*mitzvot*" (good deeds) and strict observance of the Law, believers can fulfill the Law through loving our neighbor. Verse 14 should be very damaging to the theology of the Torah Observant of the MJM. This verse contradicts their understanding that believers need to keep Torah for sanctification purposes. Love fulfills the Law, strict observance to the Law cannot and will not ever fulfill the Law. It is quite ironic that the very purpose of the Torah Observant is to fulfill the Law through their strict observance of the Law. Their great desire is to fulfill the Law because they believe this is Yeshua's directive for them and yet this verse says they can easily fulfill the Law through loving their neighbor rather than by keeping Torah.

"Fulfilled" (*pleroo*) means to "make full, complete, accomplish, bring to completion and fulfill. This meaning [of completion] may be found in a temporal sense of finishing or bringing to a conclusion..." [3] This is the idea here where love fulfills or completes the Law or even accomplishes the goal of the Law. However, *pleroo* is found to be in the present tense. This means the action of completing is a continuous action in the present. Therefore, as we share our love for our neighbor in the present we fulfill and complete the whole Law. This is a continuous life long process of fulfilling the Law through love. Every act of love that we as believers complete fulfills the Law.

Since this is biblically true, why would any believer want or desire to go back to a system of worship that only puts them under the Law and can never fulfill the Law? Especially, when Yeshua simply states that the way to fulfill the Law is to love our neighbor! This is the freedom that the Lord called us to. In fact, some of the ancient Rabbis understood this theme of love fulfilling the Law. David Stern reports in his commentary,

> "Rabbi Simlai said, '613 commandments were given to Moses... David came and reduced them to eleven (Psalm 15), Isaiah to six (Isaiah 33:15), Micah to three (Micah 6:8), and Isaiah again to two – "Observe justice and do righteousness" (Isaiah 56:1). Then Amos came and reduced them to one, "Seek me and live" (Amos 5:4) – as did Habakkuk, "The righteous one will live by his trusting" (Habakkuk 2:4).' (Makkot 23b – 24a, abridged)." [4]

Rabbi Simlai reduced the 613 commandments of the Law down to one simple phrase "seek and trust the Lord!" It is obvious that if followers of God are seeking Him and living by trust in Him then they most certainly love Him. It is God's love that permeates throughout the Bible and He is the One who showed and continues to show us how it is done.

Yeshua had this goal in mind of fulfilling the Law through love rather than through strict obedience (although He certainly was able to keep the Law flawlessly). However, His ultimate act of love actually fulfilled and completed the Law like no one else could do. In Matt. 5:17, we saw Yeshua in His first coming completely fulfilled the Law. It states, *"Think not that I am come to destroy the law, or the prophets: I am not come to destroy, but to fulfill."* Yeshua could not come to destroy the Law or the

Prophets. Their words written down are His words! Why would He come to destroy His own words? This is not possible. So what did He come to do in His first advent? Completely fulfill the Messianic mission the Law and the Prophets wrote about.

"Fulfilled" (*pleroo*) is found in the aorist tense which means it is an action in the past. He came to fulfill what was written of Him and He did it. As He ascended into heaven, He fulfilled the Law and the Prophets through His unconditional love for all of us. Sha'ul in this verse simply wanted the Galatians to follow in Yeshua's footsteps of love to fulfill the Law rather than by any other means.

Sha'ul also wanted the Galatians who were keeping Torah to notice his quote of Lev. 19:18. If they truly wanted to keep Torah then they should listen to the Torah especially when Lev. 19:18 states, "... *but thou shalt love thy neighbor as thyself: I am the LORD."* Sha'ul's application in verse 14 is implied in Leviticus. If they truly want to keep Torah and follow God's commands, then they need to love their neighbor and fulfill the Law! The Rabbis even agree: "R' [Rabbi] Akiva said that this [love] is the fundamental rule of the Torah (Rashi; Sifra)." [5]

Yeshua most certainly agreed with these statements when confronted by the lawyer in Matt. 22:34-40. The lawyer asked Yeshua which commandment in the Law was the greatest. Yeshua replied that loving the Lord God was the greatest and the second was similar: love your neighbor as yourself. Out of all the 613 commandments of the Law, love took first place. Without love in a person's heart there is no fulfillment of the Law. It is just as Yeshua concluded: that the whole Law and the Prophets hung on these two commandments of love. Love is the Law, love within the freedom of our calling.

5:15 "Bite" (*dakno*) is a word that is "...used in the Septuagint primarily to translate the Hebrew word *nashakh*, which describes the 'bite of serpents'... Its' only usage in the New Testament is a figurative reference to fighting within the Galatians church (Gal. 5:15)." [6] This fighting within the congregations involves constant battling between congregants for *dakno* is found to be in the present tense. The "biting" of one another is a continuous action in the present tense. Presumably, these members were fighting and devouring one another over the new teaching they had received from the Legalizers.

"Devour" (*katesthio*) means "to eat, swallow, devour... Metaphorically, of things such as fire...to consume or destroy one another."[7] Keener reports that the ancients used this metaphor of "being eaten" by others as a grotesque description of a horrible fate of an inconceivable wickedness. [8] In verse 15, the idea is consuming or destroying one another because they were at odds over major congregational issues such as the Legalizers' teaching on the Law. Sha'ul taught Titus in 3:9, *"But avoid foolish questions, and genealogies, and contentions, and strivings about the law; for they are unprofitable and vain."* The Galatians needed to listen to Sha'ul's advice to Titus that they should not be disputing and causing strife over the Law but they should love one another as God loved them.

Sha'ul used strong language ("bite" and "devour") to describe how fleshly the Galatians were misbehaving. This behavior was very dangerous because they were consuming one another. "Consumed" (*analisko*) means "to take away, destroy, consume." [9] When one is so consumed and determined to keep the Law as the Legalizers taught, it is very easy to forget that loving your neighbor is much more important to the Lord. We need to remember that one purpose of the Law is to reveal how utterly sinful we are, even to the point of destroying one another's faith just like the Galatians were doing.

There were obviously two sects fighting within the Galatian congregations. One, the Torah Observant group who agreed with the Legalizers and tried to fulfill the Law for sanctification reasons while walking in the flesh. The second, the New Covenant Freedom group who recognized their walk with the Lord should be out of love and grace and in the power of the Ruach Kodesh. Both seemed to be causing division within the congregations through their dissent and were commanded by Sha'ul to cease their evil ways because they would destroy each other and the congregations. Instead of destroying one another they were to love one another for this was the greatest command of Torah.

5:16 Instead of destroying one another through the desires of their flesh the Galatians should love one another by walking in the Ruach. If they would only walk in the Spirit, then they would not carry out their fleshly desires. "Walk" (*peripateo*) means to "go about, walk around, walk, live, and conduct oneself... Thus in the New Testament *peripateo* takes on particular significance and denotes the general life-style – ethical, moral, religious. Through the Spirit's work believers can live/walk as godly people, pleasing to God..." [10] Here, literal "walking" is not the meaning but the theological significance is described through the spiritual life-style of the believer.

"Walk" is a verb found in the present tense and active voice. The active voice reveals the subject of the "walking" is the doer of the action. The doers of the action of walking with the Ruach are the Galatians. Hence, the emphasis and the responsibility here relies upon the Galatians, not God. The present tense shows a continuous action in the present. The Galatians were to continuously live and conduct themselves in Godly ways. To summarize, *peripateo* means "you continuously walk." God told the Galatians that they must yield themselves to the power of the Ruach in all their thoughts, desires, actions and lives so that they would not yield to the power of the flesh and continue to destroy each other.

The Hebrew equivalent word for "walk" which has the same broad meaning is *halach (halachah* is the more accepted spoken word used in Judaism). *Halachah* in Judaism means "the way of walking" or "the path of life." This day-to-day way of life includes the understandings of Biblical law, Talmudic law, rabbinic law, Jewish customs and traditions. The *Halachah* is a comprehensive guide to all aspects of human life, both corporeal and spiritual. Its laws, guidelines, and opinions cover a vast range of situations and principles, in the attempt to realize what is implied by the central Biblical commandment to "be holy as I your God am holy." [11] To say the least about *halachah*, it is believed to be the most important aspect of Judaism. It is the determiner of how one lives life in Judaism. The unfortunate aspect of *halachah* is that it is just as diverse within Judaism as denominations are within Christianity! However, one day in the future, *halachah* for the Jewish people will come from only one source – the Messiah Yeshua!

This future time is spoken of in Ezekiel 36:27. It states, *"And I will put my spirit within you, and cause you to **walk** in my statutes, and ye shall keep my judgments, and do them.* [Bold emphasis is mine]" God is speaking here prophesying that He will save the Jewish people, indwell them with the Ruach Kodesh and help them to walk in His commands. Here, walking in His commands is equivalent to walking in the Holy Spirit. "Walk" is the same word *halach* that means "the way of life." This new way of living by the Ruach Kodesh for the Jewish people on a whole will only occur at the end of Jacob's Trouble (or commonly known as the Tribulation Period) and the beginning of the Messianic Millennial Kingdom. Let us take a look at the context of this verse to prove this statement.

Ezekiel 36 discusses the prophecy of the Lord in that He will gather all the Jewish people back to the Land of Israel and judge all the other nations who treated Israel poorly. Verses 22-24 tell us that God will vindicate His name by gathering all the Jewish people from around the world back to the Land of Israel. This is the prophecy regarding the return of the Jewish people to the Land of Israel. Since 1989, one million Jewish people from Russia have returned to the Land. Even to this day, God continues to call the Jews from all over the world to come home. There are now approximately 6 million Jewish people living in Israel.

Verses 25-28 show us that God will then cleanse the Jewish people from their sin and idols. They will be saved at the end of Jacob's Trouble through the indwelling of the Ruach Kodesh so that they can walk in the newness of life and actually keep the (what I call the "new and improved") Torah of the Messianic Millennial Kingdom. There will not be any more destroying of one another but there will be walking in the new *halachah* of the Lord!

5:17 Although the future Kingdom will be filled with righteousness, justice and peace, the believers of that time period will still be wrought with the sin nature. Unfortunately, believers of today have to deal with this same war that bombards our bodies from within each and every day of our lives. This war is between the flesh and the Spirit. The problem, of course, is that the result of this war can cause us not to perform God's will for our lives.

"Flesh" (*sarx*) has already been defined in this commentary as the sinful nature that is corrupt and at enmity with God. [12] Ultimately, this is the reason why the flesh and the Ruach are in direct opposition to one another. The sinful nature is bad and causes us to do the things that are contrary to God's will. The Ruach, on the other hand, is good and wants to lead us down the path to God's will. When we lose this constant battle from within it reveals that we have given ourselves over to the power of the sinful nature. When we win this constant battle it is indicative of having given ourselves over to the power of the Ruach. Therefore, a believer is either led by the Spirit and under His control or led by the sinful nature and under its' control.

Sha'ul's point is that since believers are called to freedom, we should not let our guard down and succumb to the flesh. In addition, believers should not even try to overcome the flesh in their own power. Nor should Messianic believers try to overcome the flesh by putting themselves under the Law. The Law actually helps and encourages the flesh to sin even more. However, we should put ourselves under the Ruach so that we could then be led by the Ruach and not be under Law.

Sha'ul never said that this battle within us would be easily won. In fact, he wrote of his own personal failures in dealing with the flesh versus the Spirit. Romans 7:14-17 declares, *"For we know that the law is spiritual: but I am carnal, sold under sin. For that which I do I allow not: for what I would, that do I not; but what I hate, that do I. If then I do that which I would not, I consent unto the law that it is good. Now then it is no more I that do it, but sin that dwelleth in me."*

Sha'ul begins in verse 14 stating that the Law is spiritual because it is the Word of God. God's Word is most definitely holy and good. The whole Bible is important for all believers to live Godly lives. Sha'ul continues to proclaim that all believers are "sold into bondage to sin." In other words, we all have the sinful nature that causes us to sin. Verse 15 tells us we are going to perform hateful deeds in this life because of our flesh. We are sometimes going to lose the inward battle between the flesh and the Ruach. This is a fact of life! Then in verse 16, Sha'ul reveals a fascinating truth. Our sins prove that the Law is good. When we sin, we agree with the Law because the purpose of the Law is to show us that we are sinners. The purpose of the Law was never to sanctify believers. In verse 17, the Law shows us even as believers we are no good and that the sinful nature indwells us. Sha'ul concludes this section with a plea unto the Lord, *"O wretched man that I am! Who will set me free...?"* The obvious answer is Adonai Yeshua Hameshiach (Lord Jesus the Messiah)! He will set us free from the power of the Law and the power of the flesh when we give ourselves completely over to the Ruach Kodesh and stop trying to keep Torah in our own power but be led by the Ruach's power. When this happens we will be able to please the Lord by faith, love and grace.

5:18 "Led" (*ago*) has many meanings including "lead, bring, guide, spend, keep, to bring forward or to drive." [13] To be led by the Ruach is to have the Ruach as the guiding force in one's life. If a believer is guided by the Ruach then it is obvious to know that they are not under Law. "Under" (*hupo*) has already been defined earlier in this book. When used with a noun found in the accusative case it figuratively signifies subordination. The "Law" is found to be in the accusative case in this verse and so we see another verse that emphatically speaks to Messianic believers to resist putting themselves under the Law. Here, being under the Law is the same as making the Law your master. When believers put themselves under the Law they put themselves under the control of the Law. So what is the problem with that?

Sha'ul says that if you are led by the Spirit then you are not led by the Law or under its power or influence. The concept of Law versus Spirit is diametrically opposed. Believers cannot be led by both. Sha'ul emphatically states in this section that believers choose who they subject and submit themselves to. They either choose the Ruach or the Law; they cannot have both as masters. This is why I said earlier it is very difficult and almost impossible to be led by the Lord to keep Torah! There is a fine line between keeping Torah for Torah's sake and following the Torah through the Lord's leading. It is so easy to fall back into keeping Torah for Torah's sake and therefore sinning against the Lord.

Yeshua certainly agrees that we can not have two masters. He taught us in Matt. 6:24, *"No man can serve two masters: for either he will hate the one, and love the other; or else he will hold to the one, and despise the other. Ye cannot serve God and mammon."* Therefore, we cannot have the Lord and the Law as our masters. We would end up hating one and loving the other. God forbid that believers could put the Law first in our lives and end up hating the Lord. Unfortunately, this is exactly what the Torah Observant movement is doing within the MJM.

The focus of life becomes so centered on Torah and being Jewish that Yeshua takes a back seat in the congregation. The Torah scroll and service become most important in congregational life that Yeshua then becomes despised and even His name is rarely mentioned. This focus overtakes Messianic lives so dramatically that some congregations have been known to verbally attack anyone who names the name of "Jesus!" Jewish lifestyle becomes so important that a person is not even allowed to use the non-Jewish name of "Jesus" at the congregation. Yeshua said we cannot have two masters, so who is your master? You must choose either the Law or the Lord. Believers need to pray for the MJM to recognize the fact that when we are led by the Ruach we are not under the power of the Law and are free from the Law.

One answer to this problem is found in one of Wiersbe's fascinating quotes, "Christ died for me to remove the *penalty* of my sin, but I died with Messiah to break its power." [14] The answer is to die to self and die to the sin nature. But how can Messianic believers do this while they are trying to keep Torah for sanctification reasons? They cannot because the Torah will not let them. It continuously places their sin ever before them so that they cannot die to self and their sin. So then what is the answer to the dilemma? Be led by the Ruach, die to self and love one another unconditionally. Gal. 2:19-20 emphatically states, *"For I through the law am dead to the law, that I might live unto God. I am crucified with Christ: nevertheless I live; yet not I, but Christ liveth in me: and the life which I now live in the flesh I live by the faith of the Son of God, who loved me, and gave himself for me."*

Although these two Scriptures have already been analyzed earlier it is important to reiterate their importance. Believers of Yeshua have died to the Law so that we might live for God. Believers of Yeshua have died to self so that Messiah can live in us so that we would live by the Ruach and not by the flesh anymore. This is why it is so important to understand that living by the Law for the Law's sake is living for the flesh and sin and is not living for the Lord!

When believers say they are Torah Observant and put the Law first in their lives, they make Yeshua second. This automatically is a sin because Yeshua needs to be first in our lives. In addition, when believers try to keep Torah with all its commands, they are in a never ending battle of dealing with their sin since one of the Law's purposes is to reveal sin in the believers' life. The resultant behavior of this lifestyle either has to be a constant daily life of confession and repentance or there has to be a great denial of sin.

I believe that a great denial of sin occurs more often in the Torah Observant movement than the constant daily confession of sin. If this denial of sin is occurring in the lives of Messianic believers who are Torah observant then they are living in the flesh and not in the Ruach. This is Sha'ul's point of this passage: do not live in the flesh but live by the Ruach. This is so important to now know because the next section of Scripture shows believers how to identify whether they are under the Law and being fleshly or whether they are led by the Spirit and being Godly.

Before we study this next section of Scripture (5:19-26), I would like to share a quote that should be very detrimental for the MJM. It needs to be prefaced that Wiersbe did not write this quote for the MJM but for Christians who are entrenched in legalism. These are believers who are trying to make their sin nature good by keeping Torah. This is truly an impossible feat. They believe they are succeeding but eventually the flesh will rebel and then all hell breaks loose in their lives. Here, Wiersbe contrasts the mindset of believers who are following the Ruach with those who are entangled in legalism. Please also note that there is usually a charismatic leader espousing legalism in these congregations and Wiersbe comments about this in his quote. He profoundly declares,

> *"It is easy to see the sequence of thought in these closing chapters [of Galatians]: 1. I have been set free by Christ. I am no longer under bondage to the law (Gal. 5:1-12). 2. But I need something – Someone – to control my life from within. That Someone is the Holy Spirit (5:13-26). 3. Through the Spirit's love, I have a*

a desire to live for others, not for self (6:1-10). 4. This life of liberty is so wonderful, I want to live it to the glory of God; for he is the One making it possible (6:11-18).

Now, contrast this with the experience of the person who chooses to live under law, under the discipline of some religious leader: 1. If I obey these rules, I will become a more spiritual person. I am a great admirer of this religious leader, so I now submit myself to his system. 2. I believe I have the strength to obey and improve myself. I do what I am told, and measure up to the standards set for me. 3. I'm making progress. I don't do some of the things I used to do. Other people compliment me on my obedience and discipline. I can see that I am better than others in my fellowship. How wonderful to be so spiritual. 4. If only others were like me! God is certainly fortunate that I am His. I have a desire to share this with others so they can be as I am. Our group is growing and we have a fine reputation. Too bad other groups are not as spiritual as we are." [15]

It is easy to see the contrast here. One group focuses on self, one's own power and how to fulfill the commandments while the other centers on the love and grace of God and how to please the Lord. One concentrates on the flesh while the other focuses on the Ruach. Wiersbe goes on to say that no matter how one looks at legalism, it is a crafty and dangerous enemy. When believers forsake grace for Law they always lose! When it comes to the Torah Observant of the MJM, he is so right.

Chapter 14

Keep The Fruit Of The Ruach
(5:19-26)

5:19 *Now the works of the flesh are manifest, which are these; Adultery, fornication, uncleanness, lasciviousness,*
5:20 *Idolatry, witchcraft, hatred, variance, emulations, wrath, strife, seditions, heresies,*
5:21 *Envyings, murders, drunkenness, revellings, and such like: of the which I tell you before, as I have also told you in time past, that they which do such things shall not inherit the kingdom of God.*
5:22 *But the fruit of the Spirit is love, joy, peace, longsuffering, gentleness, goodness, faith,*
5:23 *Meekness, temperance: against such there is no law.*
5:24 *And they that are Christ's have crucified the flesh with the affections and lusts.*
5:25 *If we live in the Spirit, let us also walk in the Spirit.*
5:26 *Let us not be desirous of vain glory, provoking one another, envying one another.*

The theme of Gal. 5 is that Messiah set us free. We should stand firm in our freedom and not let the Law become our masters again. Why? Because putting ourselves under the Law will only increase the desires of the flesh and ultimately cause us to be fleshly and sin. Sha'ul encouraged all of us to be led by the Ruach so that we will not be under Law. Those who continuously desire to be justified by the Law have fallen from grace and have lost fellowship with the Lord. This is why I encourage all those who are trying to be justified by the works of the Law to give up and put themselves under God's grace and His Ruach. The Scripture says it is impossible to keep all of the Law so why should anyone try? You can most certainly still enjoy and explore the Jewish Roots of our faith and even live and worship in a Messianic Jewish lifestyle. But taking this Jewish lifestyle to the extreme where we start believing we need to keep the Law to please God is where we get into much trouble with the Lord.

In chapter thirteen of this commentary, we were called by the Lord to this freedom from the Law. We were commanded to walk by the Ruach and not by the flesh recognizing there is a great inward battle between the two. In 5:19-26, Sha'ul revealed the deeds of the flesh and the fruit of the Ruach to provide believers a litmus test on how we should currently live. Sha'ul exhorted us to live and walk by the Ruach not by the flesh.

5:19-21 As Sha'ul begins listing the works of the flesh, he announces that they are evident. "Manifest" (*phaneros*) means "visible, clear, plain, and known... the acts of the sinful nature are 'plain' to all." [1] Sha'ul's point is to direct the Galatian believers to the obvious contrast between the lists of the flesh and the Ruach. These sins of the flesh should be easily identified in one's life by discerning believers. The obvious problem with the Galatian congregations was that some were not discerning believers and hence the reason for the lists.

Lightfoot has categorized these 15 deeds of darkness into 4 groups. He declared,

> *"The sins here mentioned seem to fall into four classes: (1) Sensual passions, 'fornication, uncleanness, licentiousness'; (2) Unlawful dealings in things spiritual, 'idolatry, witchcraft'; (3) Violations of brotherly love, 'enmities, variance, emulations, wrath, strife, seditions, heresies, envyings, murders'; (4) Intemperate excesses, 'drunkenness, revellings."* 2

Whether we classify these deeds of the flesh into four groups or keep them as individual bad works does not affect the fact that Sha'ul's list of fleshly deeds are evil in God's eyes and if we are acting in the flesh we must immediately confess our sin and repent.

As Sha'ul concludes his list of evil, he remarks, *"and such like."* This phrase obviously includes any other similarly sinful act not mentioned in his list. There are many to add like "gossip" but this was not necessary for Sha'ul has firmly made his point. The results of believers walking in the flesh can be devastating. The results of Messianic believers keeping Torah for all the wrong reasons can be just as devastating. Not only can one turn away from God and worship idols but one can horribly treat their fellow neighbor as well. Quite the difference is Yeshua's command to love God and love your neighbor.

After listing the obvious deeds of the flesh, Sha'ul dramatically warns the Galatian congregations, *"that they which do such things shall not inherit the kingdom of God."* The meaning of this phrase has been hotly debated by believers for millennia. Some believe it is talking about believers who lose or forfeit their salvation. Others think it is speaking of "professed believers" who have only fooled themselves and are not "true believers". Still others say this verse is not speaking of salvation but of the rewards for believers in heaven. Let us take a closer look at this phrase.

The question remains, "Who are *they*?" I believe the context of the book and verse 21 dictate who "they" are. They are the ones who so quickly deserted Yeshua for a different good news message (1:6), who sought to be perfected by the flesh and the works of the Law (3:3), who turned back again to the weak and worthless elemental things of the Law (4:9, 21), who subjected themselves again to the yoke of slavery of the Law (5:1) and who have been severed from fellowship with Yeshua and have fallen from His grace (5:5). Sha'ul specifically warned the Galatian believers in verse 21 (and throughout the book) not to practice evil because God would then judge them.

Therefore, "they" are the Messianic believers who received the false teaching of the Legalizers and put themselves back under the workings of the Mosaic Law for the purposes of salvation and/or sanctification. Most of those Messianic believers probably did not even know they were practicing the deeds of darkness because they were so focused on keeping Torah! It is the same today with our MJM; most Messianic believers do not know that their zealous desire to please God through keeping Torah is equated with performing deeds from the flesh and not from the Ruach.

"Do" (prasso) means to "do, accomplish, commit, practice, observe, act, and be." [3] The verb is found to be in the present tense which shows a continuous practicing performed in the present. The revealed idea here is that those Messianic believers who continually practice the deeds of the flesh (which is equated with keeping Torah for salvation and/or sanctification's sake) shall be judged by God and will not receive their inheritance in the kingdom. If they repent from these actions and turn to the New Covenant way of walking in the Ruach, then the Lord will bless them. But until such time they shall not inherit the kingdom of God. What exactly does "inherit the kingdom of God" mean?

This is where most of the heated debate has occurred. "Inherit" (kleronomeo) means to "inherit, be an heir, acquire, obtain, receive and share in." [4] The verb is found to be in the indicative mood, future tense and active voice. This means the statement is a positive and clear cut statement where the subject is the doer of the action in the future. Therefore, the wayward Messianic believers who continue to practice the deeds of the flesh in the present will not receive their inheritance in the future. The key here is the fact that believers will not receive their inheritance based on performing bad works. Can this be discussing salvation? No, because the inheritance is based on performance and salvation can only be based on faith in Yeshua. I believe this inheritance is the rewards that Yeshua will give out at the Bema Seat Judgment.

Dr. Paul Benware beautifully summarized the reality of the believer's future inheritances. He profoundly stated,

> *"The Scriptures speak of two future inheritances: one because we are children of God and one because we are faithful children of God. The first inheritance is the future aspect of our salvation and is the guaranteed inheritance of all believers. The second inheritance*

> *is based on merit and may or may not be received by the believer. A believer can, therefore, possess the first inheritance but not possess the second one. These two differing ideas about our future inheritance are based on the way in which the words are used in the Scriptures. The words involved (Grk. kleronomeo, kleros, kleronomia) speak of an inheritance that is guaranteed to all believers in Jesus Christ and of an inheritance that is conditioned upon the good deeds, as well as the avoidance of sin, of the believer."* [5]

The fact that there are two inheritances waiting for believers in heaven is an awesome illumination of Scripture. What is equally intriguing is that the same Greek words are used to describe both inheritances. So how does one go about determining which inheritance is being discussed in any given verse? The obvious answer is the same one professors of Biblical institutions have been sharing with their students for thousands of years: context, context, and more context!

Dr. Benware continued his discussion concerning this reality. He asserted,

> *"When it is seen that there are actually two inheritances that the believer in Christ has a relationship with, then other portions of Scripture become clearer. One inheritance comes to the believer because of his position as a child of God, but the other is a reward and depends on living faithfully for the Lord*

Jesus. When the Word announces the possible loss of inheritance, the issue is not the loss of the believer's salvation and entrance into hell. It rather has to do with the loss of reward. Several familiar Scriptures deal with this possible loss [including Gal. 5:21]." 6

It has already been established that the inheritance discussed in Gal. 5:21 was one based on continuously practicing deeds of the flesh. Therefore, the context is discussing the second inheritance of receiving rewards rather than the first inheritance of salvation. At this point, it is obvious to conclude that those Messianic believers who turned away from being led by the Ruach to being led by the Law and continue such practices will forfeit many possible future rewards given by Yeshua at the Bema Seat since they are carelessly not avoiding these sins of performing deeds in the flesh.

5:22-23 Herein lies Sha'ul's exhortation for the Galatians: understand and respond to their freedom from the Law by not serving the flesh but living their lives according to the fruit and the power of the Ruach. The word "but" (*de*) beginning this section shows the contrast of the fruit of the Ruach with the deeds of the flesh. The fruit of the Ruach is the result of believers who have yielded themselves unto the Lord and are walking and living in the Ruach's power. The following list of the fruit becomes the litmus test for all believers. We should be asking ourselves on a daily basis whether our words and actions measure up to Sha'ul's list. Are we being loving, joyful, peaceful, patient, kind, good, faithful, gentle and in self-control?

A most interesting observation is found concerning the word "fruit" (*karpos*). *Karpos* is in the singular and yet there are a total of nine fruit found in these verses. How can this be? Wuest declared, "The word *fruit* is singular, which fact serves to show that all of the elements of character spoken of in these verses are a unity, making for a well-rounded and complete Christian life." 7

This idea is very similar to the unity of the Lord. We believe in one God and yet He has a triune nature of Father, Son and Holy Spirit. Hence we believe in a three-in-one God. The fruit of the Ruach can be seen as a nine-in-one fruit. It would follow that if a believer showed love in the Ruach at any one moment, then the rest of the fruit could be experienced simultaneously as well. If a believer was being patient then they could have gentleness as well. If one were joyous then they could also have peace, etc, etc.

"Love" is listed first of all the fruit of the Ruach. Yeshua told Israel that the whole Law and the Prophets hung on two commandments: to love God and love your neighbor (Matt. 22:34-40). Wuest concludes that "*God is love*" (1 John 4:16). According to Rom. 5:5, the love of God is abundantly poured out into our hearts. The most famous passage of Scripture that defines love is 1 Cor. 13:4-8. 8 Some of the aspects found in this list are equated with love and are found in the list of the fruit of the Spirit (patience and kindness). Of faith, hope and love, love is found to be the greatest trait to obtain (1 Cor. 13:13). The very reason why we can love in the first place is because God first loved us by sending His Son Yeshua to be our propitiation (1 John 4:10)!

Wuest states that "joy" has a spiritual basis in the Lord. 9 Even though we have tribulation, we can receive the Word from the Lord with the joy of the Ruach Kodesh (1 Thess. 1:6). 1 Thess. 5:16 tells us to *"rejoice always."* We are to have joy in the good times and joy in the tough times. The third fruit of the

Spirit is a "peace" that only God can give to our hearts. [10] This peace surpasses all understanding and guards our hearts and minds in Yeshua (Phil. 4:7). We can experience this peace in lieu of our lives falling apart all around us.

The old saying "patience is a virtue" is most definitely true. Wuest defines "longsuffering" as patience and "gentleness" as being kind. He comments that "longsuffering" is patience and steadfastness of the soul even under provocation. The idea here is to have patience when we are provoked in any way and not have ungodly responses of anger or revenge. "Gentleness" is having a kind quality that penetrates the whole nature. [11] When someone is evil or harsh to us, we need to respond with kindness. In Col. 3:12, among other traits, we are to put on gentleness just like we put our coats on.

"Goodness" is the quality of knowing that which is right and moral. In Luke 6:33-35, Yeshua encourages us to take our good deeds above and beyond what the world performs and love our enemies despite what they do to us. "Faith" here does not necessarily mean faith or belief by itself but includes dependability, loyalty, devotion and being true to the Lord. Wuest believes that faithfulness is only produced in the life of a yielded believer. [12] "Meekness" means to be gentle and mild. Yeshua said that the gentle at heart would be blessed and inherit the earth (Matt. 5:5). Yeshua is our perfect example of being gentle (Matt. 11:29). Wuest also believes "temperance" is having the strength and mastery over oneself, our desires, needs and wants. [13] Sometimes Hasatan even tempts us when we lack in self-control (1 Cor. 7:5).

At the close of verse 23, Sha'ul declares that there is no law or command that teaches against the fruit of the Ruach. What exactly does this mean? Lightfoot answered that the "Law exists for the purpose of restraint, but in the works of the Spirit there is nothing to restrain; compare 1 Tim. 1:9...Thus then the Apostle substantiates the proposition stated in verse 18, 'If ye are led by the Spirit, ye are not under law.' [14] In other words, the Law was created to restrain the Jewish people and yet today we who are Messianic believers are not to place ourselves under the Law. If we do, then the deeds of the flesh will become evident in our lives and we become spiritually restrained. If we place ourselves under the Ruach's control, then we will see the fruit of the Ruach greatly flow in our lives. The Law will not and cannot restrain this great out-flowing unless we allow it to control our lives. Sha'ul is obviously encouraging us not to allow the Law to control and restrain the Spirit in our lives. This is why the Torah Observant of the MJM need to chose the Ruach over the Law.

Concerning this statement "*against such there is no law*" Wuest proclaimed, "This mild assertion to the effect that there is no law against such things, has the effect of an emphatic statement that these things fully meet the demands of the law." [15] Since the Law has nothing in its commandments against the fruit of the Spirit then keeping the fruit fully meets the demands of the Law. When Messianic believers live and walk in the power of the Spirit they are keeping and fulfilling the Law! Therefore, we are able to fulfill the Torah by being led by the Spirit rather than being led by the Law. We should therefore keep the fruit of the Spirit rather than keep the Law.

5:24 Sha'ul now makes a profound statement to the Galatians. Some of the congregants were living according to the freedom Messiah gave them and others were keeping Torah. Some were producing the fruit of the Ruach while others were performing the deeds of the flesh. He cuts to the chase and zings them all with a theological statement that Messiah has already provided the victory we need to live according to the Ruach. All believers can have victory over the flesh because we have already crucified the flesh.

"Crucified" (*stauroo*) means "to put to death or crucify on a cross." 16 It refers to the agonizing death of individuals who were crucified on the cursed tree. Here in verse 24, *stauroo* refers to believers putting their flesh to death so that they will not follow its' passions and desires. The interesting part of *stauroo* is that it is found to be in the aorist tense and the active voice. The aorist tense shows that the simple action was performed in the past while the active voice reveals the believers are the doers of the action of crucifying their flesh. This putting of their flesh to death was an act that was performed in the past by the believers themselves. When did this occur? The flesh was crucified at the moment of salvation. Since Messiah had victory over His crucifixion and death, we can have victory over our crucified flesh. The reason we do not live in this victory already won by Messiah is because we allow our flesh to be resurrected in our lives!

Romans 6:1-7 shows this same idea in the *mikveh* (water baptism). When believers are immersed in water this symbolizes our death to our "old man," the sin nature. When we rise up out of the water this symbolizes our resurrection to our "new man," (the Ruach in us) so that we can walk in the newness of life by the Ruach. Verse 6 even declares that our "old man" was crucified with the Lord as He was crucified so that we would no longer be slaves to our sin and could lead a victorious life in the Spirit.

Luke would certainly agree with Sha'ul as he penned Luke 9:23, *"And he said to them all, If any man will come after me, let him deny himself, and take up his cross daily, and follow me."* As Yeshua shared with His *talmidim* (disciples) that He was going to suffer, be killed and resurrect on the third day, He encouraged them to deny self, take up their own crosses and follow Him. This is exactly what Sha'ul is admonishing every believer to do since we have crucified the flesh.

This section of Scripture reveals there is a continuous powerful war going on inside of each and every believer of Yeshua. This war is between the Ruach and the flesh (sin nature) and we are urged to allow the Ruach to reign in our lives. The victory was already won at the moment of salvation; however, we must continue the fight each and every moment of every day against the flesh by living and walking in the Spirit.

5:25 The Greek grammar helps to properly understand this verse. Wuest nicely sums up the first phrase, "The word *Spirit* is dative of reference. The word *if* is the conditional particle of a fulfilled condition. That is, 'in view of the fact' or 'seeing that' we live with reference to the Spirit." [17] In other words, the phrase "if we live by the Spirit" can be translated "in view of the fact we have started and continue in the new spiritual life by the Ruach." Sha'ul is telling the Galatians, despite this wonderful beginning in the Ruach you should "*also walk in the Ruach.*"

"Walk" (*stoicheo*) has a somewhat similar meaning to the "walk" of 5:16 although it is a different Greek word. *Stoicheo* means "to proceed in a row, to walk by rule, to walk in a rule of life." [18] Here the idea of "walk" is to proceed down the straight and narrow path of spiritual life being led by the Ruach (much like the prior chapter's discussion of "*halachah*"). We are not to veer to the right or to the left following our flesh towards Torah Observance for sanctification or the deeds of darkness summarized in verses 19-21.

An interesting side note is observed in the fact that "walk" is found to be in the subjunctive mood. This indicates that "*let us also walk in the Spirit*" is not a command or even a positive and clear cut statement. Rather it is a doubtful or hesitant statement meaning the Galatians may or may not "walk in the Spirit" although they had begun to live by the Spirit. Living by the Spirit does not necessitate that we automatically walk by the Spirit. The responsibility here falls upon believers. Wuest emphatically summarized, "The responsibility of the saint is to desire to live a Christlike life, to depend upon the Holy Spirit for the power to live that life, and to step out on faith and live that life..." [19] This is excellent advice for not only the Torah Observant of the MJM but for all believers.

5:26 It may seem to the casual reader of this section of Scripture that this verse may be out of place. It does not seem to run with the flow of this passage at all. However, Sha'ul's warning here seems to be a restatement of verse 15 where he told the Galatians to stop fighting among themselves lest they destroy each other. Here, we have another warning for these two groups (New Covenant Freedom and Torah Observant) to stop antagonizing and challenging one another. Did not the Scripture encourage all believers to love one another and walk in the Ruach?

"Vain glory" (*kenodoxos*) means to be self-conceited and proud. *Kenodoxos* "referred to people who boasted without reason or people who were eager for glory." [20] Sha'ul encouraged all believers that we should not boast in anything except in the cursed tree of our Lord and Savior (Gal. 6:14). Galatians 6:3 states: *"For if a man think himself to be something, when he is nothing, he deceiveth himself."* Once believers become prideful, then we also become deceived and the truth is not in us. Then when pride hits our hearts, we can expect only one thing – destruction (Prov. 16:18)! The reason is that when we become prideful we take the glory away from God and assign it to ourselves.

Obviously, our Lord does not want us to take the glory away from Him but to give it to Him! It is very easy to become boastful and prideful when one is trying to keep Torah for sanctification reasons. Why is it so easy? Following Torah puts the focus on the *person* trying to keep it instead of focusing on Yeshua. Once we place the focus on ourselves this opens the stronghold for Hasatan and his pride. Therefore, it is not only easy for the Torah Observant to stray from the Lord but for all believers once we become boastful and prideful.

"Provoking" (*prokaleo*) means to "provoke, challenge and irritate." [21] Sha'ul is trying to be the peacekeeper between these two groups within the Galatian congregations that seem to be fighting over whether they all should be Torah Observant or New Covenant Freedom. It seems they are prideful of their theological positions and are challenging and provoking one another to change their minds. Sha'ul saw this as devouring and destroying one another and hence a dramatic problem for the congregations that needed to be resolved in a different fashion.

"Envying" (*phthoneo*) refers to being jealous of or resentful of another. [22] Again, being resentful or jealous is detrimental to the spiritual well-being of the congregation and Sha'ul wanted it immediately stopped. These three words: vain glory, provoking and envying are opposite of what the Scriptures encourage us to be. These three could have been added to the list of the deeds of the flesh.

Sha'ul encouraged other congregations that were having the same types of problems as the Galatians. In Romans 14 and 1 Corinthians 8, he exhorted the believers to love one another and not tear each other down, bear each other's burdens and for the stronger believers to uphold the weaker ones. If believers engaged in these responsibilities then they would most certainly be walking and living in the

Ruach. This last section of Scripture similarly exhorted the Galatians to live and walk by the Ruach and stop living by the flesh. The characteristics of each lifestyle were easily identified by Sha'ul. Each and every day we should be checking our thoughts, words and deeds against these lists to see where we stand. Hopefully, we will be found living and walking in the Ruach and not following the deeds of the flesh.

Chapter 15

You Reap What You Sow
(6:1-10)

6:1 *Brethren, if a man be overtaken in a fault, ye which are spiritual, restore such an one in the spirit of meekness; considering thyself, lest thou also be tempted.*
6:2 *Bear ye one another's burdens, and so fulfil the law of Christ.*
6:3 *For if a man think himself to be something, when he is nothing, he deceiveth himself.*
6:4 *But let every man prove his own work, and then shall he have rejoicing in himself alone, and not in another.*
6:5 *For every man shall bear his own burden.*
6:6 *Let him that is taught in the word communicate unto him that teacheth in all good things.*
6:7 *Be not deceived; God is not mocked: for what-so-ever a man soweth, that shall he also reap.*
6:8 *For he that soweth to his flesh shall of the flesh reap corruption; but he that soweth to the Spirit shall of the Spirit reap life everlasting.*

6:9 *And let us not be weary in well doing: for in due season we shall reap, if we faint not.*
6:10 *As we have therefore opportunity, let us do good unto all men, especially unto them who are of the household of faith.*

In chapter 5, we found that Messiah called us to freedom from sin and freedom from the Law. Not only did Yeshua call us to freedom, He gave us the Ruach to empower us to live in this newfound freedom. Some of the Galatians were bewitched into believing that Torah Observance was detrimental for salvation and/or sanctification. Sha'ul plainly tells us all that this is not the good news message he taught the Galatians. He then calls all believers to test their actions against his lists of the deeds of the flesh and the fruit of the Ruach to find out where we truly are spiritually. All are encouraged to not only live by the Ruach but walk by the Ruach.

In chapter 6, Sha'ul contrasts the way the spiritual believer and the legalist would deal with a weaker brother caught in sin. Keener simply contrasted the two: "The gentleness that comes from the Spirit (5:23) is the proper way to correct faults; conversely, the legalist who is obsessed with addressing his or her own spirituality by fleshly means will have little patience with the spiritual needs of others." [1] Wiersbe additionally contrasted the legalist with the spiritual believer,

> "The legalist is not interested in bearing burdens. Instead, he adds to the burdens of others (Acts 15:10)...The legalist is always harder on other people than he is on himself, but the Spirit-led Christian demands more of

> *himself than he does of others that he might be able to help others... Legalists do not need facts and proof; they need only suspicions and rumors. Their self-righteous imaginations will do the rest...The spiritual man would seek to restore the brother in love, while the legalist would exploit the brother."* 2

The contrast is actually quite easy to see. The legalist cares only for self, uses others for gain, adds burdens to people's lives, tries to control others and uses the Law to boast in their own flesh. On the other hand, the spiritual believer cares for others, helps others, bears burdens and encourages believers to follow the Ruach to glorify God's name. The Godly are walking in the Ruach while the legalists walk in the flesh. Each will reap what they sow and the results become easily identified within the body of Messiah.

6:1 Sha'ul begins chapter 6 by exhorting the Galatian believers to lovingly restore anyone caught in sins. It is obvious that the one performing the restoring would be the one walking by the Ruach and experiencing the fruit of the Ruach. The one caught in sin is obviously the one walking in the deeds of the flesh and needs to be restored to proper fellowship with the Lord. Everyone, whether spiritual or fleshly, needs to understand that we are all quite able to fall into horrendous sin and we need to be careful in our restoration process lest we be tempted as well. Keener noted,

> *"A variety of ancient sources, including Greek and Jewish wisdom traditions and the Dead Sea Scrolls, stressed wise reproof for the other person's good, and often stressed examining*

oneself before correcting others. Judaism (unlike Greek culture) considered humility one of the greatest virtues, even for the most noble." [3]

This is exactly what Sha'ul is saying: be humble in restoring an erring brother back to the Lord because we could be the next straying brother who would greatly desire gentle restoration rather than forceful and unloving judgment.

"Be overtaken" (*prolambano*) means "take before, overtake, anticipate, forecast, surprise." [4] Here, the idea of being overtaken and surprised is conveyed. Those Galatian believers who put themselves under the Law were finding themselves overtaken by their sin despite the fact of their zealous beliefs of trying to live above sin through the works of the Law. They failed to recognize that following the workings of the Law was going to increase consciousness of sin and the ensuing judgment as well!

The interesting part of *prolambano* is that it is found to be in the passive voice. The passive voice shows the Torah Observant were the receivers of the action of being overtaken. This reveals they were clearly caught off guard in relation to their trespasses. Once again, it is more than probable that these Messianic believers were so influenced by their zealousness to keep Torah that they were surprised and overtaken by their increase of personal sins. Therefore, it is certainly a good idea to have spiritual believers close by who rightly divide the Word of God to help in restoration.

"Restore" (*katartizo*) means to "make complete, restore, repair, complete, and perfect. [5] Sha'ul encouraged the spiritual ones of the Galatian congregations to help restore, make complete and cause maturity in the weaker believers who were caught in their trespasses. The idea here is to forgive the weaker ones, teach them the Word and what God requires from them in application. They are to gently exhort the weaker to follow the Word, confess their sins, repent from their evil ways (deeds of the flesh) and walk with the Ruach. While performing this spiritually stronger act, they were to look at themselves lest they also be tempted to sin like the weaker ones.

"Considering" (*skopeo*) means to "look at, examine carefully, hold something as a goal or model." [6] As stronger believers are ministering to weaker ones, they are to mind their thoughts and attitudes while speaking in gentleness. They are to look at, consider and examine themselves carefully while not having a judgmental attitude. Why? They, as the spiritual ones, can easily fall into temptation and sin as well. The spiritual are not to be the Judge because Yeshua is the Judge. They are to be loving and gentle in restoring the erring brother back to spiritual health. Therefore, the spiritually stronger believers under grace need to gently restore the weaker believers who are under the Law and have been overtaken by their sin.

6:2 Instead of calling for harsh judgment against the Torah Observant who seek to please God through works, Sha'ul requests for bearing one another's burdens. "Bear" (*bastazo*) means to "pick up, lift up, sustain, bear or carry." [7] *Bastazo* is found in the imperative mood and present tense. This reveals a command to continuously bear the burdens in the present. So Sha'ul's request is actually a command for the strong believers to continuously carry the burdens of the weaker ones. Wuest believes that,

> *By bearing another's burdens, Paul does not mean simply the enduring of these burdens in an enforced, reluctant manner as in 5:10*

"where the same word is used, but the assuming of those burdens in a willing, helpful, sympathetic way, despite the fact that the bearing of them may involve unpleasantness and heartache." [8]

In other words, the spiritually stronger under grace are to gently and lovingly restore and bear the burdens of the spiritually weaker ones who place themselves under the Law and who unknowingly perform the deeds of the flesh! Wuest probably had no idea that he was describing the essence of the problem with the MJM and the Torah Observant.

I have ministered to many Messianic believers who have left the Torah Observant group because their faith became shipwrecked while zealously pursuing the works of the Law and trying to please the Lord with their *mitzvot* (good deeds). What happened? In their fleshly attempt to draw closer to the Lord through the Law, they actually drew further and further away from the Lord. Although they sensed the spiritual distance between them and the Lord, they pushed further into keeping the Law because this is what they were taught to do by their Messianic Rabbis. They believed if they kept following the Law then they would ultimately succeed! Unfortunately, the ironic roller coaster ride ended with a deadly crash and the correct realization that they cannot keep the Law. Unfortunately, they come away from this experience as wounded soldiers of Messiah with a great need of spiritual healing and yet not able to trust anyone from the MJM. Hence, they turn to the Universal Body of Messiah unwilling to continue their exploration of the riches and blessings of the MJM from the New Covenant Freedom perspective.

Once the stronger bears the burdens of the weaker then they "fulfill the Law of Messiah." "Fulfill" (*anapleroo*) means "make complete, to perform, to supply, fulfill, carry out." 9 *Anapleroo* is found to be in the aorist tense and active voice. This shows that the spiritual ones bearing burdens are performing the action of fulfilling Messiah's Law in the past. Once they perform the "bearing" (which is supposed to be a continuous process in the present) action they have fulfilled the Law of Messiah. One question that desperately needs an answer is, "What is the Law of Messiah?"

Dr. Fruchtenbaum defines the Law of Messiah as such:

> *"The Law of Moses has been disannulled and we are now under a new law. This new law is called the Law of Christ in Galatians 6:2 and the Law of the Spirit of Life in Romans 8:2. This is a brand new law, totally separate from the Law of Moses. The Law of Christ contains all the individual commandments from Christ and the Apostles applicable to a New Testament believer."* 10

In other words, the Law of Messiah is all the teachings and commandments found in the New Covenant Writings (the New Testament).

The answer to the next question should be most damaging to the Torah Observant's theology: "Why is there a need for the Law of Messiah if the Law of Moses is for today?" Hebrews 7:12 states, *"For the priesthood being changed, there is made of necessity a change also of the law."* This section of Scripture in Heb. 7 clearly states because of the change from the Levitical priesthood to Melchizedek's priesthood, it was imperative that the Law of Moses was changed to the Law of Messiah! When Messiah died on the tree for our sins and resurrected He inaugurated the New Covenant. In the New Covenant, the priesthood was changed from Levitical to Melchizedekian and the Law of Moses was changed to the Law of Messiah. Since Messianic believers are under the New Covenant with these new changes, then why do so many from the Torah Observant movement continue to believe they need to keep Torah and be under Moses' Law?!

It is important at this point to show that Messiah's Law is a different Law than Moses' Law even though many of the commandments found in the two Laws are similar. Dr. Fruchtenbaum made four observations from his comparison of the Law of Messiah with the Law of Moses. He asserted,

"First, many commandments are the same as those of the Law of Moses. For example, nine of the Ten Commandments are also in the Law of Christ. But, second, many are different from the Law of Moses. For example, there is no Sabbath law now (Rom. 14:5; Col. 2:16) and no dietary code (Mark 7:19; Rom. 14:20). Third, some commandments in the Law of Moses are intensified by the Law of Christ. The Law of Moses said: love thy neighbor as thyself (Lev. 19:18). This made man the standard. The Law of Christ said: love one another, even as I have loved you (John 15:12). This makes the Messiah the standard and He loved us enough to die for us. Fourth, the Law of the Messiah provides a new motivation. The Law of Moses was based on the

conditional Mosaic Covenant and so the motivation was: do, in order to be blessed. The Law of Christ is based on the unconditional New Covenant and so the motivation is: you have been and are blessed, therefore, do." [11]

Another very obvious difference is that the Law of Moses has a total of 613 commandments while the Law of Messiah has a total of over 1,000 commandments. Based on this evidence, surely these two Laws are different with the Law of Moses becoming inoperative when the Law of Messiah began. Actually, the way to fulfill the Law of Moses is by fulfilling the Law of Messiah! So if the Torah Observant still have a great desire to keep and fulfill the Law of Moses in their lives, then keep the Law of Messiah and there will be success! This can be done as Sha'ul encouraged us all through his letters to the congregations: by living and walking in the Ruach, living by faith in Yeshua, loving God and your neighbor and (in 6:2) bearing one another's burdens.

To summarize, the first two verses of this section of Scripture encourage spiritual believers to restore the weaker brethren who are caught in sins. Some of these weaker brethren are Legalizers who believe they must keep Torah for their salvation and/or sanctification. They are the ones whose deeds of the flesh are evident because the Law ultimately and publicly reveals these trespasses. The spiritual are not to judge but rather bear the weaker ones' burdens thus fulfilling the Law of Messiah through their love rather than unsuccessfully trying to fulfill the Law of Moses through their obedience.

6:3 Pride goeth before the fall. If believers think they are something in this world or the spiritual world, then they are prideful. When believers start thinking they are God's gift to their congregations then all they are truly doing is comparing themselves with their brethren. Once we begin to think this way we become deceived.

It is good to be reminded that each and every believer is nothing. We are nothing, that is, without Yeshua Hameshiach! With Him, we are everything! Without Him, we are hopelessly lost in our walk with the Lord and heading for disastrous discipline. With Him, we are joyously found and heading to eternal bliss in heaven. In addition, one needs to remember the context of this section. If one believes they are spiritually superior then ministering to the weaker Legalizers will come across as fleshly pride and not as being loving and gentle. Instead of bearing burdens and fulfilling Messiah's Law, one will become the judge. Sha'ul encouraged the Corinthians in the same way, *"Wherefore let him that thinketh he standeth take heed lest he fall."* (1 Cor. 10:12). All ministry of reconciliation should be performed without pride in a humble, gentle and loving way.

6:4 Spiritual believers should not compare themselves with the weaker believers caught in sin and hence fall into judging others. But the spiritual should only compare themselves with themselves. They should examine their own *mitzvot* and determine by the Lord's standards whether they are worthy or not. "Prove" (*dokimazo*) means "to try, scrutinize, prove, test and examine...The intent of *dokimazo* is primarily to eliminate the dross and recover the valuable or genuine remains. That which has endured this process or trial is the 'accepted' or 'approved.'" [12] The spiritual are to scrutinize their good deeds of reconciliation and test whether they have performed them in love and gentleness. If not, then they have no right to "rejoice."

"Rejoicing" (*kauchema*) refers "to the object of boasting, ground of glorying, exultation... contrasted to *kauchesis* (2746), the act of boasting." [13] Wuest concurs,

> *"The word [kauchema] is not connected with the word glory (doxa) which is used of God's glory. It means glory in the sense of exultation, self-congratulation. It does not however have the idea of an excessive or unjustified estimate of one's self that the English word boasting has."* [14]

This kind of "rejoicing" is a Godly type of boasting, glorying in or exulting when one examines their good works and finds them performed in love, gentleness and the rest of the fruit of the Ruach.

In addition, Sha'ul could be building a case against the Legalizers whose goal is to sign up as many Messianic believers to their theology so that they can boast in their accomplishments. For in 6:13, he says the Legalizers just want to boast about how many believers they exhorted to circumcision. Sha'ul, in contrast, would boast about nothing except Yeshua's death on the tree (6:14).

6:5 Sha'ul encourages all believers to be responsible for themselves whether they are spiritually strong or weak. "Burden" (*phortion*) refers to the burdens of life's responsibilities, obligations and duties. [15] If anyone is caught in sin then the stronger believers of the congregation should lovingly and gently restore that one back to fellowship with the Lord. They should bear one another's burdens but also bearing in mind that all need to be responsible for themselves. Bearing another's burdens does not mean to completely take away the burden but to help the weaker one through their problems and issues. The Torah Observant who have fallen into sinful ways should be restored back to fellowship with the Lord but if they are unresponsive and not desirous to listen then they are responsible for themselves.

6:6 A few years ago, I heard a television preacher with a big ministry in Los Angeles read this verse and then embark on a 30 minute tirade on how his audience needed to donate $ 250,000 to his ministry in the next hour or he was not going to continue to teach them. This could hardly be called "teaching" in anyone's estimation. However, this verse is controversial in that some believers think the Lord commands them to donate to their teacher's financial support.

"Communicate" (*koineneo*) simply means to "share, partake in and participate...It carries the basic idea of commonness, something held jointly by two or more parties." [16] *Koineneo* is in the first position in the Greek sentence and is found to be in the imperative mood. The first position is emphatic and the imperative mood shows a command. Thus, Sha'ul writes for those who are taught the Word of God to emphatically share all "good things" that are common or held jointly between them and their teachers. The question remains, "What are these 'good things?'"

Zodhiates found that "good things" (*agathos*) has a variety of meanings as an adjective such as good and benevolent, profitable and useful. Good is in respect to operation or influence on others such as being useful, beneficial or profitable. When *agathos* is found in the plural (which is the case here) it refers to things good and useful, benefits and/or blessings. [17] Once the Greek word study and grammar analysis is performed the obvious meaning of the verse arises. Those who are taught the Word are commanded to share with their teachers all the benefits, blessings and results derived from making application of the Word to their lives. In addition, the context is bearing the burdens and restoration of those that have left God's grace and are following Torah with the Legalizers. When the stronger help the weaker to overcome these great burdens then they are to share the victories with their teachers so everyone can rejoice!

6:7 Do not be deceived! It is actually quite simple for believers to be deceived from doing the right thing. "Not" (*me*) is in the first position in the Greek and hence is emphatic so that the phrase should read, "Be NOT deceived!" "Deceived" (*planao*) means to "lead astray, mislead or deceive." [18] *Planao* is found to be in the present tense. This shows a continuous action in the present. Thus the understanding is, "Do not be continuously deceived in the present!" It is obvious that Sha'ul commanded the Galatians to stop receiving the teaching of the Legalizers for God is not mocked.

"Mocked" (*mukterizo*) means to "turn up the nose at, treat with contempt, mock, ridicule or deride." [19] *Mukterizo* is also found in the present tense which suggests that God is not continuously being mocked by their behavior. Wuest puts it this way,

> *"The thought which Paul wishes to press home to the Galatians is that it is vain to think that one can outwit God by reaping a harvest different from that which a person has sown... Paul therefore warns the Galatians against being led astray by the Judaizers, and reminds them that they cannot outwit God in doing so, for it will lead to disaster in their lives and chastening from the hand of God."* [20]

In other words, God is not mocked in that He is not deceived or fooled about anyone's behavior but on the contrary He knows exactly what is happening.

Believers who treat God with contempt through their actions are truly only fooling themselves; God is not mocked by their conduct. Therefore, whatever one sows one will reap.

"Soweth" (*speire*) means "to sow (as seed), scatter, spread, and disperse." [21] "Reap" (*therisei*) means "to reap, harvest and gather." [22] The obvious metaphor here is the sowing of deeds whether good or bad. If one sows good works then there will be rewards. If one sows bad deeds then there will be judgment. The idea of sowing and reaping has Jewish Roots in the *Ketuvim* (the Writings). Prov. 22:8-9 states, *"He that soweth iniquity shall reap vanity: and the rod of his anger shall fail. He that hath a bountiful eye shall be blessed; for he giveth of his bread to the poor."*

As Sha'ul encouraged the Galatians to stop being deceived by the Legalizers and their teaching of Torah observance for salvation and/or sanctification purposes, he proclaimed an age old Jewish proverb that the recipients would easily recall. Those who followed Torah for Torah sake in the flesh would reap God's present and future judgment. Those who followed the Ruach in grace and love would reap God's present and future blessings. This is just another warning of Sha'ul for today's MJM. Messianic believers must listen and obey this new directive!

6:8 If one sows from the flesh then one shall reap corruption. "Corruption" (*phthora*) means, "destruction, ruin, deterioration, corruption and loss...However, this destruction is also a spiritual danger, a moral disintegration resulting from living unrighteous." [23] Wuest comments on this moral disintegration:

"In this context, these words refer to the

> *Galatians who in following the teachings of the Judaizers, catered to the desires of the evil nature. All false systems of religion are so adjusted that they appeal to the fallen nature of man, satisfying his religious instinct for worship, while at the same time allowing him to go on in his sin."* 24

I have been warning the MJM in similar fashion all along in this commentary. The Legalizers in Sha'ul's day and today teach Messianic believers to keep Torah. If they try to keep Torah and find they come up short, they are told to try harder! This false system of religion forces Messianic believers to try in the flesh which is appealing to the sin nature. This brings about a false sense of spiritual security and even causes more sin. Each believer then is walking in the flesh rather than living in the Ruach. Ultimately, God brings about a spiritual crash of corruption and destruction so that there can be repentance.

Those who sow to the Ruach shall reap great blessings and rewards. The obvious connection here is to Gal. 5:19-25. If one sows to the flesh, then one's deeds will be fleshly and one will not only lose potential rewards in the Kingdom but reap judgment and corruption (verses 19-21, 6:8). If one sows to the Ruach, one's character traits will reflect the fruit of the Ruach (verses 22-25), one's deeds will be Godly and the eternal blessings will flow.

6:9 It is an easy thing to lose heart and become weary while ministering in the MJM. So many Messianic believers are deceived in their ignorance of their personal walk with the Lord when they try to keep Torah for Torah's sake. They truly do not recognize that what they are saying and doing is contrary to the Bible. They also do not know that their confident assertions of Torah mean nothing without the close personal fellowship with Yeshua. It is a difficult thing to teach someone the truth who does not want to hear it.

Sha'ul said it the best concerning certain men who teach strange doctrines in 1 Tim. 1:6-7, *"From which some having swerved have turned aside unto vain jangling; desiring to be teachers of the law; understanding neither what they say, nor whereof they affirm."* Sha'ul makes it very clear that those who confidently teach to keep the Law to please our Lord, do not know what they are talking about and are teaching strange doctrines contrary to the Scriptures! What more does the Torah Observant need to hear until they repent? Those of us who are trying to reach the Torah Observant with this message of love and grace must continue in perseverance because in due time we shall reap God's blessings. Not only should we persevere but we should be patient as well. Yacov encourages all believers to be patient like the farmer (husbandman) in 5:7 of his letter, *"Be patient therefore, brethren, unto the coming of the Lord. Behold, the husbandman waiteth for the precious fruit of the earth, and hath long patience for it, until he receive the early and latter rain."*

6:10 Sha'ul restated verse 9 in the positive. In verse 9, he negatively stated to not grow weary and not lose heart in doing good. In general, "doing good" should be done to all people. However, the specific "doing good" was reaching out to the Legalizers and those who were greatly affected by them. "Doing good" was to help them understand God's grace and love, to bear their burdens and restore the erring brother. In verse 10, the positive aspect is "doing good" to all people especially believers while we have the opportunity to do so.

"Opportunity" (*kairon*) means "time, a fixed time, season, or opportunity...The temporal sense (a distinct point in time) dominates the New Testament understanding." [25] The idea here is not to procrastinate but take whatever opportunity comes our way to do good. "Do" (*ergazomai*) means to "work, be active, accomplish, carry out and perform." [26] *Ergazomai* is found in the present tense suggesting a continuous work being accomplished in the present. Wuest advises, "The exhortation is not merely to do good to others when the opportunity presents itself, but to look for opportunities to go good to others." [27] This attitude should be a continuous one of believers who are living and walking in the Ruach. Actually, all of Judaism does not seem to have a problem with "doing good." Performing "*mitzvot*" (good deeds) is the backbone of the faith. The problem with doing good deeds is that most Jewish people are heavily relying on their actions to get their names written in the Book of Life. Unfortunately for them, the only way to have our names written in the Book of Life is to believe in Yeshua.

This section of Scripture puts the fruit of the Ruach into action. Biblically, there are no "couch potatoes" in the Universal Body of Messiah. True believers who are living and walking with the Ruach reap what they sow and enjoy the fruit of their labors. We are additionally fulfilling the Law of Messiah by bearing one another's burdens, restoring the erring brother, humbling ourselves and performing *mitzvot* to all people and to our brethren in the faith. Messianic believers are encouraged to reach out to our Torah Observant brethren who have sown to their flesh the idea of "keeping Torah." We must not lose heart nor grow weary in this outreach, for in due time we shall reap what we sow, so continue to sow the good seed of God's love and grace!

Chapter 16

Walk In The Lord, Not In the Flesh

(6:11-18)

6:11 *Ye see how large a letter I have written unto you with mine own hand.*
6:12 *As many as desire to make a fair show in the flesh, they constrain you to be circumcised; only lest they should suffer persecution for the cross of Christ.*
6:13 *For neither they themselves who are circumcised keep the law; but desire to have you circumcised, that they may glory in your flesh.*
6:14 *But God forbid that I should glory, save in the cross of our Lord Jesus Christ, by whom the world is crucified unto me, and I unto the world.*
6:15 *For in Christ Jesus neither circumcision availeth any thing, nor un-circumcision, but a new creature.*
6:16 *And as many as walk according to this rule, peace be on them, and mercy, and upon the Israel of God.*
6:17 *From henceforth let no man trouble me: for I bear in my body the marks of the Lord Jesus.*

6:18 *Brethren, the grace of our Lord Jesus Christ be with your spirit. Amen.*

In Sha'ul's closing chapters 5 and 6, he made practical exhortation of his doctrinal exposition of chapters 3 and 4. The major theme of these closing chapters (and of the whole book) is that Messiah has set all believers free. He set us free from the Law and from our sinful ways. We are not bound to the Law to live under the Law, but we are bound to Messiah to live under grace. Living under the Law brings about fleshly desires, subjection to slavery, quenching of the Ruach and the sowing of eventual spiritual corruption. Living under grace brings about filling of the Ruach, loving servitude, the fruit of the Ruach and the reaping of eternal rewards.

Sha'ul gave the Galatians a choice between grace (living for the Lord) or the Law (living for Torah). Wiersbe put it this way, "They [the Galatians] had to choose between bondage or liberty (Gal. 5:1-12), the flesh or the Spirit (5:13-26), and living for self or living for others (6:1-10). Now he presents a fourth contrast: living for the praise of men or the glory of God (6:11-18)." 1 Within this fourth contrast, Sha'ul makes reference to the Legalizers' character traits verses the spiritual believers' character traits. Then He encourages all to walk in the Lord and not in the flesh. We are to live for the Lord's glory and not for our own.

6:11 It is believed that early on in Sha'ul's ministry someone forged a letter in his name. 2 Thess. 2:1-2 reveals an implication of this forgery: *"Now we beseech you, brethren, by the coming of our Lord Jesus Christ, and by our gathering together unto him, That ye be not soon shaken in mind, or be troubled, neither by spirit, nor by word,* **nor by letter as from us,** *as that the day of Christ is at hand."* [Bold emphasis is mine]. To combat any forgeries, Sha'ul made it a custom to finish off each letter with his own hand writing (2 Thess. 3:17). Here in verse 11, Sha'ul shows off his large handwritten letters to prove his handwriting style. Sha'ul then summarizes the characteristics of the Legalizers, the ones who have attacked the simplicity and purity of the good news message and the ones who probably forged an epistle in his name.

6:12 Sha'ul begins his contrast of the Legalizers versus himself with a word play. The Legalizers wanted to make a good showing in the flesh through the Galatians' circumcision which involves the cutting of the flesh. Therefore the Legalizers were fleshly in pursuit of the cutting off of the flesh! Herein lies the Legalizers' character trait of being fleshly. They greatly desired to make a good showing in the flesh that the Lord was left out. "Make a fair show" (*euprosopeo*) means to make a fair and good appearance, to be concerned with an external showing and to exhibit a good face. 2 The Legalizers not only wanted to impress themselves but to amaze the Jewish community with their numbers of circumcision conversions. This was a bad motive because the Legalizers desired to please man rather than God! Not only were the Legalizers fleshly in their desires against the Galatians but they tried to compel them to circumcision.

"Constrain" (*anankazo*) means to force, compel and constrain. It denotes the outward influence or pressure exerted by someone upon another. 3 Therefore, the Legalizers tried to exert pressure and influence over the Galatians to receive circumcision. The idea of manipulation can be applied to this situation because the Legalizers used wrong motives. Thus far we have seen the Legalizers' wrong motives of selfishness and being fleshly. Kiehl writes concerning this issue, "In other words, the Judaizers were not concerned about the spiritual welfare of the Galatians, but rather about their own standing in the Jewish community." [4] Another bad motive in their compelling of the Galatians to receive circumcision was to escape being persecuted for Messiah's cursed tree.

As was discussed earlier in this book, the Legalizers who followed and attacked Sha'ul's ministry consisted of Messianic Jews and unsaved Jews. These Messianic Jews were obviously believers of Yeshua but also believed that all Messianics (Jewish and Gentile) needed to keep the Law and be circumcised for sanctification reasons. The reason why the Jewish Community at large would not persecute these Messianic Jews is because they kept positioning the Law at the forefront of their lives. Yeshua obviously came second.

The idea here was to make themselves as similar to the Jewish Community as possible so they would not be persecuted for their secondary belief in Yeshua. They desired to please the Jewish Community and the leadership by zealously converting Messianics to their and the Jewish Community's cause. It did not matter to the Jewish Community whether these Messianic Jews believed in Yeshua, as long as they continued to do their bidding. Lightfoot put it this way,

> "And so they attempted to keep on good terms with them by imposing circumcision on the Gentile converts also, and thus getting the credit of zeal for the law. Even the profession of Jesus as Messiah by the Christians was a less formidable obstacle to their intercourse with the Jews than their abandonment of the law." [5]

Thus, in today's MJM, we have the same problem. Many within in the Torah Observant movement seek to become the fourth branch of Judaism and to be accepted by the at large Jewish Community. For this to occur, many from the Jewish Community have to see them as being "real" practicing Jewish people. To be "real" practicing Jewish people they have to show their Torah observance. Therefore, Torah observance takes precedence over the Lord's teaching of New Covenant freedom. Sha'ul dealt with this problem 2,000 years ago! He encouraged the Legalizers and their *talmidim* to repent from their ways because Yeshua gave us freedom. He exhorted them to return (*shuvah*) to the simplicity of the good news message. We do not need to be accepted by anyone other than Yeshua. We have been freed from the Law and sin. Others may teach us that Torah Observance is important to please God, but it is not true!

6:13 Sha'ul continues his contrast of the Legalizers with himself. He conveys another character trait of the Legalizers to be hypocrisy. Those who zealously teach about keeping the Law should do it themselves! Sha'ul says that they do not even keep the Law themselves. "Keep" (*phulasso*) is found to be in the indicative mood and present tense. This means a positive and clear cut statement occurs continuously in the present. Therefore, the Legalizers do not keep the Law on a continuous basis in the present. This idea does not involve the impossibility of keeping the Law (which is of course true) but shows the Legalizers' hypocrisy of not thoroughly practicing all aspects of what they preach.

Lightfoot concurred, "The allusion here is not to the *impossibility* of observing the law, the distance from Jerusalem for instance preventing the due sacrifices, for this would argue no moral blame; but to the *insincerity* of the men themselves, who were not enough in earnest to observe it rigorously." [6] It can be said that these Legalizers enjoyed putting the yoke of slavery upon the Galatians and yet were not personally bound by their own teachings.

Finally, the last bad motive of the Legalizers is revealed. They desired to have the Galatians circumcised so that they could boast in their flesh! Here is the same play on words with circumcision and the cutting of flesh as in verse 12. "Glory" (*kauchaomai*) is the verb form of the noun *kauchema* found in 6:4. *Kauchaomai* means to,

> "boast or glory"...Paul's usage of kauchaomai suggests a somewhat flexible meaning involving both positive and negative connotations. Negatively, boasting is self-centered, self-reliant, and proud. Arrogance might also be a facet of its meaning, because it ignores the work of Christ and gives credit to one's own abilities. Positively, boasting is permissible, but only if it complements the message of the gospel (2 Corin. 12:1ff)." [7]

The desire to boast in one's work additionally reveals another character trait of the Legalizers. Bragging involves the negative connotation of boasting and is obviously more centered on self than the Lord. These Legalizers and their followers are the spiritually weak of the Galatian congregations in need of restoration. Although some of them are believers of Yeshua, their actions reveal a dramatic immaturity so much so that it would be difficult for anyone to know they have any faith at all. It would also be hard to distinguish them from the unsaved Jewish community. Wiersbe's conclusion concerning the Legalizers is similar: "Their reverence for the law was only a mask to cover their real goal: winning more converts to their cause. They wanted to report more statistics and get more glory." [8]

In summary, Sha'ul revealed the Legalizers to have ungodly character traits and bad motives of being fleshly: manipulating, caring for self rather than others, compromising to escape persecution, being hypocritical in their Torah observance and bragging over their *mitzvot* (good deeds). There is a dramatic difference between those who are fleshly and ungodly and those who are spiritual as we see Sha'ul contrast the Legalizers with himself.

6:14 Sha'ul reveals that he would never boast unless it was in the Lord's death on the cursed tree. It is important for Sha'ul to show the Galatians this contrast so they know who to believe and what teaching to follow. The Legalizers boast to the Jewish community about the numbers of circumcision or Torah observance converts which reveals no true concern for the people. Sha'ul's concern is for the inward certainty as opposed to the outward impression. Sha'ul shows great humility because he does not desire to boast of all the converts he has led to the Lord. But rather, he would only boast of the Lord's death for the world. This same world had been crucified to Sha'ul and he crucified to the world.

"Crucified" (*stauroo*) is found to be in the indicative mood and perfect tense. This means the statement of Sha'ul being crucified to the world and vice versa is positive and clear cut. There is no underlying mysterious meaning here. The perfect tense shows a completed action with lingering results in the present. Therefore, it is used metaphorically to mean that Sha'ul and the world are nailed together so that he can continuously share the good news message with the world. Sha'ul's mission was given to him by Yeshua since the Road to Damascus experience. Plain and simple, Sha'ul's life is all about sharing Yeshua with the world. This is the only thing he can boast in and truly he is only boasting about God's power working in and through him.

6:15   Once again we have another shocking statement from Sha'ul that taken out of context causes much confusion. Most Messianic believers read this and they are shocked! How can Sha'ul say that circumcision means nothing when the Lord commanded circumcision to Avraham?! Circumcision is the Jewish rite of passage into the Avrahamic Covenant!

The Greek understanding makes this situation even worse! "Thing" (*ischuo*) means "to be strong, i.e., to have strength, ability, power, both physical and moral...The equivalent of to have efficacy, to avail, have force and value." [9] Sha'ul is repeating his statement in 5:6 essentially stating there is no power, effect, strength or value in circumcision or uncircumcision. The context here is not denying the Jewish importance of circumcision; but rather it is revealing circumcision and uncircumcision have no power, effect or value when it comes to salvation or sanctification. What is spiritually more important to God? The answer is faith working in love (5:6) and the new creation (6:15). So Messianics, please keep your *kippot* on; there is no need to fret! You can still have your sons circumcised. However, we all need to know that this very act is not spiritually significant to God when it comes to salvation or sanctification.

What is much more important than circumcision? The new creature! "Creature" (*ktisis*) means "to bring into existence, to produce something not previously existing." [10] The new creation is thus brought into existence when a person hears the good news message of Yeshua, confesses sin, repents from sin and receives Yeshua as Lord and Savior of their lives. God the Father immediately indwells with the Ruach Kodesh and the person becomes a new person.

Romans 6:5-7 states, *"For if we have been planted together in the likeness of his death, we shall be also in the likeness of his resurrection: knowing this, that our old man is crucified with him, that the body of sin might be destroyed, that henceforth we should not serve sin. For he that is dead is freed from sin."* The "old man" in us, who has a propensity to sin, was crucified with Yeshua when people receive Yeshua. Since Yeshua crucified the "old man" in us, we have been freed from the power sin has over us and therefore can truly live for God in Yeshua (Rom. 6:11). The MJM must hear this message! There is nothing added like Torah observance or circumcision to live this kind of Godly lifestyle. Yeshua wants our hearts and our motives to be right before Him! We must live life by faith working in love and the new creation.

Unfortunately, we in the MJM tend to resurrect our old Jewish ways of keeping Torah for Torah's sake and this gets in the way of living spiritual Godly lives the way the Scriptures prescribe. There is obviously another answer to this dilemma. 2 Cor. 5:16-18 state,

"Wherefore henceforth know we no man after the flesh: yea, though we have known Christ after the flesh, yet now henceforth know we him no more. Therefore if any man be in Christ, he is a new creature: old things are passed away; behold, all things are become new. And all things are of God, who hath reconciled us to himself by Jesus Christ, and hath given to us the ministry of reconciliation..."

We must recognize that we are new creatures in Messiah to do His will in His power. The old ways of sin and some of the Jewish customs that get in the way of the new life should be put away. Finally, we should be reconciled to Messiah. This means for the Torah Observant to recognize their mistake of keeping Torah for Jewish sake and know that God wants their hearts and motives to be right with Him. This is what Sha'ul said to the Galatians in the first century and this is what he is saying to us today. Therefore, we must continue this message of reconciliation to a Messianic Jewish world no matter what happens to us. We need to be the light of the Lord to show the straight and narrow path back to Yeshua.

6:16 Those who walk by this rule will receive peace and mercy from the Lord. The rule that all believers need to walk by is boasting in Messiah and what He has done for us. Life here on earth is not about what we have done for the Lord such as being circumcised or observing Torah or even performing good deeds. Life is all about humbling oneself, living by faith and walking in the Ruach. In other words, the rule is the theme of Galatians: live life in freedom from sin and the Law. Our life is all about Him and those who walk this way will be blessed with peace and mercy. The question remains, "Who are the 'as many' in this verse?"

"As many" are the Messianic Gentile Galatian believers who were not swayed by the Legalizers to drop God's grace in their lives and live by the Torah including receiving circumcision. If they understood Sha'ul's instruction that circumcision and following Torah is not as important to God as walking in grace and the Ruach, then they would receive peace and mercy. I can be confident that "as many" are the *Gentile* believers in Galatia because the Legalizers would only exhort the Gentiles to be circumcised since almost every Jewish male was already circumcised in the first century. However, it is possible the Legalizers could come across some Jewish believers who were not circumcised. I have met one or two in my lifetime so it is possible there were some uncircumcised in Galatia.

Those Gentile believers who did not follow the Legalizers' teaching on Torah and circumcision but walked by the rule of God's grace would receive His peace and mercy. "Walk" (*stoicheo*) was earlier defined in section 5:25. It means to proceed in a row and walk by a rule of life. *Stoicheo* is found to be in the future tense and can be interpreted as "will walk." This idea includes not only those Gentile believers who were currently walking and would continue to walk in the rule but those future Gentile believers who repented of their Torah Observant ways and returned to God's rule of the simplicity of the good news.

Those Gentile believers of Galatia had to walk by the rule to be able to receive peace and mercy. "Rule" (*kanon*) refers to a "rule, standard, limit or measuring rod. The term was also utilized figuratively in reference to a 'rule, law, standard, and criterion." [11] Wuest concurs with this definition as he states, "*Rule* is from *kanon* which here means 'a principle.' The principle here is the Cross and all that goes with it in the New Testament economy, including of course the ministry of the Holy Spirit which is so much in evidence in this last section of Galatians." [12] In summary, those Gentile believers of Galatia who turned away from the Legalizers' teaching and walked with the Lord by His principle of freedom in Messiah will receive peace and mercy.

Sha'ul proclaims that those who follow this principle, peace and mercy will be upon them and the Israel of God. This section of Scripture is one of the most misinterpreted verses of Christendom. There are believers who teach "Replacement Theology" and think this verse is a proof text for their belief. Replacement Theology is defined on Wikipedia's website as, "Super sessionism and replacement theology or fulfillment theology are Christian interpretations of New Testament claims, viewing God's relationship with Christians as being either the "replacement" or "fulfillment" or "completion" of the promise made to the Jews (or Israelites) and Jewish Proselytes." [13] Stern explains the situation more concisely in his discussion of Gal. 6:16,

> *"This controversial verse, with its expression, unique in the New Testament, "the Israel of God," has been misinterpreted as teaching what Replacement theology wrongly claims, namely, that the Church is the New Israel which has replaced the Jews, the so-called "Old Israel," who are therefore now no longer God's people. But neither this verse nor any other part of the New Testament teaches this false and anti-semitic doctrine."* [14]

To believe the Church has replaced Israel and the Jewish people as God's chosen people and that she now receives all the blessings and promises God promised to Israel is a false and anti-Semitic doctrine. Stern surmises the unfortunate consequences of this age old belief: "The consequence of this wrong interpretation has been immeasurable pain for the Jews. The conclusion was reached that the Church is now the "New Israel" and the Jews, the so-called "Old Israel," no longer God's people. If the Jews are no longer God's people, isn't it appropriate to persecute them?" [15]

Church History teaches us that this persecution of the Jewish people was believed to be not only appropriate but deemed necessary by Martin Luther, the father of the reformation. Toward the end of his life, Martin Luther wrote a book entitled, "On the Jews and Their Lies." Throughout his ministry he tried to help the Jewish people see the light of Yeshua. After many years and no converts, he deduced the Jewish people were beyond reach and wrote in his book that is was okay to burn down Jewish establishments and treat the Jewish people harshly without cause. Wikipedia summarizes his book,

> *"In the treatise, Luther writes that the Jews are a "base, whoring people, that is, no people of God, and their boast of lineage, circumcision, and law must be accounted as filth." Luther wrote that they are "full of the devil's feces ... which they wallow in like swine," and the synagogue is an "incorrigible whore and an evil slut". He argues that their synagogues and schools be set on fire, their prayer books destroyed, rabbis forbidden to preach, homes razed, and property and money confiscated. They should be shown no mercy or kindness, afforded no legal protection, and these "poisonous envenomed worms" should be drafted into forced labor or expelled for all time. He also seems to advocate their murder, writing "[we] are at fault in not slaying them."* [16]

Luther distributed copies of his book to all the Kings of the known world. Years later, Hitler read a copy and using Luther's ideas embarked on his holocaust of the Jews.

Another unfortunate situation is that most of today's Protestant churches within the Body of Messiah believe in Replacement Theology (or some part of Replacement Theology). This is another reason why it is so important to teach the Jewish Roots of the Bible so that the Body of Messiah is not deceived by strange doctrines and ignorant of her Jewish connection.

Why do Replacement theologians believe this is truth? They believe the Greek word for "and" (*kai*) in 6:16 is understood epexegetically meaning "even, that is, or in other words." In fact, the New International Version, which seems to be the preferred Bible within the current American Body of Messiah, interprets 6:16 as *"Peace and mercy to all who follow this rule,* **even** *to the Israel of God."* [Bold emphasis is mine] So let us analyze this situation to see if Replacement Theology and the NIV are correct or not.

The phrase we are looking at in 6:16 is *"peace be on them, and mercy, and upon the Israel of God."* "Them" refers back to "as many" who will walk by this rule who we found out were the Gentile believers of Galatia who refused to follow Torah and be circumcised. "And" (*kai*) means "and, even, also, both, indeed, namely, but, then, yet, so, for, that is, or. *Kai* is a frequently used conjunction usually meaning 'and'; however, it can also be an adverb meaning 'even' or 'also' (as in Romans 8:17)." [17] Although *kai* has many meanings, the main definition is "and." If anyone is to interpret a secondary meaning they must have a good reason such as context or Greek grammar. For example, Rom. 8:17 uses *"kai"* to mean "then and also" instead of "and." The context here dictates this and the use of the contrasting "and" (*de*) helps interpreters to insert a secondary meaning of "then" or "also" instead of "and." There is no such reason found in Gal. 6:16 and therefore the proper interpretation is "and"!

In fact, there are better reasons to believe the primary definition of *kai* should be "and" and nothing else. There is a strange word sequence in this verse. The word for word Greek rendering is *"kai hosoi to kanoni touto stoichesousin, eirene ep' autous kai eleos, kai epi ton Israel tou theou."* The direct word for word English translation is, "And as many as by the rule this shall walk, peace upon them and mercy, and upon the Israel of God." The KJV translates this verse accurately: *"And as many as walk according to this rule, peace be on them, and mercy, and upon the Israel of God."* Most other versions of the Bible place "mercy" and "peace" together as "peace and mercy" when in fact they are separated. The meaning is certainly the same: peace and mercy will be upon those who walk by this rule. However, by placing "and mercy" between "them" and "the Israel of God," Sha'ul reveals he is writing about two separate groups.

In addition, "upon" (*epi*) is used twice as a preposition connected with "them" and with "the Israel of God." If "upon" was only used once then an interpreter can say the two groups are one and the same. The insertion of the second "upon" would be redundant and useless unless of course the reason was to reveal two groups rather than one. I believe that is exactly why Sha'ul did it. These two points unequivocally show that "them" and "the Israel of God" should be treated as two separate groups and not one and the same!

Replacement theologians additionally redefine the "Israel of God" to mean "the Church." First, let us look at the word "Israel." Zodhiates defines "Israel" (*Israel*) as a transliteration of the Hebrew *Yisrael*. Yacov (Jacob) was given this name after he wrestled with God. In the New Covenant, it was spoken only in reference to his posterity as the House of Israel, the people of Israel or the sons of Israel. [18] "Israel" is used 73 times in the New Covenant with the word never meaning anything else other than the nation of Israel or the Jewish people! So why this one time in Gal. 6:16 do Replacement theologians believe it means "the Church" when there is no Greek grammar or context to suggest making this translational change?!

Maybe the answer lies in the peculiar phrase "the Israel of God." This phrase is only used once in the New Covenant writings and is not typically used in

Judaism. Since this phrase is mysterious and has no real Jewish history, the Replacement theologians may have tried to capitalize on this mystique and infer a metaphor for "the Church." However, it is much better to interpret within the context of this section. It has already been determined that the "as many" and the "them" are the Gentile believers of Galatia. Since "Israel" means Israel and the Jewish people and "of God" can easily refer to believers of Yeshua, I propose that "the Israel of God" are the Messianic Jewish believers of Galatia!

Another logical biblical deduction would be that Sha'ul would want to include all believers in this blessing of peace and mercy. And so he does by including the Jewish believers with the Gentile believers. This is not the first time Sha'ul divides believers into the two groups of Gentiles and Jews (see Eph. 2:11-16 which also connects the circumcision argument to the division of the two groups). Therefore, the "Israel of God" are the true Jewish people of God – the Messianic Jewish believers of Yeshua!

Sha'ul wrote of a similar situation in Rom. 2:28-29, *"For he is not a Jew, which is one outwardly; neither is that circumcision, which is outward in the flesh: But he is a Jew, which is one inwardly; and circumcision is that of the heart, in the spirit, and not in the letter; whose praise is not of men, but of God."* A true Jewish person is one who has believed in Yeshua and been circumcised of the heart in the Ruach Kodesh. A true Jewish person is not necessarily one who has been physically circumcised in the flesh. The obvious contrast here is with Jewish people who rely upon their Judaism to save them. Sha'ul is teaching that those Jewish people who enter into the Avrahamic Covenant by receiving circumcision and believe they are saved because of it are truly not saved and are not true Jews! No, a true Jew is a

Jewish person who believes in the Jewish Messiah and therefore can be called the "Israel of God."

David Stern sees an allusion to the main synagogue prayer called the *Amidah* with Sha'ul's writing style of verse 16. [19] The *Amidah* is a congregational prayer where everyone stands and silently prays and is believed to be used in the first century. The last section of the *Amidah* begins with, "Grant peace, goodness, blessing, grace, kindness and mercy upon us and upon all Israel your people." [20] Although there are similarities between these phrases, the very apparent major differences show that at best Sha'ul made some sort of writing style application of the *Amidah* to the verse. Sha'ul's intention is not designing a new prayer for first century congregations but a statement of encouragement to follow the Lord's rule! The congregational *Kaddish* prayer is similar. The *Kaddish*, an Aramaic prayer originating in Second Temple times, ends with the phrase, "May He who makes peace in His high places make peace upon us and upon all Israel, and say amen." [21] Again, there are writing style similarities but not enough to claim the *Kaddish* is the key to unlocking the understanding of the verse.

A major problem develops if one adopts the interpretation of Replacement Theology of this verse. If one believes that God replaced Israel with the Church where she now receives all His blessings and promises, then this understanding contradicts with a few attributes of God! God is a faithful, truthful and immutable God. When God made promises to the Jewish people He has to completely fulfill them, He cannot change His mind about them nor can He just forget about them. The gifts and calling of God are irrevocable (Rom. 11:29). If God did not keep His promises to the nation of Israel, then why do believers of Replacement Theology think God would keep His promises to the Church? Therefore, to believe in Replacement Theology is to believe the Bible and God have contradictions and this is far from the truth.

Suffice to say, 6:16 is a power packed verse full of Jewish Roots. Sha'ul's goal was to encourage all believers to walk by the rule of freedom and not by Torah Observance focused on rules and regulations (like circumcision) that have no spiritual bearing on our walk with the Lord. Yeshua, not the Law, should be our focal point in all aspects of life. Sha'ul was so concerned over this theological point that he cried out in verse 17 for everyone to stop causing him trouble over it. He had had enough troubles in his life already.

6:17 Sha'ul was sufficiently fatigued with those who attacked his ministry especially the Legalizers who followed him from city to city trying to destroy God's work. Sha'ul is also speaking of those who physically attacked him. "Marks" (*stigma*) means "mark, brand, and tattoo... A *stigma* is a mark or tattoo pricked or branded upon the body as a means of identification...Slaves also bore a physical mark signifying their status and the name of their owner." [22] What a wonderful word play Sha'ul used here. Slaves were branded like cattle showing their status and the name of their owner. Sha'ul was similarly branded like these slaves with the physical beatings he sustained from his enemies. These brandings showed he was an ambassador, apostle and a slave of Yeshua. Not only did the sufferings prove Sha'ul's status of his owner Yeshua, but he recognized that God had a hand in them.

In Acts 9:15-16, the Lord speaks to Ananias concerning Saul, *"But the Lord said unto him, Go thy way: for he is a chosen vessel unto me, to bear my name before the Gentiles, and kings, and the children of Israel: For I will shew him how great things* **he must suffer for my name's sake**.*"* [Bold emphasis is mine] The Lord called Sha'ul to preach the good news of Yeshua to all peoples and to suffer for the truth as well. The marks of Yeshua were the beatings, whippings, stonings, sufferings and persecutions of living for the Lord. I believe Sha'ul was saying that he had enough of the sufferings for a lifetime and it was time to stop causing him more trouble.

6:18 This was Sha'ul's typical closing in his letters. God's grace be with your spirit. "Grace" (*charis*) was defined in 1:3 and refers to God's demonstration of His favor, mercy and kindness to all of mankind. This means that grace is given without stipulations, cannot be earned and is not deserved. It is a gift from God. By grace we are saved and by grace we should live our lives to the fullest in the Ruach. We should live our lives by grace alone with nothing added. This is the message from Sha'ul to the Galatians and to all believers as well.

In summary, Sha'ul finished his letter to the Galatians continuing the theme of freedom by showing a contrast between himself and the Legalizers. The Legalizers had evil motives behind their teaching and ministry. Sha'ul, on the other hand, only had Godly concern for the Galatian Messianic believers wanting them to walk with the Lord and not with the Law. Nothing in the Law was to get in the way of walking in the new creation rule. The most important aspect of a believer's life is to walk with the Lord, be filled by the Ruach, have the fruit of the Ruach, and live by faith and God's grace. If believers do this, then God's *shalom* and *chesed* (mercy) will be with us.

We additionally found that anti-Semitism has reared its ugly head in the Church through the form of "Replacement Theology." Obviously, not all who believe in Replacement Theology are anti-Semitic. However, the false teachings of Replacement Theology helped to bring about horrific anti-Semitic acts against the Jewish people. The idea that "the Church" has replaced Israel as God's covenant people is absurd and unbiblical. Our study of Gal. 6:16 does not support the theories of Replacement Theology or the NIV interpretation. In fact, it does support the idea that believers can be separated into one of two groups: Messianic Jewish believers or Messianic Gentile believers. It also supports the biblical truth that God is not done with Israel and continues to have a reconciliation plan for "the apple of His eye."

If the Replacement theologians asked themselves the following questions and truly searched for God's answers, then much Jewish pain could have been averted. These questions are for all believers as well: "Are we living in Yeshua's freedom?" "Are we living by the Ruach?" "Are we living by faith and not the Law?" "Are we living by God's grace?"

Chapter 17

Summary

This commentary was specifically written for the MJM and any believer who is in interested in learning their Jewish Roots. The MJM has branched off into two groups. The Torah Observant group is the larger of the two and it tends to dominate and control most aspects of the MJM. The New Covenant Freedom group is much smaller but slowly growing in size. The Torah Observant believe that all Messianics need to keep Torah for either salvation and/or sanctification reasons. Granted, most in this group tend to believe that following Torah is for sanctification reasons rather than for salvation. There is a great zeal to please the Lord but it is misguided down the road of following the Torah for Torah's sake. The New Covenant Freedom group believes that salvation and sanctification are by God's grace through faith alone. One can only be saved and sanctified by faith in Yeshua Hameshiach. Adding anything to faith in Yeshua's death and resurrection, like Torah observance, is false teaching and is as Sha'ul proclaimed "accursed."

Sha'ul wrote the book of Galatians to Messianic Jewish and Gentile believers to warn them not to go down the Torah Observant road to spiritual destruction and corruption. In 1:4, Sha'ul told us that Yeshua delivered us out of this present evil age which includes Torah observance. In 1:6, he claimed keeping Torah for Torah's sake was a different gospel than the gospel of grace and should not be followed. Those who preach Torah Observance for sanctification are strictly warned of their cursing in 1:8-9 as Sha'ul proclaimed, "...*let him be accursed.*"

Sha'ul calls these teachers of Torah Observance "false brethren" who tried to guide the Galatian believers from their new-found liberty in Yeshua into the Law's bondage (2:4-5). Now we know that not all of today's teachers of Torah observance are false brethren. However, one does need to find out why they teach Torah observance for sanctification when this is clearly against the Scriptures. Sha'ul even corrected the Messianic Jews who acted hypocritically toward the Gentile believers by not eating and fellowshipping with them (2:11-14). He strongly proclaimed in 2:16 that all believers were not and cannot be justified by the works of the Law but only by faith in Yeshua. In 2:19-20, Sha'ul taught us that we through the Law have died to the Law so that we can live for God. We cannot spiritually live for God through the keeping of Torah. We no longer live but Messiah (and not the Law) lives in us.

In 3:1-3, Sha'ul calls the Galatians "foolish" for being swayed by the Legalizers into keeping Torah. We cannot become perfect or mature through the Law but only by following the Ruach. Sha'ul then boldly exclaimed that anyone who is of the works of the Law is under God's curse (3:10)! But when we believe and have faith in Yeshua, the curse of the Law is lifted (3:13). Then Sha'ul teaches us in 3:19 the main purpose of the creation of the Law. It was added to define and reveal personal sins until the Messiah came to die for all those sins. Before Messiah came we were all kept in custody under the Law. But after He came the Law was no longer needed to keep us in that custody (3:23-25). Our tutor, the Law, showed us that the way to Messiah is through faith because it is impossible to come to Him through works (3:24).

In 4:5-7, Sha'ul says Yeshua redeemed everyone who was under the Law and changed us from being slaves to the Law to becoming sons and heirs of God. Since we have become personally known by God, then why would we ever desire to be enslaved again by the weak and worthless elemental things of the Law (4:9-10)?! Sha'ul even begs the Galatians to become like himself – free from the spiritual bondage of the Law (4:12). He even wonders why those Galatians who wanted to be under the Law did not truly listen to the Law that condemns them (4:21).

Sha'ul boldly declares that Messiah has set us free from the Law which is the yoke of slavery so that we should continue to stand firm in our freedom (5:1). In 5:3-4, Sha'ul states that anyone who tries to keep even one point of the Law is obligated to keep all the Law. Anyone who tries to keep the whole Law fails and sins in the process. This then severs their fellowship with Messiah and they fall from God's grace. In 5:7-8, Sha'ul says the Legalizers were not called by God and through their false teaching hindered the Galatians' walk in truth. We were all called to freedom from the Law so that we could fulfill the Law through loving our neighbor as ourself (5:13-14). Sha'ul encourages us to walk by the Ruach and not by the flesh following the Law (5:16-18). If we are truly born again, then we should live and walk by the Ruach and not by the Law (5:24-25).

In 6:2, Sha'ul declares that if believers bear one

another's burdens then we will actually fulfill the Law of Messiah. He says nothing of keeping the Law to fulfill the Law! In 6:7-8, Sha'ul states that whatever a man sows, this he will reap. If believers sow to the Law then they will reap from their flesh, but if believers sow to the Ruach then of the Ruach they will reap. He reports to the Galatians in 6:12-13 that the Legalizers are hypocrites and do not even keep the Law themselves! He even states that circumcision and uncircumcision is nothing to the Lord. What is important to the Lord is the new creation; that we share the wonderful good news message of Yeshua who died for our sins and resurrected on the third day to free us from going to hell, to free us from the power of sin, to free us from the bondage of the Law and to free us from ourselves. Is it any wonder with all these warnings and teachings of Sha'ul to not keep the Law for sanctification reasons that any believer would still want to be Torah Observant?! The Torah Observant group within the MJM must listen to Sha'ul's plea and fervently take heed the Lord's warnings found in the book of Galatians.

This book was not only written for the MJM as a friendly exhortation for correction of poor doctrine and practice but also written in commentary form for all believers who are interested in their Jewish Roots. Simply put, Sha'ul being Jewish wrote all of his epistles with a Jewish mindset. Much of his Jewish writing was not fully explained to the recipients of his letters because they would have already known it. For example, there was no need to explain the spiritual truths of the Passover Seder as everyone already knew of it. However, most of today readers do not have this Jewish understanding of the Scriptures. Therefore, there was much investigation into Jewish and Gentile sources, Hebrew and Greek word studies and Greek grammar to bring the Jewish Roots to life.

The major theme of Galatians is very simple – Messiah has set us free! Messianic Jews and Gentiles are called to freedom from the bondage of the Law, the power of sin and the strength of self. We have died to the Law's bondage, sin's power over us and self's strength so that we can live a Spirit-led life for God. To be Godly we must live by faith, grace and love and not by Law, sin and self.

Within this framework of freedom, Sha'ul discussed four additional themes: grace versus Law; faith versus works; Spirit versus flesh; and Jesus versus Jewishness. For believers to be living in freedom we need to follow grace, faith, the Spirit and Jesus rather than keeping the Law and the works of the Law, remaining fleshly in our sin and obsessing in bondage to Jewishness.

A nice summary of the book of Galatians can be developed by adding all the chapter titles of this dissertation together (with some needed insertions). One needs to follow the truth of the good news message or face the consequences. Sha'ul is a great example of how the good news transforms us from Legalizers to graceful believers. The truth of the good news is through grace and not the Law. The good news confronts and challenges us to live by faith and not by works of the Law. Righteousness comes by faith and not through the Law. Avraham was blessed by God receiving righteousness through faith. Following the Law does not bless but brings God's cursing. Why the Law then? It helps to define sin and reveal how evil sin truly is. We were slaves under the Law because of our sin. But Messiah redeemed us from sin and the Law and made us sons of God. We are now to maintain that freedom from the Law. We should listen to the Law. It tells us we are children of the free woman and not children of the bondwoman. Messiah has set us free so we should stand firm in our freedom and not be subject again to the Law. Messiah not only set us free but called us to freedom so we could love one another and walk by the Ruach. Instead of keeping Torah and being fleshly we should keep the fruit of the Ruach and be Godly. All believers need to know that we will reap what we sow. If we sow to the Ruach then we will reap to eternal rewards. If we sow to the Law and the flesh, then we will reap corruption. So we are encouraged and commanded to walk with the Lord and not with the Law or in our flesh. To do this, we need to know that we have *"Freedom in Messiah."* So we are free indeed! May *shalom* and the *chen* (grace) of our *Adonai Yeshua Hameshiach* be with you always. Amen.

Endnotes

Chapter One

[1] Jonathan Cahn. "Return to Simplicity of Faith" article in The Messianic Times newspaper, Nov. 2003.

[2] Rich Robinson and Ruth Rosen. "The Challenge of Our Messianic Movement, Part 2" article in Havurah (Jews for Jesus Magazine), Fall, 2003.

[3] Stan Telchin. "Messianic Judaism is not Christianity." (Grand Rapids: Chosen Books, 2004), 28-29.

[4] Flavius Josephus. "The Complete Works of Flavius Josephus." (Grand Rapids: Kregel Publications, 1960, 1978, 1981), 252.

[5] J.B. Lightfoot. "St. Paul's Epistle to the Galatians." United States of America: Hendrickson Publishers, Inc., Third Printing – August 1995), 11.

[6] Encyclopedia Judaica CD Rom Edition Version 1.0. (Judaica Multimedia (Israel) Ltd., 1997), located in section entitled, "Asia Minor."

[7] David Stern. "Jewish New Testament Commentary." (United States of America: Jewish New Testament Publications, Inc., Fifth Edition, 1996), 532.

[8] Spiros Zodhiates. "The Complete Word Study Dictionary New Testament." (Chattanooga, TN: AMG Publishers, 1992, 778.

Chapter Two

[2] Encyclopedia Judaica CD Rom Edition Version 1.0. (Judaica Multimedia (Israel) Ltd., 1997), located in section titled, "Apostle."

[3] Craig Keener. "The IVP Bible Background Commentary New Testament." (Downers Grove, IL: Inter-Varsity Press, 1993), 520 refers to 414.

[4] Thoralf Gilbrant and Tor Inge Gilbrant, Editors. "The Complete Biblical Library, Greek – English Dictionary, Vol. 16." 1 (Springfield, MO: World Library Press, 1989), 491.

[5] David Stern, 520 refers to 39.

[6] Spiros Zodhiates, 478.

[7] Walter Elwell, Editor. "The Concise Evangelical Dictionary of Theology." (Grand Rapids, MI: Baker Book House, 1991), 193.

[8] Walter Elwell, Editor, 193.

[9] Encyclopedia Judaica CD Rom Edition Version 1.0, located in sections titled, "Divine Presence: The Kavod of the Lord" and "Divine Presence: The Nature of the Kavod."

[10] David Stern, 520.

[11] Spiros Zodhiates, 665.

[12] Thoralf Gilbrant and Tor Inge Gilbrant, Editors. "The Complete Biblical Library, Vol. 8: Study Bible, Galatians – Philemon." (Springfield, MO: World Library Press, 1989), 21.

[13] Encyclopedia Judaica CD Rom Edition Version 1.0, located in section titled, "Oral Law."

[14] David Stern, 521.

[15] Thoralf Gilbrant and Tor Inge Gilbrant, Editors. "The Complete Biblical Library, Greek – English Dictionary, Vol. 11." (Springfield, MO: World Library Press, 1989), 220.

Chapter Three

[1] Spiros Zodhiates, 1204.

[2] Craig Keener, 521.

[3] Barry Berger, Director of Missions Emeritus, CJF Ministries. Jewish Evangelism Training (JET) Manual, (CJF Ministries, 2000 – 2005).

[4] F.F. Bruce."The New International Greek Testament Commentary, The Epistle to the Galatians." (Grand Rapids, MI: William B. Eerdmans Publishing Company, 1982), 95.

[5] David Stern, 526.

[6] Craig Keener, 522.

Chapter Four

[1] David Stern, 526.

[2] Warren Wiersbe. "Be Free, A New Testament Study – Galatians." (Colorado Springs, CO: Chariot Victor Publishing, 1975), 41.

[3] F.F. Bruce, 111.

[4] Craig Keener, 365.

[5] Craig Keener, 522.

[6] Spiros Zodhiates, 565.

[7] J. B. Lightfoot, 107.

[8] Arnold Frutchenbaum. "Israelology: The Missing Link in Systematic Theology." (United States of America, Ariel Ministries, 1989), 651.

[9] "The Willowbank Declaration On The Christian Gospel and the Jewish People, Preamble." Developed and adopted on April 29, 1989. Sponsored by the World Evangelical Fellowship. http://www.appleofhiseye.org/willowbank.html

[10] Craig Keener, 523.

[11] J. B. Lightfoot, 109.

Chapter Five

[1] David Stern, 528.

[2] Merrill Tenney. "The Zondervan Pictorial Bible Dictionary." (Grand Rapids, Michigan: Regency Reference Library, Zondervan Publishing House, 1963), 47-48.

[3] Craig Keener, 523.

[4] Warren Wiersbe, 50.

[5] David Stern, 528-529.

[6] Craig Keener, 523.

[7] Craig Keener, 523.

[8] Warren Wiersbe, 52.

[9] Spiros Zodhiates, 698.

[10] David Stern, 531.

[11] Rich Robinson and Ruth Rosen. "The Challenge of Our Messianic Movement, Part 2" article in Havurah (Jews for Jesus Magazine), Fall, 2003.

[12] Craig Keener, 524.

[13] Thoralf Gilbrant and Tor Inge Gilbrant, Editors; Erich Kiehl, Commentator. "The Complete Biblical Library, Vol. 8: Study Bible, Galatians – Philemon." (Springfield, MO: World Library Press, 1989), 39.

[14] Spiros Zodhiates, 464.

[15] Kenneth Wuest. "Galatians in the Greek New Testament." (Grand Rapids, Michigan: William B. Eerdmans Publishing Company, 1962), 78.

[16] Kenneth Wuest, 79.

[17] Thoralf Gilbrant and Tor Inge Gilbrant, Editors. "The Complete Biblical Library, Greek – English Dictionary, Vol. 13." (Springfield, MO: World Library Press, 1989), 272-273.

[18] Kenneth Wuest, 79-80.

[19] Kenneth Wuest, 80.

[20] Kenneth Wuest, 80-81.

Chapter Six

[1] Warren Wiersbe, 71.

[2] Thoralf Gilbrant and Tor Inge Gilbrant, Editors. "The Complete Biblical Library, Greek – English Dictionary, Vol. 11." (Springfield, MO: World Library Press, 1989), 451.

[3] Thoralf Gilbrant and Tor Inge Gilbrant, Editors. "The Complete Biblical Library, Greek – English Dictionary, Vol. 11."(Springfield, MO: World Library Press, 1989), 544-545.

⁴ Kenneth Wuest, 84.

⁵ Spiros Zodhiates, 642.

⁶ Thoralf Gilbrant and Tor Inge Gilbrant, Editors. "The Complete Biblical Library, Greek – English Dictionary, Vol. 16." (Springfield, MO: World Library Press, 1989), 26-28.

⁷ Warren Wiersbe, 66-67.

⁸ Thoralf Gilbrant and Tor Inge Gilbrant, Editors. "The Complete Biblical Library, Greek – English Dictionary, Vol.12." (Springfield, MO: World Library Press, 1989), 181.

⁹ Warren Wiersbe, 68.

¹⁰ Thoralf Gilbrant and Tor Inge Gilbrant, Editors. "The Complete Biblical Library, Greek – English Dictionary, Vol. 15." (Springfield, MO: World Library Press, 1989), 188.

¹¹ Thoralf Gilbrant and Tor Inge Gilbrant, Editors. "The Complete Biblical Library: The Old Testament. Hebrew – English Dictionary, Aleph - Beth." (Springfield, MO: World Library Press, 1989), 287-288.

¹² Warren Baker and Eugene Carpenter. "The Complete Word Study Dictionary Old Testament." (Chattanooga, TN: AMG Publishers, 2003, 69.

¹³ Craig Keener, 525.

¹⁴ Warren Baker and Eugene Carpenter, 100.

¹⁵ Warren Baker and Eugene Carpenter, 997.

Chapter Seven

¹ Spiros Zodhiates, 531.

² Thoralf Gilbrant and Tor Inge Gilbrant, Editors. "The Complete Biblical Library, Greek – English Dictionary, Vol. 16." (Springfield, MO: World Library Press, 1989), 370-372.

³ Warren Wiersbe, 70.

⁴ Kenneth Wuest, 95.

5 Craig Keener, 526.

6 Thoralf Gilbrant and Tor Inge Gilbrant, Editors. "The Complete Biblical Library: The Old Testament. Hebrew – English Dictionary, Aleph - Beth." (Springfield, MO: World Library Press, 1989), 283-284.

7 Thoralf Gilbrant and Tor Inge Gilbrant, Editors. "The Complete Biblical Library, Greek – English Dictionary, Vol. 13." (Springfield, MO: World Library Press, 1989), 19-21.

8 Kenneth Wuest, 96.

9 Thoralf Gilbrant and Tor Inge Gilbrant, Editors. "The Complete Biblical Library, Greek – English Dictionary, Vol.15." (Springfield, MO: World Library Press, 1989), 234-240.

10 Warren Wiersbe, 70.

11 Warren Baker and Eugene Carpenter. "The Complete Word Study Dictionary Old Testament." (Chattanooga, TN: AMG Publishers, 2003), 1171, 876, 332 respectively.

12 Thoralf Gilbrant and Tor Inge Gilbrant, Editors. "The Complete Biblical Library, Greek – English Dictionary, Vol.12." (Springfield, MO: World Library Press, 1989), 458.

13 Ibid.

14 Thoralf Gilbrant and Tor Inge Gilbrant, Editors. "The Complete Biblical Library, Vol. 8: Study Bible, Galatians – Philemon." (Springfield, MO: World Library Press, 1989), 49.

15 Thoralf Gilbrant and Tor Inge Gilbrant, Editors. "The Complete Biblical Library, Greek – English Dictionary, Vol. 13." (Springfield, MO: World Library Press, 1989), 169.

16 Craig Keener, 526.

17 Thoralf Gilbrant and Tor Inge Gilbrant, Editors. "The Complete Biblical Library, Greek – English Dictionary, Vol. 16." (Springfield, MO: World Library Press, 1989), 91-92.

Thoralf Gilbrant and Tor Inge Gilbrant, Editors. "The Complete Biblical Library: The Old Testament. Hebrew – English Dictionary, Gimel - Zayin." (Springfield, MO: World Library Press, 1989), 442-446.

18 F.F. Bruce, 173.

19 Warren Wiersbe, 77-78.

20 Kenneth Wuest, 102.

21 Thoralf Gilbrant and Tor Inge Gilbrant, Editors. "The Complete Biblical Library, Greek – English Dictionary, Vol. 13." (Springfield, MO: World Library Press, 1989), 354-355.

Chapter Eight

1 Joseph Thayer. "A Greek-English Lexicon of the New Testament." (Baker Book House: Grand Rapids, Michigan, 1977), 665.

2 Kenneth Wuest, 104.

3 Rabbi Nosson Scherman & Rabbi Meir Zlotowitz, General editors. "The Chumash." (Mesorah Publications, Ltd: Brooklyn, NY, 1993, 1994), 1113.

4 Thoralf Gilbrant and Tor Inge Gilbrant, Editors. "The Complete Biblical Library, Greek – English Dictionary, Vol. 11." (Springfield, MO: World Library Press, 1989), 515.

5 Spiros Zodhiates, 306.

6 J.B. Lightfoot, 147.

7 David Stern, 551.

8 Thoralf Gilbrant and Tor Inge Gilbrant, Editors. "The Complete Biblical Library, Greek – English Dictionary, Vol. 16." (Springfield, MO: World Library Press, 1989), 459-460.

9 Thoralf Gilbrant and Tor Inge Gilbrant, Editors. "The Complete Biblical Library, Greek – English Dictionary, Vol. 16." (Springfield, MO: World Library Press, 1989), 139.

10 Thoralf Gilbrant and Tor Inge Gilbrant, Editors. "The Complete Biblical Library, Greek – English Dictionary, Vol. 16." (Springfield, MO: World Library Press, 1989), 140.

11 Kenneth Wuest, 110.

12 J.B. Lightfoot, 149.

13 Kenneth Wuest, 110.

14 Thoralf Gilbrant and Tor Inge Gilbrant, Editors. "The Complete Biblical Library, Greek – English Dictionary, Vol. 16." (Springfield, MO: World Library Press, 1989), 370-372.

15 Kenneth Wuest, 111.

Chapter Nine

[1] Thoralf Gilbrant and Tor Inge Gilbrant, Editors. "The Complete Biblical Library, Greek – English Dictionary, Vol. 16." (Springfield, MO: World Library Press, 1989), 371-372.

[2] Thoralf Gilbrant and Tor Inge Gilbrant, Editors. "The Complete Biblical Library, Greek – English Dictionary, Vol. 12." (Springfield, MO: World Library Press, 1989), 573.

[3] Thoralf Gilbrant and Tor Inge Gilbrant, Editors. "The Complete Biblical Library, Greek – English Dictionary, Vol. 14." (Springfield, MO: World Library Press, 1989), 323.

[4] Thoralf Gilbrant and Tor Inge Gilbrant, Editors. "The Complete Biblical Library, Greek – English Dictionary, Vol. 16." (Springfield, MO: World Library Press, 1989), 371-372.

[5] Craig Keener, 529.

[6] Thoralf Gilbrant and Tor Inge Gilbrant, Editors. "The Complete Biblical Library, Greek – English Dictionary, Vol.12." (Springfield, MO: World Library Press, 1989), 458.

[7] Thoralf Gilbrant and Tor Inge Gilbrant, Editors. "The Complete Biblical Library, Greek – English Dictionary, Vol. 16." (Springfield, MO: World Library Press, 1989), 339-340.

[8] David Stern, 99.

[9] Craig Keener, 529.

[10] Craig Keener, 529.

[11] Thoralf Gilbrant and Tor Inge Gilbrant, Editors. "The Complete Biblical Library, Greek – English Dictionary, Vol. 14." (Springfield, MO: World Library Press, 1989), 310-313.

[12] Thoralf Gilbrant and Tor Inge Gilbrant, Editors. "The Complete Biblical Library, Greek – English Dictionary, Vol. 11." (Springfield, MO: World Library Press, 1989), 620-625.

[13] Thoralf Gilbrant and Tor Inge Gilbrant, Editors. "The Complete Biblical Library, Greek – English Dictionary, Vol. 11." (Springfield, MO: World Library Press, 1989), 466.

[14] Thoralf Gilbrant and Tor Inge Gilbrant, Editors. "The Complete Biblical Library, Greek – English Dictionary, Vol. 15." (Springfield, MO: World Library Press, 1989), 381, 383

15 Thoralf Gilbrant and Tor Inge Gilbrant, Editors. "The Complete Biblical Library, Greek – English Dictionary, Vol. 15." (Springfield, MO: World Library Press, 1989), 78.

16 Wiersbe, 94; Stern, 557; Lightfoot, 171; Wuest, 122-123; Erich Kiehl. The Complete Biblical Library, Vol. 8: Study Bible, Galatians – Philemon. (Springfield, MO: World Library Press, 1989), 63.

17 Craig Keener, 530.

18 Kenneth Wuest, 123.

Chapter Ten

1 Thoralf Gilbrant and Tor Inge Gilbrant, Editors. "The Complete Biblical Library, Greek – English Dictionary, Vol. 12." (Springfield, MO: World Library Press, 1989), 44-45.

2 Kenneth Wuest, 125.

3 Craig Keener, 530.

4 Thoralf Gilbrant and Tor Inge Gilbrant, Editors. "The Complete Biblical Library, Greek – English Dictionary, Vol. 12." (Springfield, MO: World Library Press, 1989), 481-482.

5 Thoralf Gilbrant and Tor Inge Gilbrant, Editors. "The Complete Biblical Library, Greek – English Dictionary, Vol. 12." (Springfield, MO: World Library Press, 1989), 356.

6 J. B. Lightfoot, 176.

7 Warren Wiersbe, 96-97.

8 Warren Wiersbe, 97.

9 Thoralf Gilbrant and Tor Inge Gilbrant, Editors. "The Complete Biblical Library, Greek – English Dictionary, Vol. 16." (Springfield, MO: World Library Press, 1989), 262.

10 Thoralf Gilbrant and Tor Inge Gilbrant, Editors. "The Complete Biblical Library, Greek – English Dictionary, Vol. 16." (Springfield, MO: World Library Press, 1989), 563.

Chapter Eleven

[1] Thoralf Gilbrant and Tor Inge Gilbrant, Editors. "The Complete Biblical Library, Greek – English Dictionary, Vol. 11." (Springfield, MO: World Library Press, 1989), 142.

[2] Rabbi Nosson Scherman & Rabbi Meir Zlotowitz, General editors. "The Chumash." (Mesorah Publications, Ltd: Brooklyn, NY, 1993, 1994), 972-973.

[3] Thoralf Gilbrant and Tor Inge Gilbrant, Editors. "The Complete Biblical Library, Greek – English Dictionary, Vol. 11." (Springfield, MO: World Library Press, 1989), 168.

[4] David Stern, 559.

[5] F.F. Bruce, 220-221.

[6] Kenneth Wuest, 133.

[7] Craig Keener, 532.

Chapter Twelve

[1] Thoralf Gilbrant and Tor Inge Gilbrant, Editors. "The Complete Biblical Library, Greek – English Dictionary, Vol. 12." Springfield, MO: World Library Press, 1989), 377.

[2] Thoralf Gilbrant and Tor Inge Gilbrant, Editors. "The Complete Biblical Library, Greek – English Dictionary, Vol. 12." (Springfield, MO: World Library Press, 1989), 378.

[3] Thoralf Gilbrant and Tor Inge Gilbrant, Editors. "The Complete Biblical Library, Greek – English Dictionary, Vol. 16." (Springfield, MO: World Library Press, 1989), 116.

[4] Thoralf Gilbrant and Tor Inge Gilbrant, Editors. "The Complete Biblical Library, Greek – English Dictionary, Vol. 12." (Springfield, MO: World Library Press, 1989), 437.

[5] Warren Wiersbe, 115.

[6] Kenneth Wuest, 136.

[7] Craig Keener, 533.

[8] Thoralf Gilbrant and Tor Inge Gilbrant, Editors. "The Complete Biblical Library, Greek – English Dictionary, Vol. 14." (Springfield, MO: World Library Press, 1989), 419-420.

[9] Warren Wiersbe, 116.

[10] Spiros Zodhiates, 841-842.

[11] Spiros Zodhiates, 841-842.

[12] Thoralf Gilbrant and Tor Inge Gilbrant, Editors. "The Complete Biblical Library, Greek – English Dictionary, Vol. 12." (Springfield, MO: World Library Press, 1989), 353.

[13] Rabbi Nosson Scherman & Rabbi Meir Zlotowitz, General editors. "The Chumash." (Mesorah Publications, Ltd: Brooklyn, NY, 1993, 1994), 75.

[14] Thoralf Gilbrant and Tor Inge Gilbrant, Editors. "The Complete Biblical Library, Greek – English Dictionary, Vol. 13." (Springfield, MO: World Library Press, 1989), 225-227.

[15] Thoralf Gilbrant and Tor Inge Gilbrant, Editors. "The Complete Biblical Library, Greek – English Dictionary, Vol. 15." (Springfield, MO: World Library Press, 1989), 123-125.

[16] Kenneth Wuest, 144.

[17] Craig Keener, 533.

[18] Thoralf Gilbrant and Tor Inge Gilbrant, Editors. "The Complete Biblical Library, Greek – English Dictionary, Vol. 16." (Springfield, MO: World Library Press, 1989), 59-60.

[19] Thoralf Gilbrant and Tor Inge Gilbrant, Editors. "The Complete Biblical Library, Greek – English Dictionary, Vol. 11." (Springfield, MO: World Library Press, 1989), 246-247.

[20] Thoralf Gilbrant and Tor Inge Gilbrant, Editors. "The Complete Biblical Library, Greek – English Dictionary, Vol. 11." (Springfield, MO: World Library Press, 1989), 374.

Chapter Thirteen

[1] Thoralf Gilbrant and Tor Inge Gilbrant, Editors. "The Complete Biblical Library, Greek – English Dictionary, Vol. 13." (Springfield, MO: World Library Press, 1989), 225-227.

[2] Thoralf Gilbrant and Tor Inge Gilbrant, Editors. "The Complete Biblical Library, Greek – English Dictionary, Vol. 16." (Springfield, MO: World Library Press, 1989), 26-28.

[3] Thoralf Gilbrant and Tor Inge Gilbrant, Editors. "The Complete Biblical Library, Greek – English Dictionary, Vol. 15." (Springfield, MO: World Library Press, 1989), 213-216.

[4] David Stern, 565.

[5] Rabbi Nosson Scherman & Rabbi Meir Zlotowitz, General editors. "The Chumash." (Mesorah Publications, Ltd: Brooklyn, NY, 1993, 1994), 661.

[6] Thoralf Gilbrant and Tor Inge Gilbrant, Editors. "The Complete Biblical Library, Greek – English Dictionary, Vol. 12." (Springfield, MO: World Library Press, 1989), 26.

[7] Spiros Zodhiates, 849.

[8] Craig Keener, 534.

[9] Spiros Zodhiates, 153.

[10] Thoralf Gilbrant and Tor Inge Gilbrant, Editors. "The Complete Biblical Library, Greek – English Dictionary, Vol. 15." (Springfield, MO: World Library Press, 1989), 156-158.

[11] www.Wikipedia.org; search for "halachah."

[12] Thoralf Gilbrant and Tor Inge Gilbrant, Editors. "The Complete Biblical Library, Greek – English Dictionary, Vol. 16." (Springfield, MO: World Library Press, 1989), 26-28.

[13] Thoralf Gilbrant and Tor Inge Gilbrant, Editors. "The Complete Biblical Library, Greek – English Dictionary, Vol. 11." (Springfield, MO: World Library Press, 1989), 65-67.

[14] Warren Wiersbe, 132.

[15] Warren Wiersbe, 114-115

Chapter Fourteen

[1] Thoralf Gilbrant and Tor Inge Gilbrant, Editors. "The Complete Biblical Library, Greek – English Dictionary, Vol. 16." (Springfield, MO: World Library Press, 1989), 406.

[2] J.B. Lightfoot, 210.

[3] Thoralf Gilbrant and Tor Inge Gilbrant, Editors. "The Complete Biblical Library, Greek – English Dictionary, Vol. 15." (Springfield, MO: World Library Press, 1989), 278-279.

[4] Thoralf Gilbrant and Tor Inge Gilbrant, Editors. "The Complete Biblical Library, Greek – English Dictionary, Vol. 13." (Springfield, MO: World Library Press, 1989), 353.

[5] Dr. Paul Benware. "The Believer's Payday." (Chattanooga, TN: AMG Publishers, 2002), 22.

[6] Paul Benware, 33.

[7] Kenneth Wuest, 159.

[8] Kenneth Wuest, 159.

[9] Kenneth Wuest, 159-160.

[10] Kenneth Wuest, 160.

[11] Kenneth Wuest, 160.

[12] Kenneth Wuest, 160.

[13] Kenneth Wuest, 160.

[14] J.B. Lightfoot, 213

[15] Kenneth Wuest, 161.

[16] Thoralf Gilbrant and Tor Inge Gilbrant, Editors. "The Complete Biblical Library, Greek – English Dictionary, Vol. 16." (Springfield, MO: World Library Press, 1989), 107.

[17] Kenneth Wuest, 162.

[18] Thoralf Gilbrant and Tor Inge Gilbrant, Editors. "The Complete Biblical Library, Greek – English Dictionary, Vol. 16." (Springfield, MO: World Library Press, 1989), 121.

[19] Kenneth Wuest, 162.

[20] Thoralf Gilbrant and Tor Inge Gilbrant, Editors. "The Complete Biblical Library, Greek – English Dictionary, Vol. 13." (Springfield, MO: World Library Press, 1989), 324.

[21] Thoralf Gilbrant and Tor Inge Gilbrant, Editors. "The Complete Biblical Library, Greek – English Dictionary, Vol. 15." (Springfield, MO: World Library Press, 1989), 304.

[22] Thoralf Gilbrant and Tor Inge Gilbrant, Editors. "The Complete Biblical Library, Greek – English Dictionary, Vol. 16." (Springfield, MO: World Library Press, 1989), 425.

Chapter Fifteen

[1] Craig Keener, 535.

[2] Warren Wiersbe, 140.

[3] Craig Keener, 535.

[4] Thoralf Gilbrant and Tor Inge Gilbrant, Editors. "The Complete Biblical Library, Greek – English Dictionary, Vol. 15." (Springfield, MO: World Library Press, 1989), 307.

[5] Thoralf Gilbrant and Tor Inge Gilbrant, Editors. "The Complete Biblical Library, Greek – English Dictionary, Vol. 13." (Springfield, MO: World Library Press, 1989), 286.

[6] Thoralf Gilbrant and Tor Inge Gilbrant, Editors. "The Complete Biblical Library, Greek – English Dictionary, Vol. 16." (Springfield, MO: World Library Press, 1989), 71.

[7] Thoralf Gilbrant and Tor Inge Gilbrant, Editors. "The Complete Biblical Library, Greek – English Dictionary, Vol. 11." (Springfield, MO: World Library Press, 1989), 545.

[8] Kenneth Wuest, 167.

[9] Thoralf Gilbrant and Tor Inge Gilbrant, Editors. "The Complete Biblical Library, Greek – English Dictionary, Vol. 11." (Springfield, MO: World Library Press, 1989), 240.

[10] Dr. Arnold Fruchtenbaum. "Israelology: The Missing Link in Systematic Theology." (Tustin, CA: Ariel Ministries, 1989), 650.

[11] Dr. Arnold Fruchtenbaum, 650-651.

[12] Thoralf Gilbrant and Tor Inge Gilbrant, Editors. "The Complete Biblical Library, Greek – English Dictionary, Vol. 12." (Springfield, MO: World Library Press, 1989), 159-160.

[13] Spiros Zodhiates, 854.

[14] Kenneth Wuest, 168.

[15] Thoralf Gilbrant and Tor Inge Gilbrant, Editors. "The Complete Biblical Library, Greek – English Dictionary, Vol. 16." (Springfield, MO: World Library Press, 1989), 451.

[16] Thoralf Gilbrant and Tor Inge Gilbrant, Editors. "The Complete Biblical Library, Greek – English Dictionary, Vol. 13." (Springfield, MO: World Library Press, 1989), 366.

[17] Spiros Zodhiates, 62-63.

[18] Thoralf Gilbrant and Tor Inge Gilbrant, Editors. "The Complete Biblical Library, Greek – English Dictionary, Vol. 15." (Springfield, MO: World Library Press, 1989), 196.

[19] Thoralf Gilbrant and Tor Inge Gilbrant, Editors. "The Complete Biblical Library, Greek – English Dictionary, Vol. 14." (Springfield, MO: World Library Press, 1989), 226.

[20] Kenneth Wuest, 172.

[21] Thoralf Gilbrant and Tor Inge Gilbrant, Editors. "The Complete Biblical Library, Greek – English Dictionary, Vol. 16." (Springfield, MO: World Library Press, 1989), 89.

[22] Thoralf Gilbrant and Tor Inge Gilbrant, Editors. "The Complete Biblical Library, Greek – English Dictionary, Vol. 13." (Springfield, MO: World Library Press, 1989), 103.

[23] Thoralf Gilbrant and Tor Inge Gilbrant, Editors. "The Complete Biblical Library, Greek – English Dictionary, Vol. 16." (Springfield, MO: World Library Press, 1989), 426-427.

[24] Kenneth Wuest, 172-173.

[25] Thoralf Gilbrant and Tor Inge Gilbrant, Editors. "The Complete Biblical Library, Greek – English Dictionary, Vol. 13." (Springfield, MO: World Library Press, 1989), 212-213.

[26] Thoralf Gilbrant and Tor Inge Gilbrant, Editors. "The Complete Biblical Library, Greek – English Dictionary, Vol. 12." (Springfield, MO: World Library Press, 1989), 584.

[27] Kenneth Wuest, 174.

Chapter Sixteen

[1] Warren Wiersbe, 152.

[2] Thoralf Gilbrant and Tor Inge Gilbrant, Editors. "The Complete Biblical Library, Greek – English Dictionary, Vol. 12." (Springfield, MO: World Library Press, 1989), 645.

[3] Thoralf Gilbrant and Tor Inge Gilbrant, Editors. "The Complete Biblical Library, Greek – English Dictionary, Vol. 11." (Springfield, MO: World Library Press, 1989), 212.

[4] Thoralf Gilbrant and Tor Inge Gilbrant, Editors. Erich Kiehl, Commentator. "The Complete Biblical Library, Vol. 8: Study Bible, Galatians – Philemon." (Springfield, MO: World Library Press, 1989), 91.

[5] J.B. Lightfoot, 222.

[6] J.B. Lightfoot, 222.

[7] Thoralf Gilbrant and Tor Inge Gilbrant, Editors. "The Complete Biblical Library, Greek – English Dictionary, Vol. 13." (Springfield, MO: World Library Press, 1989), 317-319.

[8] Warren Wiersbe, 155.

[9] Spiros Zodhiates, 788.

[10] Thoralf Gilbrant and Tor Inge Gilbrant, Editors. "The Complete Biblical Library, Greek – English Dictionary, Vol. 13." (Springfield, MO: World Library Press, 1989), 418.

[11] Thoralf Gilbrant and Tor Inge Gilbrant, Editors. "The Complete Biblical Library, Greek – English Dictionary, Vol. 13." (Springfield, MO: World Library Press, 1989), 236.

[12] Kenneth Wuest, 179.

[13] www.Wikipedia.org; search for "Replacement Theology."

[14] David Stern, 571-572.

[15] David Stern, 574.

[16] www.Wikipedia.org; search for "On the Jews and Their Lies."

[17] Thoralf Gilbrant and Tor Inge Gilbrant, Editors. "The Complete Biblical Library, Greek – English Dictionary, Vol. 13." (Springfield, MO: World Library Press, 1989), 210.

[18] Spiros Zodhiates, 783.

[19] David Stern, 572.

[20] Dr. John Fischer. "Siddur for Messianic Jews." (Palm Harbor, FL: Menorah Minstries, 1988), 59.

[21] Pastor Jeremiah Greenberg. "Messianic Shabbat Siddur." (Miami, FL: Messianic Revival Ministries, June 1996, 2nd Edition), 28.

[22] Thoralf Gilbrant and Tor Inge Gilbrant, Editors. "The Complete Biblical Library, Greek – English Dictionary, Vol. 16." (Springfield, MO: World Library Press, 1989), 118.

Bibliography

Baker, Warren and Carpenter, Eugene. *The Complete Word Study Dictionary Old Testament*. Chattanooga, TN: AMG Publishers (2003).

Bean, E. William. *New Treasures, A Perspective of New Testament Teachings Through Hebraic Eyes*. Minneapolis, Minnesota: Cornerstone Publishing (1995, 1999).

Benware, Dr. Paul. *The Believer's Payday*. Chattanooga, TN: AMG Publishers (2002).

Berger, Barry, Director of Missions Emeritus, CJF Ministries. *Jewish Evangelism Training (JET) Manual*. CJF Ministries (2000 – 2005).

Bruce, F.F. *The New International Greek Testament Commentary, The Epistle to the Galatians*. Grand Rapids, MI: William B. Eerdmans Publishing Company (1982).

Cahn, Jonathan. "Return to Simplicity of Faith" article in *The Messianic Times* newspaper (Nov. 2003).

Cohn-Sherbok, Dan, General editor. *Voices of Messianic Judaism*. Baltimore, MD: Messianic Jewish Publishers (2001).

Cohn-Sherbok, Dan. *The Jewish Faith*. Valley Forge, Pennsylvania: Trinity Press International (1993).

Daube, David. *The New Testament and Rabbinic Judaism*. Peabody, MA: Hendrickson Publishers (May 1998).

Edersheim, Alfred. *Sketches of Jewish Social Life*. Peabody, MA: Hendrickson Publishers, Inc. (1995, 2nd Edition).

Editorial Board. *The Interpreter's Bible, Volume X*. New York and Nashville: Abingdon Press (no date).

Elwell, Walter, Editor. *The Concise Evangelical Dictionary of Theology*. Grand Rapids, MI: Baker Book House (1991).

Fischer, Dr. John. *Siddur for Messianic Jews*. Palm Harbor, FL: Menorah Minstries (1988).

Frutchenbaum, Arnold. *Israelology: The Missing Link in Systematic Theology*. United States of America, Ariel Ministries (1989).

Kac, Arthur W. *The Spiritual Dilemma of the Jewish People Its Cause and Cure*. Grand Rapids, MI: Baker Books (1983, 2nd Edition).

Keener, Craig. *The IVP Bible Background Commentary New Testament*. Downers Grove, IL: Inter-Varsity Press (1993).

Kolatch, Alfred J. *The Jewish Book of Why*. Middle Village, NY: Jonathan David Publishers, Inc. (1981).

Kolatch, Alfred J. *The Second Jewish Book of Why*. Middle Village, NY: Jonathan David Publishers, Inc. (1985, 2000).

Lightfoot, J.B. *St. Paul's Epistle to the Galatians*. United States of America: Hendrickson Publishers, Inc., Third Printing (August 1995).

Matthews, Victor H. *Manners and Customs in the Bible*. Peabody, MA: Hendrickson Publishers, Inc. (1988, 1991).

Metzger, Bruce M. and Coogan, Michael D. *The Oxford Companion to the Bible*. New York and Oxford: Oxford University Press (1993).

Neusner, Jacob. *The Mishnah Introduction and Reader*. Philadelphia, PA: Trinity Press International (1992).

Plaut, W. Gunther, Editor. *The Torah A Modern Commentary*. New York: The Union of American Hebrew Congregations (1981).

Robinson, Rich, and Rosen, Ruth. "The Challenge of Our Messianic Movement, Part 2" article in *Havurah (Jews for Jesus Magazine)* (Fall, 2003).

Robinson, Rich and Naomi Rose Rothstein, Editors. *The Messianic Movement: A Field Guide for Evangelical Christians*. San Francisco, CA: Purple Pomegranate Productions (2005).

Ryrie, Charles C. *Basic Theology*. Colorado Springs, CO: ChariotVictor Publishing (1986).

Scott Jr., J. Julius. *Jewish Backgrounds of the New Testament*. Grand Rapids, MI: Baker Books (1995).

Scherman, Rabbi Nosson and Zlotowitz, Rabbi Meir, General editors. *The Chumash*. Mesorah Publications, Ltd: Brooklyn, NY (1993, 1994).

Stern, David. *Jewish New Testament Commentary*. United States of America: Jewish New Testament Publications, Inc., Fifth Edition (1996).

VanGemeren, Willem A. *New International Dictionary of Old Testament Theology and Exegesis, Vol. 1-5.* GrandRapids, Michigan: Zondervan (1997).

Vine, W. E. *Vine's Complete Expository Dictionary of Old and New Testament Words.* Nashville, Camden and New York: Thomas Nelson Publishers (1985).

Walton, John H., Matthews, Victor H., & Chavalas, Mark W. *The IVP Bible Background Commentary Old Testament.* Downers Grove, Illinois: InterVarsity Press (2000).

Wiersbe, Warren W. *The Bible Exposition Commentary Pentateuch.* Colorado Springs, CO: Victor (2001).

Wiersbe, Warren. *Be Free, A New Testament Study – Galatians.* Colorado Springs, CO: Chariot Victor Publishing (1975).

Wilson, William. *Wilson's Old Testament Word Studies.* McLean, VA: MacDonald Publishing Co. (No date).

Wuest, Kenneth. *Galatians in the Greek New Testament.* Grand Rapids, Michigan: William B. Eerdmans Publishing Company (1962).

Zodhiates, Spiros. *The Complete Word Study Dictionary New Testament.* Chattanooga, TN: AMG Publishers (1992).

Encyclopedia Judaica CD Rom Edition Version 1.0. Judaica Multimedia (Israel) Ltd., (1997).

The Willowbank Declaration On The Christian Gospel and the Jewish People, Preamble. Developed and adopted on April 29, 1989. Sponsored by the World Evangelical Fellowship. http://www.appleofhiseye.org/willowbank.html

Wikipedia Encyclopedia. http://en.wikipedia.org/wiki/Main_Page